C0-AVA-817

CONTINUED ON BACK END PAPER

English
Grammar
and
Composition

REVISED EDITION
WITH SUPPLEMENT

7

JOHN E. WARRINER

JOHN H. TREANOR

SHEILA Y. LAWS

SPECIAL CONTRIBUTORS

Desmond Nunan
composition

Francis Griffith
speaking and listening

Donald W. Lee
vocabulary

HARCOURT BRACE JOVANOVICH

New York   Chicago   San Francisco   Atlanta   Dallas   and   London

THE SERIES:

▶ **English Grammar and Composition 7**
English Grammar and Composition 8
English Grammar and Composition 9
English Grammar and Composition 10
English Grammar and Composition 11
English Grammar and Composition: Complete Course

Test booklet and teacher's manual for each title above

CORRELATED BOOKS OF MODELS FOR WRITING:
Composition: Models and Exercises 7
Composition: Models and Exercises 8
Composition: Models and Exercises 9
Composition: Models and Exercises 10
Composition: Models and Exercises 11
Advanced Composition: A Book of Models for Writing

AUTHORS: John E. Warriner has taught English for 32 years, in junior and senior high schools and in college. He is also a coauthor of the *English Workshop* series. John H. Treanor is well known as a teacher of workshops and extension courses, a lecturer, and a writer of numerous articles on the teaching of English. Sheila Y. Laws has taught English in secondary schools and college. She is a coauthor of the *Harbrace College Workbook:* Forms 6A and 6B.

SPECIAL CONTRIBUTORS: Desmond Nunan, Director of Curriculum for the West Chester Schools, West Chester, Pennyslvania has taught English for twelve years. He is the author of *Composition: Models and Exercises 7.* Francis Griffith, who holds a doctor's degree in education from Columbia University and includes in his experience advanced courses from the National University of Ireland, was for many years Chairman of English and Speech in a Brooklyn, New York, high school. Donald W. Lee, Associate Professor of English at the University of Houston, is a coauthor of the *Harbrace Vocabulary Workshop.*

ISBN 0-15-311950-0

Preface

It is the continuing conviction of the authors of the *English Grammar and Composition* series that the foremost responsibility of the English teacher is to improve his students' competence in speaking and writing. This is a demanding task, one that calls for the best tools and strategies the teacher can muster. Even the most successful teacher does not accomplish it to his complete satisfaction; certainly no textbook can guarantee to make writers out of nonwriters in a few easy steps. What an English textbook can do is provide for teacher and student the necessary materials in a convenient form.

In preparing this new edition, the authors have carefully maintained the basic character of a series which received wide acceptance in its previous editions.

The approach is always businesslike and efficient. Everything that will help the teacher to bring his students to an improved level of competence has been included; everything that will not help has been carefully excluded. The presentation is always direct and clean-cut. Uncluttered by extraneous matter—decorative art, fringe topics of the curriculum, and discursive, motivational talks to the student—the texts state clearly and exactly what the student is to learn and then provide the abundance of exercise material which is essential to his learning it. Omission of the nonessential leaves more space for the essential. Motivation is a necessary element in all good teaching, but the only truly effective motivation is that which comes from an enthusiastic and experienced teacher face-to-face with his own class. In general, motivation is left to the teacher, unencumbered by methods imposed by the text.

Texts in the series follow a unit organization. All instructional materials on a topic are placed together in the same chapter or group of chapters. They are not distributed throughout the book. For example, all instruction in verb usage is in one chapter; all punctuation rules and exercises are together in a unit of several consecutive chapters. Teachers like the unit organization because it is efficient in permitting concentration on one skill at a time, and because it simplifies the student's problem when he wishes to look up a topic on his own. This type of organization also makes the books completely flexible. With two or three necessary exceptions, the text imposes no sequence; any chapter may be taught as a separate unit without regard for what immediately precedes or follows. This flexibility assures that the books will fit any course of study, whatever its organizing principle. The clarity and conciseness of the rules and explanations are enhanced by the typography: the important rules are printed in red; the tab-keys are a reference aid.

With complete units on grammar, usage, composition, mechanics, and oral English, the books cover all important areas of language study, with the natural exceptions of reading and literature.

Grammar

The *English Grammar and Composition* series teaches traditional grammar. The English profession is beginning to feel the impact of linguistic research and to ponder the relative values of several different grammars of English. In the opinion of the authors, the concepts of these new grammars are not yet clearly enough defined for general use in the schools; insofar as a knowledge of grammar is an aid in speaking and writing, traditional grammar's view of the English sentence appears to the authors to be as useful as any other view.

There is little time in the crowded English curriculum for the teaching of grammar as an end in itself. *English*

Grammar and Composition 7 covers only that grammar which in simplicity and usefulness is appropriate to students in the seventh grade. Since in so many communities the seventh grade is the first year of junior high school, to which students bring a wide variety of educational experience, the seventh-grade teacher is wise to assume that he must start from scratch. Book 7 begins with the study of subject and predicate, then takes up the parts of speech, the prepositional phrase, and objects and subject complements. Verbals and the subordinate clause are left to grade eight. They are left out not because seventh graders never use them, but because there are more fundamental concepts that must be established first. The concentration is upon the simple sentence. The concepts and terms are those which can be applied at this level to usage and composition.

Usage

Like all books in the *English Grammar and Composition* series, Book 7 devotes a large amount of space to establishing good usage habits. Throughout the series, usage is taught in full recognition of the fact that language fashions are constantly changing, that dialects differ in different parts of the country, and that there are usage levels which reflect social and educational backgrounds. The book recognizes also, however, that at any one time there does exist a standard of usage to which the majority of educated people everywhere do conform. The attitude toward usage is sanely liberal but not so permissive as to ignore this standard. Any textbook is a selection. The criterion of selection in the entire series has been utility.

Composition

In the previous edition of Book 7, the composition section was expanded and a new chapter on the whole composition was added. The student learns the importance of careful planning even in the personal-experience theme. In this new edition of Book 7, a supplement, "Topics to Write About," has been included. Students are asked to look at cartoons and photographs that tell a story or suggest an idea and then to put these stories and ideas into words. Students are also asked to interpret information provided in charts and graphs. Thus, the student learns not only to plan a composition, but to find numerous topics by looking around him.

One learns to write through frequent practice. As he practices, the student tries to follow sound composition precepts presented in his text and to imitate the models of good writing provided for him. A general English textbook is necessarily limited, however, in the amount of space it can devote to the reproduction of models. Teachers desiring additional examples of good writing will find them in the series *Composition: Models and Exercises*, which accompanies the *English Grammar and Composition* series. *Composition: Models and Exercises 7* contains approximately 200 pages of carefully selected models, systematically arranged with appropriate analyses and writing assignments.

Mechanics

Book 7 concentrates on those punctuation rules which function in the writing of seventh graders. The basic rules for the use of capital letters are covered. The spelling chapter teaches the most useful rules, gives practice in distinguishing common homonyms, and provides a selected list of 200 spelling words, as well as 50 spelling demons—a spelling program for the year.

Speaking and Listening

Chapters on speaking and listening give the teacher material he needs for refining his students' skills in these two important areas. Both chapters emphasize good manners. Students are given concrete practice in the improvement of such daily speech activities as making social introductions, initiating and carrying on a conversation, using the telephone, and giving directions. They study how to prepare and deliver a talk. In their study of the often neglected skill of listening, they learn to listen purposefully, and critically in a variety of common listening situations.

Dictionary, Library, and Vocabulary Development

Under the general heading "Aids to Good English," these chapters provide the teacher with materials for teaching the efficient use of the dictionary and of library and reference tools. The chapter on vocabulary development shows the student how to enlarge his vocabulary through context clues, word analysis, a knowledge of common prefixes and suffixes and the study of companion forms of a word. A list of 300 vocabulary words provides a vocabulary program for the whole year.

Teaching Tests and Manual

A separate booklet of tests is available from the publisher at a small cost. Written by a teacher with extensive experience in preparing English tests, the booklet provides an easily scored test for each testable chapter in *English Grammar and Composition 7*. When kept in the teacher's possession until the class is ready for a test, these tests provide a sound basis for evaluating student achievement.

A complete *Teacher's Manual*, including a suggested course of study, teaching aids, supplementary material, and an answer key, is available upon request from the publisher.

J. W.

ACKNOWLEDGMENTS   The authors and publishers wish to acknowledge the valuable assistance given by many teachers who contributed in many ways to the preparation of this series. Special thanks are due to Mr. Henry Aronson, International School of The Hague, Netherlands; Dr. John Arscott, Coordinator, Senior Division, West Essex High School, North Caldwell, New Jersey; Mrs. Margaret R. Bonney, Lexington High School, Lexington, Massachusetts; Mrs. Louise Brock, Tuckahoe Junior High School, Richmond, Virginia; Mrs. Kenneth Brown, Hand Junior High School, Columbia, South Carolina; Mr. Lewis Browne, Myers Park High School, Charlotte, North Carolina; Mrs. Margaret Christianson, Point Loma High School, San Diego, California; Mr. W. Griffith Couser, Melrose High School, Melrose, Massachusetts; Miss Jean E. Crabtree, Garden City Senior High School, Garden City, New York; Mr. Peter Evarts, Assistant to the Director, Teacher Education Program, Oakland University, Rochester, Michigan; Miss Anna Fort, Deal Junior High School, Washington, D.C.; Mrs. Betty Gray, Abington Junior High School, Abington, Pennsylvania; Mrs. Helen Hiller, Former Chairman of English Department, Macomb's Junior High School, Bronx, New York; Mr. Robert U. Jameson, The Haverford School, Haverford, Pennsylvania; Mr. Raymond Kavanagh, Levittown Memorial High School, Levittown, New York; Mrs. Gladys Kronsagen, Glenbard Township High School, Glen Ellyn, Illinois; Miss Alice Liberto, Miami Edison Junior High School, Miami, Florida; Mrs. Archibald McClure, John Adams High School, South Bend, Indiana; Mrs. Ruth McKinney, A. C. Flora High School, Columbia, South Carolina; Miss Rita Morgan, James Madison High School, Vienna, Virginia; Miss Geraldine Oliver, Fairview High School, Dayton, Ohio; Mr. Orville Palmer, Educational Testing Service, Princeton, New Jersey; Mrs. Helen Slonin, Baldwin Junior High School, Baldwin, New York; Miss Julia Tygart, Miami Edison Junior High School, Miami, Florida; Mr. Arthur Weisbach, Summit High School, Summit, New Jersey.

Contents

PART THREE: MECHANICS

PART FOUR: SENTENCE STRUCTURE

PART FIVE: COMPOSITION

PART ONE

Grammar

CHAPTER 1

The Sentence

Subject and Predicate;
Kinds of Sentences

All people need to express their thoughts and feelings to others. Expression may take many forms other than words. For example, a smile on the face may show happiness. A shrug of the shoulders may express uncertainty. A siren indicates a fire or an accident. An arrow points out a one-way street.

Of course, the two most common forms of communication—speaking and writing—depend on words. When words are combined in a meaningful arrangement, or pattern, communication takes place. The patterns used in speaking and writing often differ. When we speak, we very often depend on gestures and facial expressions to help communicate thoughts and ideas. But when we write, we have only words and punctuation. To make ideas clear and easy to read, we must construct good sentences and punctuate them properly.

3

Look at the following groups of words spoken at one end of a telephone conversation:

> Yes.
> Sure.
> This afternoon.
> I'll bring my skates.
> Don't be late.

Although you know each word in the first three lines, you do not know exactly what is meant because in each case the thought is incomplete. Some words—those of the other speaker—are missing. The first three lines do not express complete thoughts; therefore, they are not sentences. The last two groups of words do express complete thoughts; they are sentences.

1a. A sentence is a group of words expressing a complete thought.

Here are four sentences. Notice the capital letter at the beginning of each sentence and the mark of punctuation at the end.

> Tokyo is one of the largest cities in the world.
> There are many legends about gypsies.
> Why did you miss the party?
> What amazing discoveries are being made today!

The following groups of words are not sentences because they do not express complete thoughts. Each one leaves something you need to know in order to understand what the writer means to say.

> after he adjusted his instruments and fired the rockets [Then what happened?]

because Tom made a perfect score on the test [What was the result?]

hiking across the Sahara [What about it?]

on his trip to Europe [What did he do on the trip?]

● EXERCISE 1. The following groups of words have no capital letters at the beginning and no marks of punctuation at the end. Some groups are sentences; some are not. Write the numbers 1–20 on your paper. Copy each sentence, adding a capital letter at the beginning and a mark of punctuation at the end. Write *NS* after the number of each group of words that is not a sentence. Do not write in the book.

EXAMPLES   1. a garden full of cucumber vines and weeds

1. *NS*

2. we found seven cucumbers and picked them

2. *We found seven cucumbers and picked them.*

1. my favorite ballerina danced the Swan Queen
2. in one corner of the cave
3. after winning the race, he felt tired but happy
4. the small and dainty poodle
5. the large dog with the vicious growl
6. dogs make good pets
7. leaped the hurdles easily
8. one of the seniors vaulted twelve feet
9. she skated gracefully in the center of the rink
10. they rode bicycles to school
11. entered the sack race and won it
12. when he saw the bus
13. arranging a bouquet of peonies

1a

14. although everyone could swim
15. because of the hurricane warnings
16. after a long delay the train started again
17. do you know the famous legend about Mrs. O'Leary's cow
18. according to the story the cow kicked over a lantern
19. setting fire to a barn
20. and started the great Chicago fire of 1871

● EXERCISE 2.   Ten of the following twenty groups of words are sentences although the capital letters and marks of punctuation have been purposely omitted. Write the numbers 1–20 on your paper. After each number, if the group of words is a sentence, copy it, adding a capital letter at the beginning and a mark of punctuation at the end. If the group of words is not a sentence, write *NS* after its number.

1. the Olympic games have a long history 2. held as early as 775 B.C. 3. at first they were memorial services 4. commemorating the Greeks who died during a four-year period 5. later they were used to help unite the Greek nations 6. the warring countries forgot their differences 7. when they met for the Olympic games 8. Olympia was chosen as the site for the games 9. which were held every four years 10. before the games began 11. the players made a trip to the statue of the god Zeus 12. praying for victory 13. each always added to his prayer one qualification 14. "only if I am the best" 15. after the games were finished 16. the winners offered prayers of thanks to Zeus 17. then a five-day festival followed 18. on their return home 19. each winner was treated like a great hero 20. and was given many gifts and honors

SUBJECT AND PREDICATE

Every sentence has two essential parts: a *subject* and a *predicate.*

1b. The *subject* of a sentence is that part about which something is being said.

In these sentences, the subjects are in heavy type.

> **Jane** cried.
> **The ferns in the forest** were all dry and brown.
> **Ernie Pyle** was a famous reporter in World War II.

In any sentence, you can find the subject by asking yourself who or what is doing something or about whom or what something is being said.

● EXERCISE 3.   Write the numbers 1–10 on your paper. After each number, write the subject of the sentence.

EXAMPLE   1. Mountain climbing is an exciting sport.
           1. *Mountain climbing*

1. Mount Everest is the highest mountain in the world.
2. Many men enjoy mountain climbing.
3. Falling rocks present a danger to climbers.
4. Snow avalanches are also dreaded by climbers.
5. Expeditions often attempt to scale Mount McKinley in Alaska.
6. Some great mountain peaks contain volcanoes.
7. The lava from a volcano is very dangerous.
8. The seeming quietness of a volcano crater is misleading.

1b

9. One volcano in Japan was silent for more than a thousand years.
10. A gigantic outburst occurred in 1888.

The subject does not always come at the beginning of a sentence—it may be in the middle or at the end. Notice the position of the subjects in the following sentences.

> Did **the pitcher** strike him out?
>
> After practicing for hours, **Timmy** bowled a strike.
>
> For centuries **the earth** was thought to be the center of the universe.
>
> Hiding in the tall grass was **a frightened rabbit.**
>
> Have **you** called your mother yet?

● EXERCISE 4. Write the numbers 1–10 on your paper. After each number, write the subject of the sentence.

1. Many stories have been written about Paul Bunyan.
2. In his North Woods one winter a blue snow fell.
3. The animals of the forest fled even farther north.
4. Because of the extreme cold, some bears became polar bears.
5. During the storm Paul discovered a blue calf.
6. The big woodsman nursed the calf back to health.
7. Soon the calf grew to be very large.
8. Its horns were forty-two ax handles and a plug of chewing tobacco apart.
9. Linked forever with Paul Bunyan was Babe, his Blue Ox.
10. With Babe's help Paul Bunyan became the greatest logger of all time.

● EXERCISE 5. Write the numbers 1–10 on your paper. Make sentences out of the following groups of words by adding subjects where there are blanks. Remember to begin each sentence with a capital and end it with a mark of punctuation. Do not write in the book.

EXAMPLE 1. —— circled the lake.
      1. *Two large birds circled the lake.*

1. Probably —— are hunting for hazel nuts.
2. —— carelessly rocked the boat back and forth.
3. —— performed in the center ring at the circus.
4. By the next day —— had returned to normal.
5. Into the water dived ——.
6. Have —— returned from Chicago?
7. On television last night —— saw an interview with the governor.
8. —— was heard in the distance.
9. Suddenly —— appeared in the sky.
10. At the stroke of twelve up rose ——.

Complete Subject and Simple Subject

The part of the sentence that you have been writing is called the *complete subject*. Among the words of the complete subject, there is always a main word. This main word is called the *simple subject*.

1c. The *simple subject* is the main word in the complete subject.

EXAMPLE The four new students arrived early.
Complete subject   The four new students
Simple subject   students

1c

EXAMPLE   A round walnut table with drop leaves
stood in the middle of the dining room.

Complete subject   A round walnut table with drop
leaves
Simple subject   table

Note that the key, or main, word of the subject (*students*, *table*) cannot be omitted. Without this word the sentences do not make sense.

The four new . . . arrived early.
A round walnut . . . with drop leaves stood in
the middle of the dining room.

● EXERCISE 6.   Write the numbers 1–10 on your paper. Copy the complete subject of each sentence. Then underline the simple subject. Remember that the subject of a sentence may come at the beginning, in the middle, or at the end of the sentence.

1. A typical five-year-old child is sometimes out-reasoned by a chimpanzee.
2. The average chimp can easily be taught to eat with a fork.
3. The friendly chimp enjoys a meal at a table.
4. In the middle of the meal, the playful rascal may put his feet on the table.
5. No self-respecting chimpanzee enjoys a cage.
6. Unexpected jailbreaks have been carried out by chimps.
7. One very cunning female dug a tunnel under the walls of her cage.
8. This particular operation required hours of patient toil.
9. The work had to be done without attracting attention.
10. Hidden in the chimp's mind are many such tricks.

Sometimes when the subject is very short, the simple and the complete subject are the same.

EXAMPLES   **Jets** break the sound barrier.

Uncle Ben owns a hardware store.

The Last of the Mohicans is a novel by James Fenimore Cooper. [*The Last of the Mohicans* is the title of a book; therefore, all the words make up the simple subject; they are also the complete subject.]

From now on in this book, the term *subject* will mean "simple subject," unless otherwise indicated.

● **EXERCISE 7.** Write the numbers 1–10 on your paper. Copy the complete subject of each sentence. Then underline the simple subject.

1. H. G. Wells was a writer of history and fiction.
2. *The Time Machine* is one of his best books.
3. The main character in that book is called the Time Traveler.
4. He journeys into the future to the year 802,701.
5. In that distant year this imaginary traveler meets two kinds of creatures.
6. One kind dwells above ground.
7. These people live peaceful but unproductive lives.
8. The other creatures live below the earth's surface.
9. Because of their dark surroundings, this second group cannot bear any light to strike their eyes.
10. These apelike creatures work machinery underground to support the dwellers of the upper world.

● **EXERCISE 8.** Write five sentences about school, your family, or your favorite sport. Underline the simple subject of each sentence. Try to make some of your subjects come in the middle or at the end of your sentences.

The Predicate

Predicate comes from a Latin word meaning "to proclaim." Thus, a predicate proclaims, or says, something about the subject.

1d. The *predicate* of a sentence is that part which says something about the subject.

In these sentences the predicates are in heavy type.

> Old Faithful **is a giant geyser in Yellowstone National Park.**
> The roller coaster **sped up and down the hills of the track.**
> Bert's father **took us bowling yesterday.**
> The hot sun **blistered the berry pickers.**

The predicate in the first sentence, *is a giant geyser in Yellowstone National Park,* says something about the subject, *Old Faithful.* In the second sentence, *sped up and down the hills of the track* tells what the subject, *roller coaster,* did. You can see that the predicates in the other sentences also tell something about their subjects.

● EXERCISE 9. Write the numbers 1–10 on your paper, and copy the predicates from the following sentences.

EXAMPLE   1. Greek myths are very interesting.
           1. *are very interesting.*

1. The Greeks worshiped many gods and goddesses.
2. Stories of Greek heroes have been passed down through the centuries.
3. Hercules was one of the most famous Greek heroes.

4. He possessed unbelievable strength.
5. The eight-month-old Hercules strangled two large serpents.
6. Hercules is famous for his twelve great labors.
7. He slew a serpentlike creature with nine heads.
8. Another labor was the cleaning of the Augean stables.
9. These stables had not been cleaned for thirty years.
10. Hercules channeled two rivers through the stables.

Just as the subject does not always come at the beginning of the sentence, so the predicate does not always come at the end. When the subject comes in the middle of the sentence, a part of the predicate usually stands before it; when the subject comes at the end of the sentence, the whole predicate stands before it.

Notice the positions of the predicates in the sentences below.

> **Late in the night we heard a noise.**
> **Quickly we jumped to our feet.**
> **Outside the tent was a baby bear.**

● EXERCISE 10. Write the numbers 1–10 on your paper and copy the predicates from the following sentences. Remember that a part or all of the predicate may come before the subject.

1. Have you read "The Ransom of Red Chief" by O. Henry?
2. A mischievous boy appears in this story.
3. The boy calls himself Red Chief.
4. One day he is kidnaped by two men.
5. Soon the kidnapers regret their deed.
6. The boy plays a number of tricks on the kidnapers.
7. For hours they defend themselves against the boy's pranks.

1d

8. The kidnapers finally receive an answer to their ransom note.
9. They must pay the father two hundred and fifty dollars.
10. For that amount the father will take the boy off their hands.

● EXERCISE 11.   To each of the following subjects, add a predicate to fill the blank or blanks marked. Write the complete sentence on your paper.

EXAMPLES   1. The tides of the oceans ——.
   1. *The tides of the oceans are influenced by the moon.*

   2. —— we ——.
   2. *One day we visited a planetarium.*

1. My favorite television show ——.
2. The path in the woods ——.
3. Finger painting ——.
4. A powerful locomotive ——.
5. The Buzzell twins ——.
6. —— our television set ——.
7. Five sailboats ——.
8. —— the little bay pony ——.
9. A four-leaf clover ——.
10. The skyline of Chicago ——.

The Simple Predicate

The predicates you have been studying are called *complete predicates*. Each complete predicate contains a *simple predicate*, which is the main word in the predicate. The simple predicate is the *verb* of the sentence.

1e. The *simple predicate*, or *verb*, is the main word or group of words in the complete predicate.

EXAMPLE   The pilot broke the sound barrier.
Complete predicate   broke the sound barrier.
Simple predicate (*verb*)   broke

EXAMPLE   Arkansas has the only diamond field in the United States.
Complete predicate   has the only diamond field in the United States.
Simple predicate (*verb*)   has

Look at the following sentences. The complete predicates are underlined, and the simple predicates (verbs) are in heavy type.

The dinosaur **is** a prehistoric animal.

The puppy **walked** across the sofa with muddy feet.

Terry **found** two birds' nests in the hedge.

The city of Washington **has** many monuments.

The simple predicate is always a verb. In this book, we will usually refer to the simple predicate as the *verb*.

● EXERCISE 12.   Copy the complete predicate of each sentence. Then underline the verb.

EXAMPLE   1. The pyramids of Egypt are among the Seven Wonders of the Ancient World.
    1. *are among the Seven Wonders of the Ancient World.*

1e

1. The ancient Egyptians worshiped their rulers, the Pharaohs.
2. They built great pyramids for the Pharaohs.
3. The pyramids supposedly preserved the Pharaohs for the afterlife.
4. Several pyramids still stand today.
5. They have many passageways.
6. One pyramid near Cairo covers almost thirteen acres.
7. Archaeologists search the pyramids.
8. They discover much about ancient Egyptian life.
9. The pyramids show the engineering skill of the Egyptians.
10. The Egyptians painted scenes of their daily life on the walls of the pyramids.

The Verb Phrase

Some verbs consist of more than one word. Even so, these verbs are still the simple predicate of a sentence. When a verb is made up of more than one word, it is called a *verb phrase*. Notice the verb phrases in these sentences.

> Kathy **is riding** the Ferris wheel.
> The carnival **has been** in town for two weeks.
> Kathy's brother **should be** here somewhere.

● EXERCISE 13.　Copy the verb or verb phrase from each of the following sentences.

1. Alaska became the forty-ninth state of the Union.
2. It was admitted to the Union in 1959.
3. Alaska is two and one-fifth times the size of Texas.
4. Statehood brought some new problems to the people of Alaska.

5. Tourists can drive to Alaska along the Alcan Highway.
6. Thousands of gold prospectors rushed to Alaska between 1897 and 1899.
7. Many of them died from exposure.
8. Others were forced into trading or farming.
9. The people of Alaska must endure extremely cold temperatures.
10. The weather during an Alaskan summer may be hot.

● EXERCISE 14. Write ten original sentences using these verbs or verb phrases.

1. roars
2. learned
3. was dancing
4. will need
5. begs
6. poked
7. demands
8. have been warned
9. shuddered
10. has teased

Finding the Subject

You have probably found that in some sentences it is easy to identify the subject at once. By now you should have no difficulty in locating the subject in these sentences:

The **movers** arrived early Saturday morning.
The math **test** was easy.

In other sentences, however, you may have trouble in locating the subject. Sometimes it is a help to find the verb first and then to ask yourself, "Who ——?" or "What ——?" Study the following examples:

In high school we will have more homework than ever.

What is the verb? Clearly, it is *will have*. Ask yourself, "Who will have?" The answer is *we*. *We* is the subject of the sentence.

Can you untie this knot?

What words in this sentence express action? *Can untie*, of course; *can untie* is the verb. Ask, "Who can untie?" *You* is the answer, and *you* is the subject of the sentence.

The peak of Mount Everest was first reached by a British party.

The verb in this sentence is not difficult to identify: *was reached*. "What was reached?" The answer is *the peak*. *Peak* is the subject of the sentence. If you thought that *Mount Everest* might be the subject, you will see the value of first finding the verb and then asking yourself, "What ——?" The answer to that question is always the subject. If you use this method, you will not be misled by other words in the sentence that look as if they might be the subject.

Diagraming Subjects and Predicates

One good way of showing that you know the parts of a sentence is to use a diagram. The diagram of a sentence is really a picture of its structure. It shows how the subject and verb fit together.

A sentence diagram begins with a straight horizontal line, divided by a short vertical line. The horizontal line is for the main parts of the sentence—the subject and verb. The vertical line separates the subject and the predicate. In making a diagram you keep the capital letters but omit the punctuation marks.

PATTERN

subject	predicate

EXAMPLES   Horses gallop.   Men think.

Horses	gallop

Men	think

Examples such as these are easy because the sentences each contain only a simple subject and a verb. Let us look at a longer sentence.

Many countries cooperate in the scientific investigation of space.

To diagram the subject and predicate of this sentence, take three steps: (1) Separate the complete subject from the complete predicate. (2) Find the simple subject and the verb. (3) Draw the diagram.

	complete subject	*complete predicate*
Step 1	Many countries	cooperate in the scientific investigation of space.

	simple subject	*simple predicate* (*verb*)
Step 2	countries	cooperate

Step 3

countries	cooperate

Following the same steps, we can diagram the simple subjects and the verbs of the following sentences.

1. Roger Maris hit sixty-one home runs in one season.

Roger Maris	hit

2. America was named for Amerigo Vespucci.

America	was named

Think of the horizontal line as the base of the sentence, holding the main words—the simple subject and the verb. The vertical line divides the sentence into its two main parts—subject and predicate.

● EXERCISE 15.   Find the simple subject and the verb in each of the following sentences. Then make a sentence diagram of the simple subject and the verb. Use your ruler for the lines. Leave plenty of space between diagrams.

EXAMPLE   1. Hot weather came early this year.

1.

weather	came

1. Some people have strange pets.
2. In city apartments, small pets are popular.
3. However, some large dogs live in cities.
4. They walk quietly along the crowded streets.
5. A Great Dane on the sidewalk may startle pedestrians.
6. Some children like hamsters as pets.
7. Wild creatures may be trained for domestic life.
8. Farm families often have a variety of animals about the place.
9. At some time in his life, nearly every youngster wants a pony.
10. A quiet, untroublesome pet is the goldfish.

Questions may seem more difficult to diagram. However, if you look carefully for the subject and verb, you will have no trouble. Remember that in a question a part of the predicate comes before the subject. Notice this question, for example:

Are you going to the banquet?

Make the question into a declarative sentence.

You are going to the banquet.

You will recognize *are going* as the verb. To find the subject, ask "Who?" The answer is *you*.

In a diagram the subject always comes first on the horizontal line.

you	Are going

● EXERCISE 16. Diagram the simple subject and verb in each of the following sentences. Use your ruler and allow plenty of space between diagrams.

1. Have you visited a wax museum?
2. The figures seem almost alive.
3. Can you imagine a house full of life-size wax "people"?
4. For many years England has specialized in wax museums.
5. Many monarchs of the past have been re-created in wax.
6. Famous criminals have been shown at the scenes of their crimes.
7. Each wax figure has real hair.
8. Even the wrinkles on the face are in the right places.
9. How can a lifeless dummy look so realistic?
10. Museum visitors repeatedly ask that question.

COMPOUND SUBJECTS AND PREDICATES

Often we wish to show that two or more subjects are performing the same action or that the same subject is doing two or more things. To do this, we connect subjects or verbs with words like *and* or *or*. Subjects or verbs connected in this way are said to be *compound*.

Compound Subjects

1f. A *compound subject* consists of two or more connected subjects that have the same verb. The usual connecting words are *and* and *or*.

EXAMPLES   **Paris** and **London** are favorite tourist attractions. [The two parts of the compound subject have the same verb, *are*.]

Costumes, makeup, scenery, and **props** are needed for the production of a play. [The four parts of the compound subject have the same verb phrase, *are needed*.]

Miss Ellis or **Mr. Schwartz** will go on the field trip with us. [The two parts of the compound subject have the same verb phrase, *will go*.]

● EXERCISE 17.   Copy the compound subjects from the following sentences. Watch for subjects in the middle or at the end of sentences.

EXAMPLE   1. The pilot and the navigator are in the cockpit.
1. *pilot, navigator*

1. Bob and Brenda were flying for the first time.
2. Their mother and father took them to the airport.

3. The stewardesses and the pilots spoke to the youngsters.
4. Bob, Brenda, and the other passengers were soon ready for the takeoff.
5. The preparations and instructions for takeoff were new to Bob and Brenda.
6. Blue sky and billowy clouds filled their window for a while.
7. On the ground below, the houses and cars looked like miniatures.
8. A good meal and interesting magazines kept them busy.
9. Soon, however, the reduced speed and the lower altitude signaled preparations for landing.
10. The children's aunt and uncle met them at the airport.

● EXERCISE 18. Make sentences by adding compound subjects to these predicates. Write the complete sentence on your paper. Use *and* or *or* to join the parts of your compound subjects.

1. —— are competing in the race.
2. —— amused the audience.
3. —— make good pets.
4. —— planned the hayride.
5. Yesterday —— sailed into the harbor.
6. —— are fun to collect.
7. Staring at us through the window were ——.
8. At the ocean —— found a starfish.
9. —— can water-ski on one ski.
10. In the attic —— were piled.

Compound Verbs

Just as a sentence may have a compound subject, so it may have a *compound verb*. When two or more verbs

1f

or verb phrases are joined by *and, or, nor,* or *but,* the combination is called a *compound verb.*

1g. A *compound verb* consists of two or more connected verbs that have the same subject.

EXAMPLES   That dog either **barked** or **whined** all night.

Bill **pitched** well but **lost** the game.

The rain **has fallen** for days and **is flooding** the low areas.

A sentence may have both a *compound subject* and a *compound verb.*

EXAMPLES   A few **vegetables** and many **flowers sprouted** and **grew** in the rich soil.

Pam and **Sue bought** peanuts and **fed** the bears.

Note that in such sentences both subjects carry out the action of both verbs.

● EXERCISE 19.   Copy the verbs and verb phrases from the following sentences.

EXAMPLE   1. The Trojan War was fought in Troy and lasted ten years.
1. *was fought, lasted*

1. Ulysses left his homeland and helped the Greeks in the Trojan War.
2. Ulysses was a crafty leader.
3. He built the Trojan horse and hid soldiers in the wooden structure.
4. The Greeks won the war and destroyed the city of Troy.

5. For twenty years Ulysses fought in Troy or wandered over the seas.
6. During one adventure his men ate the lotus plant and refused to leave the island.
7. The lotus has been called a plant of forgetfulness.
8. The men forgot their homes and former lives.
9. Finally, Ulysses dragged his men to the ship and tied them to the deck.
10. In a later adventure Ulysses and his men blinded a one-eyed giant and barely escaped from the giant's island.

● EXERCISE 20. Make sentences by adding compound verbs to these subjects. Try to use some compound verb phrases. Write the complete sentence.

1. The trained seal ——.
2. At the fair we ——.
3. The doctor ——.
4. Last week my next-door neighbor ——.
5. The birds ——.

● EXERCISE 21. Make two columns on your paper, headed *Subject* and *Verb*. After the number of each sentence write its subject and verb in the proper columns. Some of the subjects and verbs are compound.

1. Ponce de Leon discovered and named Florida.
2. The Rockies and the Appalachians are two great mountain chains.
3. Many sportsmen hunt and fish in Colorado.
4. Many famous racehorses have been raised or trained in Kentucky.
5. Each year many people rush to New Orleans for Mardi Gras.
6. The bright lights and tall buildings of New York City thrill and delight tourists.

1g

7. Boiling springs, mud volcanoes, and petrified forests can be found in Yellowstone National Park.
8. The Carlsbad Caverns are located in New Mexico and have the largest natural cave room in the world.
9. *Kansas* comes from a Sioux Indian word and means "south wind people."
10. An education in colonial history awaits the visitor to New England.

Diagraming Compound Subjects and Verbs

To diagram a compound subject, you place the subjects on parallel lines. Notice that the connecting word is put on a dotted line between the parallel subject lines.

EXAMPLE   Sharks and eels are dangerous.

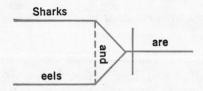

A compound predicate is diagramed in a similar way. The two verbs go on parallel lines with the connecting word on a dotted line between them.

EXAMPLE   The cowboy swung into the saddle and rode away.

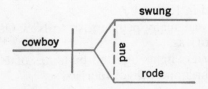

A sentence with both a compound subject and a compound verb combines the two patterns.

EXAMPLE Paul Revere and William Dawes saw the lantern in North Church and warned the Americans of the approach of the British troops.

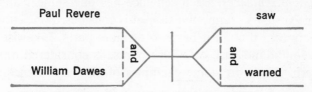

● EXERCISE 22.   Diagram the subjects and verbs in the following sentences. Many of them are compound. Use your ruler and leave plenty of space between diagrams.

1. Everyone knows and loves the bears at the zoo.
2. Cubs and adults entertain the onlookers.
3. They stand on their hind legs and beg appealingly for peanuts.
4. The koala is a native of Australia and looks like a teddy bear.
5. This little bear measures about two feet long and has large, hairy ears and gray fur.
6. Some bears are extremely large and can be vicious.
7. The polar bear may stand fourteen feet tall and can kill a human being with a slap of his great paw.
8. Visitors should not taunt or mistreat the animals at the zoo.
9. Signs and guides plainly warn visitors of the danger.
10. Some children and adults disregard the warning and later find themselves in trouble.

SIMPLE AND COMPOUND SENTENCES

1h. A *simple sentence* is a sentence that has one subject and one verb.

The sentences you have been studying so far are *simple sentences*. Each sentence has one subject and one verb. (A compound subject is considered one subject, even though it has two or more parts. Likewise, a compound verb or a verb phrase is considered one verb.) Here are some examples of simple sentences:

> A good, soaking rain would help the farmers.

> Hank and Larry are the best players on the junior varsity team.

> Susan read *Johnny Tremain* and reported on it last week.

1i. A *compound sentence* is a sentence that contains two or more simple sentences, usually joined by a connecting word.

When two or more simple sentences are joined into one sentence, they form a compound sentence. The words *and, but, or, nor, for,* and *yet* are used to combine simple sentences into a compound sentence. Here are some examples:

> In the last fifty years man has conquered many contagious diseases, **but** the common cold persists.

> Citrus fruits and green vegetables should be a part of everyone's diet, **for** they supply needed vitamins.

Mrs. Norell called the children to supper, **but** John refused to leave the ball game, **and** Nancy didn't hear.

● EXERCISE 23. Write the numbers 1–10 on your paper. Read the following sentences carefully. If a sentence is simple, write *simple* after its number. If it is compound, write *compound* after its number. Be prepared to explain your answers.

1. Evelyn ordered a strawberry soda, and her mother had a cup of coffee.
2. The pine tree is native to many parts of America.
3. Seals and porpoises are great performers.
4. The farmers worked all night, but the rain still destroyed some of the wheat crop.
5. In Europe students attend high schools voluntarily, and they usually pay admission fees.
6. *Circus* comes from a Greek word and originally meant "ring" or "circle."
7. William McKinley, James Garfield, Abraham Lincoln, and John Kennedy were assassinated while in office.
8. To the east of the United States is Europe, and to the west is Asia.
9. Keith and Dick did not join the gang or sign the petition.
10. Did you read the book or see the movie?

Diagraming Compound Sentences

Learning to diagram a compound sentence may help you to see how its parts are related. The diagram of a compound sentence is like the diagrams of two simple sentences put together.

The first step is to find the subject and verb in each part of the compound sentence. Then make a diagram

1
h-i

for the first part of the sentence. Write the subject and the verb on the horizontal line with a vertical line between them. Below that diagram, make a diagram for the second part of the compound sentence. Join the two diagrams by a dotted line drawn from the verb in the first part to the verb in the second part. On the dotted line, write the word that connects the two parts.

EXAMPLE   Crocodiles look slow, but they can move swiftly.

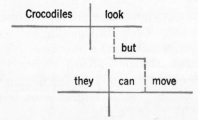

● EXERCISE 24.   Diagram the subjects and verbs in the following compound sentences. First diagram the two parts; then join the verbs with a dotted line on which you write the connecting word.

1. Tony collects foreign stamps, and Louise is starting a shell collection.
2. Napoleon was a brilliant general, but he made several costly mistakes.
3. The President of the United States is elected for a four-year period, and he may serve only two terms.
4. In the bottom of the trunk was a faded ball gown, and on top of the dress were pictures of my grandmother as a young girl.
5. Is history still your favorite subject, or do you prefer science this year?

6. The giraffe has a long neck and legs, but it is a very graceful animal.
7. Two problems remained, and I did both of them in a hurry.
8. The older Thompson boy became a marine biologist, and the younger one is in television.
9. Miss Bonnard always speaks French in class, and her third-graders are soon speaking French too.
10. Shall I answer, or will you?

CLASSIFYING SENTENCES BY PURPOSE

The following examples illustrate the main kinds of sentences: those that make statements, those that give orders or make requests, those that ask questions, and those that express strong feeling. Sentences may be classified according to these purposes.

> A storm warning has been issued. [a statement]
> Get into the storm cellar. [an order]
> Are you afraid of the storm? [a question]
> Here comes the tornado! [an expression of excitement]

1j. Sentences may be classified according to their purpose.

(1) A *declarative sentence* is a sentence that makes a statement.

EXAMPLES   Our school colors are purple and gold.
            We will learn a new cheer tomorrow.

A declarative sentence makes a statement. It is used more frequently than all of the other kinds combined. It is always followed by a period.

1j

(2) An *imperative sentence* is a sentence that gives a command or makes a request.

EXAMPLES   Be quiet during the play.

Please give me another piece of melon.

Don't miss the bus!

An imperative sentence may be followed by a period or an exclamation point. Ordinary requests take a period. Commands and strong requests take an exclamation point.

The subject of a sentence that is a command or a request is the word *you*, understood but not expressed. The first sentence means: *You* be quiet during the play. The second means: *You* please give me another piece of melon. The understood *you* may refer to one person or to a group of persons.

Sometimes an imperative sentence consists of only one word, as in the following:

Stop! [The subject *you* is understood.]

Hurry! [The subject *you* is understood.]

The word *you* is still the understood subject when the person spoken to is addressed by name, as in:

Mary, [you] please answer the door.

(3) An *interrogative sentence* is a sentence that asks a question.

EXAMPLES   What time does the next plane for San Francisco leave?

How much did the skates cost?

An interrogative sentence is always followed by a question mark. Notice that in an interrogative sentence a part of the verb always comes before the subject.

(4) An *exclamatory sentence* is a sentence that expresses strong feeling. It exclaims.

EXAMPLES   Imagine the look on his face when he won first prize!

How terrifying that movie was!

An exclamatory sentence is always followed by an exclamation point.

● EXERCISE 25.   Decide whether the following quotations are declarative, imperative, interrogative, or exclamatory sentences. Write the numbers 1–10 on your paper. After each number write the kind of sentence it is. (Be careful of the spelling of declar*a*tive, imper*a*tive, interrog*a*tive, and exclam*a*tory: notice the *a* before the *t* in each word.) Then write the proper mark of punctuation to follow the sentence.

EXAMPLE   1. If Winter comes, can Spring be far behind—SHELLEY

1. *Interrogative ?*

1. Kindness gives birth to kindness—SOPHOCLES
2. Take time for all things—FRANKLIN
3. Where are the snows of yesteryear—VILLON
4. Genius is one percent inspiration and ninety-nine percent perspiration—EDISON
5. What a piece of work is man—SHAKESPEARE
6. Seize the present day—HORACE
7. What greater or better gift can we offer the republic than to teach and instruct our youth

—CICERO
8. The only way to have a friend is to be one

—EMERSON
9. A useless life is an early death—GOETHE
10. Keep true to the dreams of thy youth—SCHILLER

● REVIEW EXERCISE A.   Some of the following groups of words are sentences; some are not. Copy the groups of words which are sentences, adding capital letters and punctuation marks. If a group of words is not a sentence, add whatever is needed (subject or verb or both) to make a sentence.

EXAMPLES   1. the students read English ballads
1. *The students read English ballads.*
2. over the glowing coals
2. *We toasted marshmallows over the glow-ing coals.*

1. wrapped the presents and put them under the tree
2. the snow fell for two days
3. just before the game
4. the boys skiing down the mountain
5. how happy the dog was to see his master again
6. a detective story keeps you guessing until the end
7. do you know the distance from the earth to the sun
8. draw a picture of a castle
9. hanging almost stationary in the sky
10. about half a mile below Niagara Falls is a great whirlpool

● REVIEW EXERCISE B. Copy the following sentences. Underline the complete subjects with one line and the complete predicates with two lines. Circle the simple subjects and verbs. If your teacher prefers, diagram the simple subjects and verbs.

1. Switzerland is the most mountainous country in Europe.
2. The Alps have about seventy peaks.
3. Can you name a famous Swiss lake?
4. The Rhine and Danube originate in Switzerland.

5. The country produces much machinery and manu-factures more than half of the world's watches.
6. Salt is the principal mineral.
7. Large amounts of chocolate and cheese are ex-ported from Switzerland.
8. Switzerland is a republic and is governed by a Federal Council of seven members.
9. One member serves as president for a one-year term.
10. In Switzerland dialects of German are spoken by most of the people, but French and Italian are also spoken.

● REVIEW EXERCISE C. Some of the following sen-tences are simple; others are compound. After each number on your paper, write *S* if the sentence is simple or *C* if it is compound. Then write the simple subjects and verbs.

EXAMPLE   1. Golf is a popular sport in Scotland.
          1. *S Golf is*

1. Several excellent golf courses in Scotland attract golfers from all over the world.
2. The rugged terrain is a challenge to the golfer's skill, and the Scots accept the challenge enthusi-astically.
3. They even play golf in cow pastures, and occasion-ally they must chase cows out of the way.
4. We think of cricket as a characteristic game of England.
5. Cricket is a little like baseball, but it is slower.
6. Cricket games are interrupted by an interval for tea, and then the play resumes.
7. Rugby, another popular British game, resembles football.

8. Have you ever watched a game of jai alai?
9. It is a game of Spanish origin and is played on an indoor court.
10. Several countries around the world have acquired America's interest in baseball.

● REVIEW EXERCISE D.   The following sentences are declarative, interrogative, imperative, or exclamatory. Copy each sentence, adding the appropriate mark of punctuation at the end. Then underline the simple subject once and underline the verb twice in each sentence. If the subject is *you* understood, add it in parentheses.

1. Flowers and insects depend on each other for life
2. Have you ever watched a bee in a garden
3. The bee flies from one blossom to another
4. Notice the pollen on his wings and body
5. He is carrying pollen from one flower to another
6. What a remarkable process pollenization is
7. Think of other ways of pollenization
8. Could the wind do it
9. Pollen of corn plants is transported by the wind
10. How many food products come from a tiny grain of pollen

CHAPTER 2

The Parts of Speech

Noun, Pronoun, Adjective

Words, which are the building blocks of language, are used in eight different ways. They have, therefore, eight different names, called *parts of speech*. These parts of speech are noun, pronoun, adjective, verb, adverb, preposition, conjunction, and interjection. In this chapter and the next one you will discover two things about each part of speech: what it is and how it is used.

THE NOUN

Look around your classroom and name the things that you see. All the objects that you have named are nouns. Many things which you associate with your classroom but which you cannot see or touch are also nouns: *interest, thought, education, instruction, cooperation.* A noun is the *name* of something, something which you may or may not be able to see or touch.

2a. A noun is a word that names a person, place, thing, or idea.

Persons	Mother, Dan, Tarzan, Mayor Dawson, teacher, brother, woman
Places	Grand Canyon, city, Nevada, kitchen
Things	train, lamp, canary, year, bread
Ideas	grief, desire, democracy, speed, bravery

● EXERCISE 1. There are twenty nouns in the following paragraph. Make a list of them on your paper. Before each noun, write the number of the sentence.

1. The *Titanic* was supposed to be an unsinkable ship. 2. The captain and the crew had great confidence in her strength. 3. The passengers, too, were convinced that the vessel was indestructible. 4. Then the liner struck an iceberg off the coast of Newfoundland. 5. About fifteen hundred persons drowned because few lifeboats had been provided. 6. Only the children, the women, and a small group of men were saved. 7. The whole world was shocked by this senseless tragedy.

● EXERCISE 2. There are twenty-five nouns in the following paragraph. Make a list of them on your paper. Before each noun, write the number of the sentence. Some nouns will be listed more than once.

1. Beowulf is a great hero of Old English literature. 2. When the king of a neighboring land needed aid, Beowulf accepted the challenge. 3. A giant named Grendel was terrifying the kingdom. 4. The monster would strike in the night, and each time would eat several men. 5. Beowulf met Grendel without any weapons. 6. With his superior strength the great warrior tore off the arm of the fiend. 7. The news of his accomplishment spread throughout the country.

Proper Nouns and Common Nouns

You may have noticed that some of the nouns you have been identifying begin with a capital letter. These are called *proper nouns*. Nouns that do not begin with a capital are called *common nouns*. A proper noun names a particular person, place, or thing. Here are some examples of proper nouns:

Persons Mr. Frankel, Alan Shepherd, Rita, Uncle Fred
Places Kansas City, Idaho, Egypt, Australia
Things Eiffel Tower, Old Faithful, Jupiter

A common noun does *not* name a particular person, place, or thing. These are common nouns:

Persons child, teacher, movie star, uncle
Places town, meadow, street, valley, gym
Things book, airplane, scissors, typewriter, shed
Ideas friendship, consideration, justice, anger

Proper nouns are always capitalized. Study the following lists of common and proper nouns until you are sure you understand why each word is classed as it is.

COMMON NOUNS	PROPER NOUNS
document	Bill of Rights
mayor	Mayor Hudson
boy	Ralph O'Neill
desert	Sahara
country	Venezuela
people	Finns

Nouns of more than one word, like *White House*, *living room*, or *Colorado River*, are considered one noun.

2a

● EXERCISE 3. List the twenty-five nouns in the following paragraph. Before each noun, write the number of the sentence. After each noun, write *C* if it is common or *P* if it is proper.

1. Early one morning Charles A. Lindbergh left Roosevelt Field in New York in his plane, the *Spirit of St. Louis*. 2. Lindbergh was attempting a nonstop flight to Paris. 3. The pilot was in the air for about thirty-three hours. 4. The plane flew through rain and fog. 5. Lindbergh finally reached the designated landing field in Paris. 6. The whole world celebrated his heroic achievement. 7. On his return to the United States aboard a cruiser, the young hero was welcomed by President Calvin Coolidge.

● EXERCISE 4. Rewrite the following sentences, substituting proper nouns for all common nouns. You may need to change some of the words which precede the noun.

EXAMPLE 1. An ambassador visited a local school and spoke about his country.

1. *Ambassador Rios visited Jackson High School and spoke about Brazil.*

1. Two boys water-skied on the lake.
2. The doctor turned right at the street beyond the department store.
3. The twins, who are from a large city, are vacationing near a lake.
4. A teacher asked a student to report on a country.
5. The architect says the building will be completed next month.
6. Our school newspaper comes out in three days.
7. The girl bought a book at the bookstore.

8. That state borders on the ocean.
9. The principal of our school toured two European countries during a summer month.
10. A man flew to a Southern city one day.

● REVIEW EXERCISE A.   The following paragraph contains twenty-five nouns, some common and some proper. List them on your paper, writing the number of the sentence before each. Capitalize all proper nouns. Some nouns will be listed more than once.

1. Tom sawyer and huckleberry finn, the chief characters in a novel by Mark Twain, have many adventures together. 2. The boys live in st. petersburg, missouri, a town on the mississippi. 3. On one occasion the two boys run off to an island and pretend to be pirates. 4. The people in their hometown think that the youngsters have been killed. 5. While their funerals are being held, tom and huck march into the church. 6. Naturally, the young scamps enjoy their trick on the mourners.

● REVIEW EXERCISE B.   Have you a keen imagination? By filling the blanks in the following paragraph with various nouns, you can produce a story. In fact, with different sets of nouns, you could make a number of different stories. Copy the paragraph, filling in the blanks with either common or proper nouns.

We were in the —— when the —— occurred. We were frightened by the —— and the ——. Finally, a —— advised us to try to get to ——. By the time we reached ——, we were so exhausted that we headed for the ——. But we could never forget the —— of the terrifying ——.

THE PRONOUN

Study the following sentences:

> When Ted met Lorraine, Ted noticed that Lorraine was carrying several books. Ted offered to help Lorraine. Lorraine thanked Ted.

> When Ted met Lorraine, **he** noticed that **she** was carrying several books. **He** offered to help **her.** Lorraine thanked **him.**

The words in heavy type take the place of the nouns *Ted* and *Lorraine*. These words are *pronouns. Pro* means "for"; a pronoun is a word used for, or in place of, a noun.

2b. A pronoun is a word used in place of a noun. It may stand for a person, place, thing, or idea.

The pronoun gives a noun a rest. Can you tell which noun each pronoun in the following sentences replaces?

> After Lois borrowed the book, **she** found **it** had not been assigned by the teacher.

> Dan, have **you** seen the new skating rink?

> Esther poured another glass of milk and drank **it.** Then **she** helped **herself** to an apple.

Personal Pronouns

There are several kinds of pronouns. The ones you will be studying in this chapter are *personal* pronouns. These are the personal pronouns:[1]

---

[1] Words like *my* and *his* (possessive forms of the pronouns *I* and *he*) are called pronouns throughout this book. Some teachers, however, prefer to think of possessive pronouns as adjectives. Follow your teacher's direction in labeling these words.

I, me, my, mine
you, your, yours
he, him, his
she, her, hers
it, its
we, us, our, ours
they, them, their, theirs

Some of the personal pronouns in the preceding list can be combined with *–self* or *–selves:*

Be careful not to cut *yourself.*
I will do it *myself.*

A pronoun combined with *–self* or *–selves* is still a pronoun.

Some other kinds of pronouns, which you will study later, are *indefinite, interrogative,* and *demonstrative.*

INDEFINITE PRONOUNS	INTERROGATIVE PRONOUNS	DEMONSTRATIVE PRONOUNS
anybody	who	this
each	whom	that
either	what	these
none	which	those
someone, etc.	whose	

● EXERCISE 5. Write the numbers 1–10 on your paper. After each number, copy the pronouns in the sentence, writing after each the noun or nouns that the pronoun stands for.

1. "I can tell you which chapters the quiz will cover," Miss Halverson told the class.
2. The driver had another cup of coffee before he continued the journey.
3. "I think the bicycle has a flat tire," reported Joe gloomily.
4. The boys decorated the gym themselves.

2 b

5. Mother asked the children to let her know when they were ready for lunch.
6. Bert asked himself how he could have missed so many shots.
7. Jane and Ida decided they would try out for the team.
8. Edward and Ronald are demonstrating their tricks of magic.
9. Mr. Kent said to let him know when George arrives.
10. Grace said she felt the part was not for her.

● EXERCISE 6.   Read these sentences aloud. Replace the repeated nouns with pronouns.

1. The plane gained speed as the plane taxied down the runway.
2. Christine finished the book and returned the book to the library.
3. When Marilyn met Arthur, Marilyn told Arthur that Marilyn knew Arthur's sister.
4. The parents of the mountain climbers prepared the parents of the mountain climbers for bad news.
5. Roger doesn't like the city, but Roger commutes to the city every day.
6. Dana asked Barbara, "Will Barbara have a soda with Dana?"
7. Lydia enjoys biology and astronomy because biology and astronomy explain many mysteries to Lydia.
8. The roses had hardly opened before the roses' petals began to drop.
9. Ben confessed, "Ben does not know what the sport of curling is."
10. When the electrician arrived, the electrician found that several power lines had been blown down.

Possessive Pronouns

Among the pronouns listed on page 43 are *his, your, our*. These words and others like them are *possessive pronouns*. They are used to show ownership or relationship.

POSSESSIVE PRONOUNS

my, mine	his	its	their, theirs
your, yours	her, hers	our, ours	

The words in heavy type in the following sentences are possessive pronouns.

> All the books that were **theirs** became **mine.**
> **Your** boat goes faster than **ours** does.
> **His** motor scooter was imported from Italy.

◆ NOTE   The possessive form of the pronoun *it* is *its.* Do not confuse *its* with the word *it's*, which means "it is."

● EXERCISE 7.   Write the numbers 1–20 on your paper. After each number, write the pronouns that occur in the sentence. Do not overlook the possessive pronouns.

1. Our house is not far from theirs.
2. The baby bruised himself when he fell.
3. They read the false document and approved it.
4. My record player is quite different from hers.
5. We must not allow ourselves to overlook injustice.
6. The record player is his, but the new records are hers.
7. He should have used his racquet instead of hers.
8. The professor told us our dog had been burying its bones in his garden.
9. You know that a single match can destroy acres of valuable timber.

10. Shall we follow her suggestion?
11. She gave herself a permanent and gave me a manicure.
12. "I will act the part left vacant by the missing member of the cast," the director said to us.
13. Marie and Pierre Curie devoted their lives to the discovery of radium and the study of how it affects human beings.
14. We must stop quarreling among ourselves if we are to finish the assignment.
15. "You must give yourselves time to adjust to the new situation," I told them.
16. Will you pick up the laundry for me, please?
17. She thought to herself that they were getting into trouble.
18. Whenever Mr. Nagel gives a talk about "contemporary history," we enjoy it.
19. "Piano lessons are definitely not for me," said Martha.
20. The decision must be ethical if we are to commit ourselves to it.

● EXERCISE 8. There are twenty pronouns in the following quotations. Write them on your paper after the number of each quotation.

1. Books think for me.—CHARLES LAMB
2. I never think of the future. It comes soon enough.
—ALBERT EINSTEIN
3. Time is but the stream I go a-fishing in.
—HENRY DAVID THOREAU
4. She wears her clothes as if they were thrown on with a pitchfork.—JONATHAN SWIFT
5. In the faces of men and women I see God.
—WALT WHITMAN

6. Life is very short, and very uncertain; let us spend it as well as we can.—SAMUEL JOHNSON
7. I wear the chain I forged in life.—CHARLES DICKENS
8. For every man the world is as fresh as it was at the first day, and as full of untold novelties for him with eyes to see them.—THOMAS HENRY HUXLEY
9. I believe in Democracy because it releases the energies of every human being.—WOODROW WILSON
10. A teacher affects eternity; he can never tell where his influence stops.—HENRY ADAMS

THE ADJECTIVE

Notice the difference in the following sentences. Which sentence is more interesting?

> A house stood on the hill.
> A **haunted** house stood on the **barren** hill.

The second sentence has additional words, *haunted* and *barren,* which make the house and its location more vivid. These words are called *adjectives.* Adjectives are used to describe nouns and pronouns. The adjective *haunted* describes or modifies the noun *house,* and the adjective *barren* modifies the noun *hill.* These adjectives make more definite your idea of what the house and the hill are like.

2c. An adjective is a word that modifies a noun or pronoun.

Most nouns, like *animal, city,* and *man,* have a very general meaning because they name a whole class of things. To make these words definite and specific, we need the adjective, a word that describes or makes

2c

clear the meaning of a noun. As you will see, adjectives are used with some pronouns as well as with nouns. Adjectives are said to *modify* the words they describe.

Adjectives answer the questions *What kind? Which one? How many?* or *How much?* The adjectives in the following phrases are in heavy type.

What kind?	**happy** children
	busy housewife
	sunny day
Which one or *ones?*	**seventh** grade
	these countries
	any book
How many or *How much?*	**full** tank
	five dollars
	no marbles

Adjectives don't always come before the word they modify; sometimes they follow it.

EXAMPLES The box is **empty**. [The adjective *empty* modifies *box*.]

They are **hungry** all the time. [The adjective *hungry* modifies *they*.]

Study the adjectives in the following sentences. An arrow shows you what word each adjective modifies.

1. This drawing was chosen the winner. [*This* tells *which one* was chosen.]

2. I visited San Francisco for several days. [*Several* tells *how many* days.]

3. The team was eager. [*Eager* tells *what kind* of team.]

4. Fort Laramie was an important stop on the way to California. [*Important* tells *what kind* of stop.]

The Article

Three small words—*a, an, the*—are the most commonly used adjectives. They are called *articles*. You use an article almost every time you write a sentence. Because of the number of articles in the exercises in this chapter, you will not be asked to mark them, however, you should remember that they are adjectives.

● EXERCISE 9.   Copy the following story, filling each blank with an appropriate adjective.

The group explored the __1__ section. They saw __2__ trees and __3__ bushes. Very often they had a __4__ time getting through the __5__ jungle. On __6__ occasions they almost gave up. But they were rewarded for the __7__ effort they put forth. During the __8__ trek through the jungle, the party discovered __9__ kinds of animals. A __10__ parrot particularly amused them. They were admiring the bird when a __11__ jaguar walked out of the undergrowth. Immediately the __12__ animals began to make __13__ noises and wasted __14__ time in getting out of the __15__ cat's way. After a day of __16__ hiking, the __17__ group finally pitched camp in a __18__ clearing. They were __19__ for their __20__ supper.

● EXERCISE 10.   There are twenty-five adjectives in the following paragraphs. Copy each adjective, and before it write the number of the sentence. Then write the word that the adjective modifies. Do not copy the articles *a, an,* or *the*.

EXAMPLE   1. "The Erlking" (Elfking) is a famous ballad by Goethe.
　　　　　1. *famous, ballad*

1. This ballad was set to music by the great composer Franz Schubert. 2. It tells of the strange ride of a father and son on a cold night. 3. The father held the small boy close to him as they sped through a dark forest. 4. The father feared that the dreadful Erlking might take the boy from him. 5. During their perilous ride, the son heard the icy voice of the Erlking. 6. But the father, to reassure him, said that the voice was the howling wind. 7. A second time the boy heard the Erlking beckoning him; again the father reassured the frightened lad. 8. But when the son heard the voice another time, the father urged the tired horse to go faster. 9. After several hours the father and son arrived in a friendly village. 10. Then the anxious father discovered that the boy had died during the last part of the terrifying trip.

11. Many ballads have sad endings like this poem by Goethe. 12. Of course, some ballads end with the main characters in better circumstances than they were at the beginning.

Proper Adjectives

A proper noun, you will recall, is one that names a particular person, place, or thing. A proper adjective is formed from a proper noun.

PROPER NOUNS	PROPER ADJECTIVES
Iceland	**Icelandic** holiday
Spain	**Spanish** dancer
Asia	**Asian** country
the Arctic	the **Arctic** climate

Notice that the proper adjective, like the proper noun, always begins with a capital letter.

● EXERCISE 11.   There are twenty adjectives, common and proper, in the following paragraphs. List them on your paper after the number of the sentence in which they occur. Do not include articles.

1. American artists have long admired the work of Leonardo da Vinci. 2. Leonardo was an Italian painter who created the famous painting, *Mona Lisa*. 3. This work by Leonardo has received much discussion because of the inscrutable smile on the face of the subject. 4. There has been endless speculation on the reason for her slight smile.

5. The painting is small and dark. 6. Some critics think that the *Mona Lisa* is a masterpiece, but many others feel that this painting has been overrated.

7. In 1911 the *Mona Lisa* was stolen from the Louvre, a French museum which was originally an elegant palace. 8. After two years it was recovered in an Italian city and was returned to the Louvre. 9. It left France legally in 1962 to be exhibited in American museums. 10. Thousands of Americans were glad to catch a glimpse of the famous lady.

● EXERCISE 12.   Change the following proper nouns into proper adjectives, and write each one in a sentence.

1. Britain
2. Canada
3. Paris
4. China
5. Mexico

Diagraming Adjectives

Diagrams show the relationships among words. The patterns on the next page show how an adjective is related to the noun it modifies.

PATTERNS

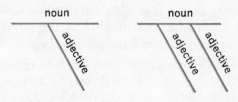

EXAMPLES   lively fish   a heavy, cumbersome box

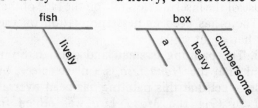

To diagram adjectives, put them on slanting lines beneath the noun they modify, in the order in which they occur in the sentence. Remember that articles are adjectives.

● EXERCISE 13.   Using the patterns given above, diagram the following groups of words. For neat work, use a ruler. In each diagram, write the noun first. Leave plenty of space between diagrams.

1. tired worker
2. clear water
3. worn-out jalopy
4. lost pet
5. a blue sweater

6. the mysterious note
7. an impossible feat
8. the three careful hikers
9. a tall, slender woman
10. many mistakes

● EXERCISE 14.   Diagram the following sentences.

1. Miss Everett sighed.
2. A big orange truck overturned.
3. The package arrived.

4. The new soldier saluted.
5. The two lost children rested.
6. Hot, dusty days have come.
7. An old fort burned.
8. The students attended.
9. A sleek, new ship was christened.
10. The tired, hungry pup returned.

THE SAME WORD AS DIFFERENT PARTS OF SPEECH

A word that is a pronoun in one sentence may be an adjective in another. Similarly, a noun may be used as an adjective. You cannot tell what part of speech a word is until you see it in a sentence. Notice how the same word is used in different ways in the pairs of sentences below.

That problem is difficult. [adjective]
That is a surprise. [pronoun]
The helmet is made of **steel**. [noun]
It is a **steel** helmet. [adjective]

● REVIEW EXERCISE C.   Locate all the nouns, pronouns, and adjectives in each sentence in the following paragraph, and write them after the number of the sentence. After each noun, write *n.*; after each pronoun, write *pron.*; and after each adjective, write *adj.* Do not list the articles—*a, an,* and *the.*

EXAMPLE   1. We located the bats in a dark cave.

    1. *We, pron.*
      bats, n.
      dark, adj.
      cave, n.

1. Bats often hang from the roofs of caves during the day and fly out at night. 2. Although they can fly, they are mammals. 3. These mysterious creatures have dim eyesight. 4. People cannot hear their high-pitched sound. 5. The sound echoes back to the bats like a radar beam. 6. This beam tells them the location of obstacles, and it also helps them to find food.

7. Many kinds of bats live in tropical regions. 8. Sixty-five varieties are found in the United States. 9. Many bats feed on insects; other larger kinds eat fruit. 10. The South American vampire bat feeds on blood.

CHAPTER 3

The Parts of Speech

Verb, Adverb, Preposition, Conjunction, Interjection

In Chapter 2 you learned about nouns, pronouns, and adjectives. There are five other parts of speech, which you will study in this chapter.

You have already learned to recognize *verbs* from your study of Chapter 1. You know that the verb is the most important word in the predicate of a sentence.

THE VERB

The verb is one of the foundation words of a sentence. Every sentence must contain a verb.

The verb gives the sentence meaning by saying something about the subject. Notice the verbs in these sentences:

I **like** homemade ice cream.

The Blakes **drove** through the Ozarks last month.

Are alligators reptiles?

3a. **A *verb* is a word that expresses action or otherwise helps to make a statement.**

Action Verbs

The easiest kind of verb to recognize is one that expresses physical or mental action. Verbs like *walk, speak, write, drive,* and *hope, believe, understand, approve* are *action* verbs.

(1) An *action verb* is a verb that expresses mental or physical action.

EXAMPLES   The owls **hooted** all night.
The lioness **played** with her cubs.
We **studied** our history at the library.

● EXERCISE 1.   Write the numbers 1–10 on your paper. After each number, write the action verb from the sentence.

1. The new High Dam near Aswan, Egypt, controls the waters of the Nile.
2. In this dry land, farmers need water from the Nile for their crops.
3. Engineers planned the dam for the purpose of irrigation.
4. The huge lake behind the dam covers the ancient land of Nubia.
5. Archaeologists hope for the preservation of some signs of Nubian art and civilization.
6. Many countries cooperated in the excavation of art treasures in this area.
7. One expedition found prehistoric rock paintings of giraffes.
8. Colossal statues of ancient kings and queens sit serenely in walls of rock.

9. Inscriptions and paintings on stone tell us of the daily life of the Nubians.
10. Modern Egyptian boats without keels resemble those of the ancient Nubians.

● EXERCISE 2. There are twenty action verbs in the following paragraph. Write them on your paper, with the number of the sentence preceding them.

1. We thought a long time about our vacation. 2. Finally, we decided on the Smoky Mountains. 3. We drove down from Ohio and reached the Smoky Mountain Park about one o'clock in the afternoon. 4. The views from the many mountain peaks thrilled us. 5. The trip to Clingman's Dome particularly excited us. 6. We climbed the ramp to the modernistic lookout tower. 7. From there we saw all the mountains around us. 8. We went back the next day. 9. This time clouds floated in on us like great ocean waves. 10. The mist dampened our skin and made us cold. 11. On our way down the mountain we noticed a large group of people. 12. We parked our car and walked over to the group. 13. There in the middle of the circle of people stood two large bears. 14. They played happily together. 15. Soon one came toward us. 16. We quickly jumped back into our car. 17. From the car we watched the antics of the bears for almost twenty minutes.

Linking Verbs

Some verbs do not express mental or physical action. They help make a statement by connecting the subject with a word in the predicate that describes or explains it. These verbs are called *linking* verbs. The most common linking verb is *be*. The following are forms of the verb *be:*

3a

am	has been	may be
is	have been	would have been
are	had been	can be
was	will be	should be
were	shall be	

Any verb phrase that ends in *be* or *been* is a form of the linking verb *be*.

> I **am** a photographer.
> He **has been** sick.
> We **would have been** early.
> Those berries **were** delicious.

In addition to the forms of *be*, there are other linking verbs. Notice how the linking verbs in heavy type in the following sentences *link* the subject with a word in the predicate.

> The bean stalk **grew** tall overnight. [The verb *grew* connects *bean stalk* and *tall*.]
>
> Harold **stayed** calm in the midst of the clamor. [The verb *stayed* links *Harold* and *calm*.]
>
> This corn **smells** fresh. [The verb *smells* connects *corn* and *fresh*.]

(2) A *linking verb* is a verb that does not show action but connects the subject with a word in the predicate.

In addition to *be*, the following verbs are commonly used as linking verbs:

taste	look	grow
feel	appear	remain
smell	become	stay
sound	seem	

Some verbs may be either action or linking verbs, depending on how they are used. The meaning of the sentence tells you which kind of verb it is.

Action   Amy **looked** through the telescope.
Linking Amy **looked** pale.

Action   We all **felt** the rough bark of the tree.
Linking We all **felt** excited before the experiment.

Action   Mother **sounded** the bell for dinner.
Linking Mother **sounded** pleased by the news.

● EXERCISE 3. There are ten linking verbs in the following paragraph. List them in order on your paper, writing the number of the sentence before each one.

1. Seeds are very strange. 2. A simple seed becomes a watermelon. 3. At first the seed remains lifeless in the ground. 4. Then it becomes larger and larger. 5. Finally, the plant is large enough to break through the ground. 6. Later the plant is recognizable. 7. On the vines the small watermelons first appear green. 8. After a few weeks the melons sound ripe when thumped. 9. Then the melon smells and tastes so good that one wishes he could buy a watermelon farm.

● EXERCISE 4. Pick out the verbs in the following sentences. If the verb is a linking verb, write after it the subject and the word in the predicate to which the subject is linked.

EXAMPLES   1. The pilot flew faster than the speed of sound.
           1. *flew*
           2. A bobcat looks ferocious.
           2. *looks, bobcat—ferocious*

1. He felt bad about his score on the test.
2. The cat's eyes looked green in the dark.

3. The climbers moved cautiously along the edge of the cliff.
4. We stayed in Hollywood for the shooting of the film.
5. Sergeant Holder felt his way carefully through the mine field.
6. The pavement smells clean after a hard rain.
7. Juneau is the capital of Alaska.
8. Sylvia cautiously tasted the strange liquid.
9. The movie previews looked silly.
10. The dancers were natives of Chile.

● EXERCISE 5.   There are twenty verbs in the following paragraphs. List them in order on your paper, writing the number of the sentence before each one. Write *action* after action verbs and *linking* after linking verbs.

1. I once visited a planetarium. 2. It was a fascinating place. 3. Before the lecture, I wandered around the building and looked at the many displays. 4. One exhibit showed various comets. 5. Another displayed a meteorite of more than thirty-four tons. 6. It fell to the earth many years ago and left a crater in the earth's surface. 7. Meteorites caused the thousands of craters on the moon, also.

8. In a few minutes a group of us went into the large lecture room. 9. The lecturer was ready for us. 10. He stood beside a large, strange-looking machine. 11. It re-created the stars, the moon, and the sun on the great dome-shaped roof of the room. 12. The lecturer dimmed the lights, and the dome appeared full of stars. 13. In fact, more stars were visible than on the clearest night. 14. The lecturer showed us the heavens of centuries ago. 15. We also got a glimpse of future skies.

16. At the end of the lecture, we were quiet and awe-struck. 17. Our universe is full of wonders!

● EXERCISE 6. Write ten original sentences, five with action verbs and five with linking verbs.

Helping Verbs

You learned in Chapter 1 that a verb may consist of one word or several words. If it consists of more than one word, it is called a *verb phrase*. A verb phrase contains one *main verb* and one or more *helping verbs*. In the following sentences the verb phrases are underscored, and the helping verbs are in heavy type.

Anita **will** <u>vote</u> in the next Presidential election.
Many Europeans **can** <u>speak</u> a second language.
Kansas **has been** <u>named</u> the Sunflower State.
The lawn **should have been** <u>tended</u> with greater care.

(3) A *helping verb* **helps the main verb to express action or make a statement.**

Here is a list of words commonly used as helping verbs. Those in the first column are all forms of the verb *be*.

am	has	might
is	have	can
are	had	could
was	do	shall
were	does	should
be	did	will
been	may	would

● EXERCISE 7. Read the following verb phrases aloud. Tell which words in each phrase are helping verbs.

1. will be seen
2. can launch
3. has been sighted
4. should have been done
5. will topple
6. may bring
7. have been hammering
8. shall hope
9. would have told
10. had been running

Sometimes the verb phrase is interrupted by another part of speech. A common interrupter is *not*. The verb phrase in a question is often interrupted by the subject. Note the separation of the verbs in the following verb phrases.

> Ken **does** not **have** a new desk.
>
> Our school **has** always **held** a victory celebration in the fall.
>
> **Did** you **watch** the launching this morning?
>
> **Can** you **make** a noise?

● EXERCISE 8.   Copy the verb phrases from each of the following sentences. Be prepared to tell which words are helping verbs.

1. Have you ever visited the Okefenokee Swamp in Georgia?
2. You would really enjoy a trip through the swamp.
3. The Okefenokee has been called "the land of the trembling earth."
4. Can you find it on a map?
5. Visitors may take boat trips through the swamp.
6. You certainly would not attempt the journey without a guide.
7. The color of the water would surprise you.
8. Its black color is caused by titanic acid.
9. The acid is secreted by the thousands of cypress trees in the swamp.
10. The water will reflect your image almost as well as a mirror.

● EXERCISE 9. Use each of the following word groups as the subject of a sentence by adding an appropriate verb phrase. Try to use as many different helping verbs as possible. Make some of your sentences questions.

EXAMPLE   1. the long hours of waiting
           1. *The long hours of waiting have ended.*
           2. my younger sister
           2. *Has my younger sister come home?*

1. the rickety boat
2. my letter from the travel agency
3. the bus to Miami
4. our science exam
5. the kidnaper of the child
6. my visitors from Germany
7. valuable mineral deposits
8. a rainy spell
9. a new portable typewriter
10. the dog in the window of the pet shop

● REVIEW EXERCISE A. There are twenty verbs in the following paragraph. List them in order on your paper, writing the number of the sentence before each one. Be sure to include helping verbs. Be prepared to tell which are action and which are linking verbs.

1. Do you enjoy sea adventures? 2. Robinson Crusoe had loved the sea for many years. 3. Finally, without his parents' knowledge, he took his first voyage. 4. The sea was rough and Robinson became seasick. 5. His ship hit a reef near an island off the coast of South America, and of all the passengers and crew only he remained alive. 6. The waves washed him ashore on the island. 7. He carefully planned his course of action—he built a raft and brought back food and

supplies from the wrecked ship. 8. Before long he had made himself quite comfortable. 9. He had a summer home and a winter home. 10. He planted vegetables and hunted game on the island. 11. Now he was especially happy. 12. For almost twenty-four years his life seemed quiet. 13. Then an unusual thing happened.

14. You should certainly read the story yourself. 15. Then you can appreciate Robinson's early life on the island as well as his life after the unusual occurrence.

● REVIEW EXERCISE B.   Write the numbers 1–20 on your paper. After each number, write the corresponding italicized word or words from the paragraph below. Identify the part of speech of the italicized word or words. Use *n.* for a noun; *pron.* for a pronoun; *adj.* for an adjective; and *v.* for a verb.

There were (1) *many* knights during the twelfth and thirteenth centuries. Only sons of the nobility (2) *could become* knights. A child (3) *began* his education for (4) *knighthood* at an early age. First he (5) *was taught* the social arts by the lady whom he served as a (6) *page*. Then (7) *he* became a squire. This was the essential (8) *part* of his training. He was taught how to handle (9) *arms*. As a squire to a lord, he (10) *accompanied* the lord and served him. In return, the lord (11) *fed* and (12) *housed* his squire. When the lord entered a (13) *great* battle, the squire followed his lord and (14) *carried* his shield. If the lord was thrown from his (15) *horse*, the squire was expected to rescue the lord and help (16) *him* back into his saddle. Finally, at the age of twenty or twenty-one the (17) *young* man was considered ready for knighthood. By (18) *this* time he (19) *had received* about (20) *fifteen* years of practical education.

THE ADVERB

You have learned that an adjective is a word that modifies a noun or pronoun. An *adverb*, too, is a modifier. By using an adverb you can make a verb, an adjective, or another adverb have a more exact or definite meaning.

A fireman ran **swiftly** past her.

He was carrying a **very** small child.

The fire blazed **too dangerously** for anyone to enter.

3b. An *adverb* is a word that modifies a verb, an adjective, or another adverb.

Just as an adjective will answer certain questions about a noun or pronoun—What kind? Which one? How many?—so an adverb will answer certain questions about the word it modifies: *Where? When? How? How often? To what extent?*

1. **Yesterday** a fire **completely** destroyed the home of a family on Hill Street. [*Yesterday* and *completely* are adverbs modifying the verb *destroyed*. *Yesterday* tells *when; completely* tells *to what extent.*]

2. A woman who lives **nearby** explained that the fire began **early** in the morning and continued **furiously** until noon. [*Nearby* is an adverb modifying the verb *lived;* it tells *where*. *Early* is an adverb modifying the verb *began;* it tells *when*. *Furiously* is an adverb modifying the verb *continued;* it tells *how.*]

3. **Rarely** does a fire last **so long.** [*Rarely*, modifying the verb *does last*, tells *how often*. *So* modifies the

3b

adverb *long*, which modifies the verb *does last*. Together the words *so long* answer the question *to what extent?*]

Here is a list of words that are often used as adverbs.

Where? here   there   away   up
When? now   then   later   soon
How? clearly   easily   quietly   slowly
How often? never   always   often   seldom
To what extent? very   too   almost   so

The word *not* is nearly always used as an adverb to modify a verb. Sometimes *not* is a part of a contraction, as in *hadn't, aren't, didn't*. When it is, the *n't* is an adverb and should not be mistaken for part of the verb.

The Form of Adverbs

Perhaps you have noted that many adverbs end in *–ly*. These adverbs are formed by adding *–ly* to adjectives: *clear—clearly, vigorous—vigorously, quiet—quietly*. But do not think that all words which end in *–ly* are adverbs. Some words ending in *–ly* are adjectives: *friendly* welcome, *timely* remark, *lonely* weekend, *kindly* man.

● EXERCISE 10.   Think of an adverb to modify each of the following verbs. Write both adverb and verb on your paper.

1. works
2. are sailing
3. sliced
4. sews
5. had been yelling

6. washes
7. grew
8. can guess
9. thought
10. scattered

● EXERCISE 11. Each sentence below contains one adverb. Write the adverb after the number of the sentence. Then write the word that the adverb modifies. Be prepared to tell what question the adverb answers.

EXAMPLE 1. Many Cherokee Indians still live in the mountains of North Carolina.
   1. *still, live*

1. In 1815 a small boy excitedly reported the discovery of gold in Georgia.
2. Many of the white settlers of the area fought greedily for the gold.
3. The Cherokee Indians had been living peacefully in the area of Georgia, North Carolina, Alabama, and Tennessee for many years.
4. The settlers completely forgot about the Indians' right to the land.
5. They quickly petitioned the government to remove the Indians from the area.
6. In spite of the fact that many Cherokees had fought bravely for the settlers, they were forced to leave their land.
7. Then began the unfortunate "Trail of Tears."
8. The Indians were hardly given a chance to collect their belongings.
9. They were quickly exiled to Oklahoma.
10. Many Cherokees can never forget the harsh treatment suffered by their ancestors.

The Position of Adverbs

Adverbs may come before or after the word they modify. Notice the position of the adverbs in these sentences:

Bud **often** complains about the cooking.
Bud complains **often** about the cooking.

When an adverb modifies a verb phrase, it frequently comes in the middle of the phrase.

> Linda did **not** know the answer to the riddle.
> Falling stars are **often** seen in September.

The adverbs above are close to the words they modify. For variety or emphasis, a writer may begin a sentence with an adverb, separating it from the word it modifies.

> **Suddenly** the door opened.

> **Finally,** after hours of climbing, we came to the end of the trail.

It is an important characteristic of an adverb that it can usually come at more than one place in the sentence. At what other places could *finally* be used in the sentence above? Adverbs often begin questions:

> **When** does your school start? [The adverb *when* modifies the verb *does start.*]

> **How** did you spend your vacation? [The adverb *how* modifies the verb *did spend.*]

● EXERCISE 12.   Copy the adverbs from the following sentences. After each adverb write the word that the adverb modifies. Remember that adverbs may modify verbs, adjectives, or other adverbs.

1. Squirrels can be seen in almost every park and forest.
2. Most squirrels do not seem to be afraid of people.
3. Often they enjoy human company.
4. They chatter noisily among themselves.
5. They search endlessly for things to eat.
6. If a person feeds a certain squirrel frequently, the squirrel may recognize him.

7. Tuft-eared squirrels are the most attractive squirrels.
8. Some of them have completely white tails.
9. How do flying squirrels get their name?
10. They can glide easily from trees to the ground by means of the loose membrane between their front and hind legs.

● EXERCISE 13.   There are twenty adverbs in the following paragraph. Copy them in order, writing the number of the sentence before each adverb. After each one, write the word it modifies. Be prepared to tell what question the adverb answers.

EXAMPLE   1. *Treasure Island* is an extremely exciting story.
        1. *extremely, exciting*

1. A very strange seaman by the name of Bill Bones stalked proudly into the inn of Jim Hawkins' father. 2. Learning that the inn was seldom crowded, Bones quickly decided that it would be an almost perfect hideout for him. 3. He carefully watched the shore by day and drank heartily in the inn at night. 4. Jim's father waited patiently for Bill Bones to pay his rent, but Bones never offered him any money after the first day. 5. Jim's father was so afraid of Bones that he could not ask his guest for the money. 6. Somewhat later Bones received the Black Spot, a very terrible symbol to a pirate. 7. The Black Spot has always been known as a death notice for pirates. 8. The Black Spot held such awful terror for Bones that he died of a stroke. 9. Jim and his mother soon opened the pirate's sea chest to get the money due them. 10. To their surprise they found there a packet which contained a map locating the treasure of the famous buccaneer, Captain Flint. 11. Jim later sailed with Long

John Silver, an extremely shrewd one-legged seaman, in search of the treasure.

● EXERCISE 14.   Copy the following paragraph. Fill each blank with an appropriate adverb.

Each fall I __1__ anticipate the first football game. I can __2__ wait for the gates to open. __3__ I run to my seat and join the __4__ cheering fans. __5__ the cheerleaders come to lead us in the school song. During the kickoff we __6__ stand to encourage the players. If the right halfback receives the ball, we __7__ count on a long run. He dashes __8__ up the field. __9__ he runs the kickoff back for a touchdown. If that happens, we cheer __10__ .

Diagraming Adverbs

Adverbs that modify verbs are diagramed in much the same way as adjectives. By using a slanting line for the adverb, you can show the relationship between it and the word it modifies.

1. An adverb modifying a verb:

PATTERN

EXAMPLES   walks briskly   got here late

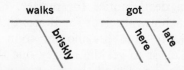

● EXERCISE 15.   Using the pattern above, diagram the following verbs and adverbs. Use a ruler for lines.

In each diagram, write the verb or the verb phrase first; then add the adverb. Leave plenty of space between diagrams.

1. laughed loudly
2. drive slowly
3. did not happen again
4. carefully recorded
5. write legibly

When an adverb modifies an adjective or another adverb, the adverb modifier appears on a slanting line below the word it modifies.

2. An adverb modifying an adjective:

PATTERN

EXAMPLES badly tarnished silver   very fast ball

3. An adverb modifying another adverb:

PATTERN

EXAMPLES   drove rather care-   could not see very
           fully   well

drove   could see

rather *carefully*   *not* *very* *well*

● EXERCISE 16.   Using the patterns above, diagram
the following groups of words. Use a ruler for lines. In
each diagram, first write the verb or the noun; then
add the modifying word or words. Leave plenty of
space between diagrams.

1. almost never find
2. stopped too abruptly
3. exceptionally fast race
4. very complete report
5. is not swimming well
6. highly skilled work-
   men

7. had been practicing
   often
8. walked too rapidly
9. spoke slowly
10. did not listen care-
    fully

DIAGRAMING SENTENCES

You are now able to diagram more complicated
sentences than you have done so far. The long horizontal line supports the subject and the verb. The
modifiers, adjectives and adverbs, are suspended below
the words they modify. The articles *a*, *an*, and *the* are,
of course, diagramed as adjectives.

PATTERN

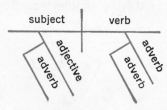

EXAMPLES The predicted rain came today.

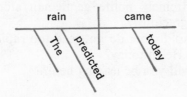

The mare and her colt were looking around rather nervously.

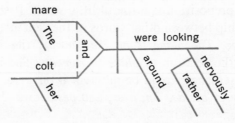

● EXERCISE 17. Diagram the following sentences.

1. The judge spoke clearly.
2. The new alarm rings softly.
3. The two dogs ran away quickly.
4. I answered very reluctantly.
5. Somewhere a rooster crowed loudly.
6. The orange moon shone brightly.
7. Five extremely tall men sauntered in.
8. The old man spoke uncertainly.
9. The whole cast performed especially well.
10. A relatively unknown candidate won easily.

● EXERCISE 18. Diagram the following sentences.

1. The last boat left yesterday.
2. My very good friend moved away recently.
3. Tomorrow I will study more carefully.
4. Jim's guests came early.
5. Never had he laughed so heartily.

6. Suddenly the huge rocket shot upward.
7. The extremely polite gentleman stood up and bowed graciously.
8. Read rapidly but do not read too rapidly.
9. How is Helen today?
10. When will you be leaving here?

THE PREPOSITION

The preposition is a useful little word. It shows relationship between other words in the sentence. In the sentence, *The plane is on the runway,* the word *on* shows the relation of *plane* to *runway.* The meaning of the sentence would be different if *on* were replaced by *over* or *beside. On, over,* and *beside* are all prepositions.

3c. A *preposition* is a word that shows the relation of a noun or pronoun to some other word in the sentence.

The following words are commonly used as prepositions.

aboard	behind	from	throughout
about	below	in	to
above	beneath	into	toward
across	beside	like	under
after	between	of	underneath
against	beyond	off	until
along	by	on	up
among	down	over	upon
around	during	past	with
at	except	since	within
before	for	through	without

In these sentences the prepositions are in heavy type.

> The man **in** the heavy coat was very hot. [The preposition shows the relation of *man* to *coat*.]
>
> The plane flew **through** the thick clouds. [The preposition shows the relation of *flew* to *clouds*.]
>
> One **of** my favorite sports is ice hockey. [The preposition shows the relation of *one* to *sports*.]

● EXERCISE 19.   In each sentence below, a preposition is missing. You are to think of three appropriate prepositions to go in the sentence. (Notice how a change in prepositions changes the relationship between words.) Write the prepositions on your paper after the sentence number. Be sure to use prepositions that make sense in the sentence.

EXAMPLE   1. The boy raced —— the street.
          1. *down, up, across*

1. We saw the cartoons —— dinner.
2. Two friends wal ed —— the river.
3. My fishing tackle is —— the box.
4. The scout crawled —— the fence.
5. I could hardly see the man —— the window.

The Prepositional Phrase

The preposition never stands alone in a sentence. It is always used with a noun or pronoun that is called the *object* of the preposition. Usually the noun or pronoun follows the preposition.

> You can press those leaves **under glass.** [The preposition *under* relates its object, *glass*, to *can press*.]

3c

The quartet sang **in harmony.** [The preposition *in* relates its object, *harmony*, to *sang.*]

A preposition may have more than one object.

Pete's telegram **to Nina and Ralph** brought good news.

The objects of prepositions may have modifiers, of course.

It happened **during the last examination.** [*The* and *last* are adjectives modifying *examination*, the object of the preposition *during.*]

All together the preposition, its object, and the object's modifiers (if there are any) make up a *prepositional phrase.*

● EXERCISE 20.   Below are several groups of words, each containing a prepositional phrase. Write the numbers 1–10 on your paper. After each number, write the prepositional phrase. Underline the preposition and circle its object.

EXAMPLE   1. the clock in the kitchen
           1. *in the* (*kitchen*)

1. a pad of paper
2. searched at night
3. a friend of mine
4. delighted by the good news
5. a bird outside my window
6. a cottage on the lake
7. one of you
8. flying far above the clouds
9. the display of books and art work
10. two among the many

● EXERCISE 21.   Write the numbers 1–10 on your paper. Find the prepositional phrases in the following sentences. Copy each preposition and its object.

EXAMPLE 1. Cal enjoyed swimming in the cool stream.
1. *in, stream*

1. Everyone except me left the schoolroom.
2. William Tell shot the apple from his son's head.
3. The captain climbed aboard his new ship.
4. After the trial, reporters interviewed the defendant.
5. Each of the astronauts wanted the assignment.
6. Under the smoothly carved stone was a message.
7. Man cannot live long without food and water.
8. Among the many candidates he is the best qualified.
9. The old castle had a deep moat around its rapidly decaying walls.
10. The covered wagon made its way toward the distant fort.

Prepositions and Adverbs

You remember from your study of Chapter 2 that the part of speech a word is depends on its use in the sentence. Some words may be used as prepositions or as adverbs.

> The cowboy got **off** his horse. [*Off* is used as a preposition. Its object is *horse*.]
>
> The cowboy rode **off**. [*Off* is used as an adverb. It tells *where* the cowboy rode.]

A preposition always has an object. An adverb never does. If you are in doubt about whether a word is used as an adverb or a preposition, look for an object.

> The posse walked **around** and then went **inside**. [*Around* and *inside* are used as adverbs. They modify the verbs *walked* and *went*.]

The posse walked **around the yard** and then went **inside the cabin.** [*Around* and *inside* are used as prepositions. Their objects are *yard* and *cabin.*]

● EXERCISE 22.   The italicized words in the sentences below are adverbs or prepositions. Decide which each is, and write *adverb* or *prep.* on your paper after the number. Be prepared to explain your answer.

1. In the story "The Most Dangerous Game," a famous hunter, Rainsford, fell *overboard* and was washed ashore on a strange island.
2. Rainsford knew that the island was greatly feared *by* all sailors who passed by.
3. *Among* seamen the place was known as "Ship-Trap Island."
4. After he had looked *around* for several hours, Rainsford located a chateau on a high bluff.
5. A man with a revolver *in* his hand answered Rainsford's knock.
6. He introduced himself *to* his guest as General Zaroff, a man who, like Rainsford, was a hunter.
7. Rainsford went *inside* and was amazed at the elegance of Zaroff's home.
8. That evening Rainsford learned *about* the kind of hunting Zaroff liked.
9. Rainsford soon wished that he could get *out* and never see Zaroff again.
10. Zaroff had tired of ordinary hunting and had cast about *for* a new kind of game—men.

THE CONJUNCTION

The next part of speech that you will study is the conjunction. The term *conjunction* comes from two

Latin words: *con*, which means "together," and *jun-gere* which means "join." A *conjunction* joins things together.

3d. A *conjunction* is a word that joins words or groups of words.

The most common conjunctions, or connecting words, are *and, but, or, nor*, and *for*.

CONJUNCTIONS JOINING WORDS

> Bill **and** Peggy
> pretty **but** useless
> rain **or** snow

CONJUNCTIONS JOINING GROUPS OF WORDS

> listened to the code **and** reported it accurately
> all alone **but** not bored
> in the newspaper **or** on the radio

CONJUNCTIONS JOINING PARTS OF COMPOUND SENTENCES

> Dad is waiting for the mailman, **and** Mother is expecting a telephone call.
> Rabbits are born blind, **but** hares can see at birth.
> These peaches should be used at once, **for** they are overripe.
> The tiny bird could not fly, **nor** could it feed itself.

● EXERCISE 23. Write sentences using conjunctions as directed.

EXAMPLE   1. Use *and* to join two verbs.
            1. *Geraldine talked and laughed excitedly.*

1. Use *or* to join two adjectives.
2. Use *but* to join the parts of a compound sentence.

3 d

3. Use *and* to join two adverbs.
4. Use *or* to join two prepositional phrases.
5. Use *for* to join the parts of a compound sentence.
6. Use *and* to join the parts of a compound subject.
7. Use *or* to join two pronouns.
8. Use *or* to join two proper nouns.
9. Use *but* to join two linking verbs.
10. Use *or* in an imperative sentence.

THE INTERJECTION

You already know that an exclamatory sentence is one which expresses strong feeling. One part of speech has the same purpose as an exclamatory sentence: the *interjection*. Like an exclamatory sentence, the interjection is usually followed by an exclamation point.

3e. An *interjection* is an exclamatory word that expresses strong emotion. An interjection has no grammatical relationship to the rest of the sentence.

> **Ouch!** That hurts!
> **Goodness!** What a haircut!
> **Look!** The moon is full.
> **Aha!** I know the trick.
> **Oops!** The glass slipped out of my hand.

Sometimes the interjection is followed by a comma:

> **Oh,** I made the same mistake again!
> The weather here, **alas,** is worse than I expected.

● EXERCISE 24.   Copy the following sentences, supplying an appropriate interjection for each blank. Try to use a different interjection in each.

1. ——! I stubbed my toe!
2. ——! I dropped the eggs.
3. ——! What a touchdown!
4. ——! What a pretty dress!
5. ——! Did you see it?
6. "——!" I exclaimed.
7. The time, ——, had come.
8. ——! It's hot!
9. "——!" I shouted.
10. ——! It's about time!

◆ NOTE In the next chapter you will learn more about the prepositional phrase, including how to diagram it. You already know how to diagram conjunctions in compound subjects or verbs and compound sentences. (See pp. 26–30.) The interjection is usually not diagramed, since it has no grammatical relation to the rest of the sentence.

In this chapter and in Chapter 2, you have been studying the eight parts of speech. At this point, you should review what you have learned about them. If you are not sure that you understand each part of speech and can identify each one in sentences, take time now to go back and study them further.

Remember that you cannot tell what part of speech a word is until you know how it is used in a sentence. The same word may be used in different ways.

EXAMPLES The **storm** ended by midnight. [*Storm* names something; it is a noun.]

The soldiers will **storm** the enemy camp. [*Storm* shows action; it is a verb.]

Play **outside** for a while. [*Outside* is an adverb modifying the verb *play*. It tells *where*.]

3e

The **outside** of the house needs paint.
[*Outside* is a noun.]

I saw the birds' nest **outside** my window.
[*Outside* is a preposition. Its object is *window*.]

Summary

RULE	PART OF SPEECH	USE	EXAMPLE
2a	noun	names	**Marie** had an **idea** about the **dress**.
2b	pronoun	takes the place of a noun	**This** is **mine**, but **I** will give **it** to **you**.
2c	adjective	modifies a noun or pronoun	We have **two attractive Danish** bowls.
3a	verb	shows action, makes a statement	Bob **had** the right of way, and he **drove** through the intersection.
3b	adverb	modifies a verb, an adjective, or another adverb	We were **so** tired that we watched the game **very quietly**.
3c	preposition	relates a noun or pronoun to another word	**After** the ball game the players got **into** a discussion **about** the umpire's decision.
3d	conjunction	joins words or groups of words	**and, but, or, nor, for**
3e	interjection	shows strong feeling	**Ouch! Help!**

● REVIEW EXERCISE C.   In each of the following sentences one word is in italics. Write the numbers 1–10 on your paper. After the proper number write the part of speech of the italicized word. Be prepared to give a reason for your answer.

EXAMPLE   1. *Sheep* are raised in Australia.
          1. *noun*

1. The sun set *in* the west.
2. Admiral Perry *reached* the North Pole in 1909.
3. *Oh!* What a brilliant diamond!
4. The teacher *carefully* prepared the science exhibit.
5. The *message* was confidential.
6. Call Charles *or* Dan to the phone.
7. Who discovered *electricity*?
8. A family of nine lives *across* the street.
9. Judith told *me* what had happened.
10. My new *woolen* socks are very warm.

● REVIEW EXERCISE D.   Write ten sentences, using the following words as directed. Underline the given word in each sentence.

EXAMPLE   1. *dance* as a noun
          1. *Are you going to the <u>dance</u>?*

1. *hike* as a verb
2. *beyond* as a preposition
3. *motor* as a noun
4. *study* as a verb
5. *under* as a preposition
6. *outdoors* as an adverb
7. *slow* as an adjective
8. *spring* as a verb
9. *down* as an adverb
10. *one* as an adjective

● REVIEW EXERCISE E. Diagram the following sentences.

1. The audience applauded.
2. We have been warned.
3. The large balloon was released.
4. The old train stopped abruptly.
5. Our yellow kite floated gracefully upward.
6. The lecturer has traveled widely and has spoken often.
7. Bill and Dana live here.
8. The new submarine proceeded very cautiously.
9. Benjamin Franklin wrote well.
10. Where are my books?

● REVIEW EXERCISE F. Diagram the following sentences.

1. Silently the lion waited.
2. Then it sprang forward noiselessly.
3. A small animal had been trapped.
4. The lion roared and attacked.
5. The prey was quickly eaten.
6. Lions and other wild animals do not kill needlessly.
7. Wild animals are often killed wantonly.
8. They must be protected, or they will disappear entirely.
9. Some species are endangered now.
10. They can never be replaced.

● REVIEW EXERCISE G. In each of the following sentences one word is in italics. Write the numbers 1–10 on your paper. After the proper number, write the part of speech of the italicized word. Be prepared to give a reason for your answer.

1. Where did you find *this* extremely well-shaped starfish?
2. I seldom miss a *summer* at the seashore.
3. There I pick up shells, starfish, *and*, occasionally, a sea horse.
4. Once I wandered down *to* the beach alone.
5. On the shore I *found* several exceptionally large fish.
6. "*Wow!*" I exclaimed to a lifeguard who was nearby. "How did these creatures get here?"
7. *He* explained that they were pilot whales, or black-fish.
8. They always travel in *schools*.
9. They follow their leader so closely that they *may be stranded* on the shore by a mistake on the part of the leader.
10. I frequently think about the unfortunate school of fish which followed the leader *too* well.

● REVIEW EXERCISE H. Write a paragraph of ten sentences. Underline adjectives, adverbs, and prepositions. You may wish to write about a story you have read, a trip you have taken, or a movie you have seen.

CHAPTER 4

The Prepositional Phrase

Adjective and Adverb Uses

In Chapters 2 and 3 you learned how individual words function as parts of speech. A group of words may also be used as a single part of speech—as a noun, adjective, or adverb. One such word group is called a *phrase*.

4a. A *phrase* is a group of related words that does not contain a subject and verb and that is used as a single part of speech.

It is important to remember that a phrase never has a subject or a verb. Phrases cannot stand alone— they must be part of a sentence.

4b. A *prepositional phrase* is a phrase that begins with a preposition and ends with a noun or pronoun. A prepositional phrase may be used as an adjective or an adverb.

Prepositions are words like *at*, *by*, *of*, and *with* that show the relation of a noun or pronoun—called the object of the preposition—to another word in the sentence. The preposition and the object and whatever modifiers it may have make up a prepositional phrase.

The groups of words printed in heavy type in the following sentences are all prepositional phrases.

Sandra has a collection **of shells.**

She started it **in Maine,** but she has gathered shells **from tropical waters,** too.

Her trip **to Puerto Rico** doubled the size **of her collection.**

● EXERCISE 1.   Find the prepositional phrases in the following sentences and write them on your paper. Underline each preposition and circle its object(s).

1. The whole world watches a flight into space.
2. A bouquet of roses was the centerpiece.
3. The water in the cellar is getting deeper!
4. The view from the mountain is spectacular.
5. Grandma brought a gift for Sandy.
6. This morning I had a dish of cereal and straw-berries.
7. Who bought the house across the way?
8. Did you see the lightning during the storm?
9. The baby left her fingerprints along the wall.
10. Betty Myers read with expression and feeling.
11. We're having a party with some friends tonight.
12. You don't know any people like them.
13. The boys told ghost stories before the campfire.
14. There is a leak underneath the sink.
15. The picture over the mantle is crooked.
16. Shhh—I'm leaving without permission.
17. They hacked a trail through the very dense jungle.

4
a-b

18. This is a secret between you and me.
19. We were riding across unusually flat plains.
20. Dad hid a surprise behind the sofa.

● Exercise 2.   Copy the following sentences, filling in each blank with an appropriate prepositional phrase.

EXAMPLE   1. The hornet stung Mr. Simpson ——.
          1. *The hornet stung Mr. Simpson without any warning.*

1. The lady —— is the wife ——.
2. —— residents were evacuated from the area ——.
3. We planted tulips —— and rose bushes ——.
4. When we peered ——, we saw cobwebs and dust ——.
5. —— we discovered a sword that once belonged ——.

● Exercise 3.   There are twenty prepositional phrases in the following paragraph. Write them in order on your paper, putting the number of the sentence before each phrase. In each phrase, underline the preposition and circle the object(s).

1. During the days of chivalry no knight surpassed King Arthur. 2. Through his strength he proved his right to the throne of Britain. 3. He removed a great sword from a solid rock. 4. Later, Arthur was given a sword with magical strength. 5. The knights who gathered around King Arthur were known throughout the land for their courage and goodness. 6. They were dedicated to the service of those in need of help. 7. Under Arthur's protection they met and feasted at Camelot. 8. When someone was in trouble, one of the knights rode to his assistance. 9. The Knights of the Round Table led adventurous lives.

ADJECTIVE PHRASES

Like an adjective, a prepositional phrase can be used to modify a noun or a pronoun. Such a prepositional phrase is called an *adjective phrase*. The adjective phrase answers the same questions that a single-word adjective answers—*What kind? Which one? How many?* (or *How much?*)

Adjective	Taylor learned an **important** lesson.
Adjective Phrase	Taylor learned a lesson **of importance.**
Adjective	Lucy chose the **striped** one.
Adjective Phrase	Lucy chose the one **with stripes.**

4c. An *adjective phrase* modifies a noun or a pronoun.

● EXERCISE 4. Write the numbers 1–20 on your paper. Each of the following sentences contains an adjective phrase. Write the phrase and the noun or pronoun it modifies after the proper number.

EXAMPLE 1. The work of Marie and Pierre Curie was invaluable.

1. *of Marie and Pierre Curie, work*

1. Marie was an obscure student with little money when she met Pierre Curie.
2. Pierre was already a scientist of great ability.
3. Marie was simply an eager young girl from Poland.
4. Her life at the university was unbelievably hard.
5. Her meals of tea and bread were hardly nourishing.

4 c

6. But her love of science kept her going.
7. The marriage of the two scientists was a true partnership.
8. Marie's years with Pierre were happy ones.
9. Long hours of laboratory work filled their days and nights.
10. Finally, their theories about a new element were proved true.
11. Their research on pitchblende uncovered the new element radium.
12. Radium, with its powerful rays, is used to fight diseases.
13. Suddenly people around the world knew the Curies.
14. The Curies disliked publicity about their discovery.
15. The laboratory near their home did not change.
16. Their dedication to their work continued.
17. The end of their long partnership came when Pierre was killed crossing a street.
18. Marie continued the work on radium.
19. Once again her devotion to science kept her going.
20. Her experiments with radium won her many honors.

An adjective phrase frequently follows another adjective phrase in a sentence. Sometimes both adjective phrases modify the same noun or pronoun.

> The portrait **of George Washington by Gilbert Stuart** is familiar to all Americans. [The two phrases, *of George Washington* and *by Gilbert Stuart*, both modify the noun *portrait*.]

Sometimes an adjective phrase modifies a noun or pronoun in another adjective phrase.

A majority **of the mammals in the world** sleep during the day. [The adjective phrase *of the mammals* modifies the noun *majority,* and the adjective phrase *in the world* modifies the noun *mammals,* which is the object of the preposition in the first phrase.]

● EXERCISE 5. The following paragraph contains twenty adjective phrases. List the phrases in order on your paper, writing the number of the sentence before each phrase. After each phrase, write the noun or pronoun it modifies. Most sentences contain more than one adjective phrase.

EXAMPLE 1. Stories about life on the frontier have always fascinated me.
  1. *about life, stories*
    on the frontier, life

1. A major character in the stories by James Fenimore Cooper about pioneer days is Natty Bumppo. 2. He is a man with great courage who honors the ways of the white man but who also respects the kind of life the Indian lives. 3. This hero of several Cooper novels prefers the life of the frontiersman. 4. When there is an advance by the white man, Natty leaves. 5. A simple life in the forest with his trusted Indian friends is all that he requires. 6. Finally, Natty reaches the end of the frontier in America. 7. His years of faithful service to his fellow man are finished, and Natty Bumppo dies. 8. The hour of his death—sunset —is appropriate. 9. His last word, like an answer to roll call, is "Here." 10. Thus ends the life of an appealing character in American fiction.

● EXERCISE 6. Think of an appropriate adjective phrase to fill the blank in each of the following sentences. Write the phrase on your paper after the number. Remember that an adjective phrase must modify a noun or a pronoun.

EXAMPLE   1. The dachshund —— is very amusing to watch.
        1. *with his short legs and long body*

1. A scream —— awakened us.
2. The shopping center —— is seldom crowded.
3. The comic strips —— are funny.
4. The painting —— won the grand prize.
5. The trip —— was exciting.
6. I found a clue to the location ——.
7. On a table —— we piled the heavy bundles.
8. The man —— is staring at the necklace.
9. My tree house is in the oak tree ——.
10. Finally someone —— threw him a life raft.

ADVERB PHRASES

When a prepositional phrase modifies a verb, an adjective, or an adverb, it is called an *adverb phrase*. An adverb phrase usually modifies the verb in the sentence. Like a single-word adverb, an adverb phrase qualifies or limits the meaning of the word it modifies. It answers the questions that an adverb does: *Where? When? How? How often? To what extent?*

Adverb	The soldier reported **there** first.
Adverb phrase	The soldier reported **to the fort** first.
Adverb	The cavalry **soon** reached the fort.
Adverb phrase	**By noon** the cavalry reached the fort.

4d. An *adverb phrase* modifies a verb, an adjective, or another adverb.

EXAMPLES   **For the first few weeks,** the education of a puppy may be difficult. [The adverb phrase *for the first few weeks* modifies the verb *may be*.]

A puppy is always ready **for a game.** [The adverb phrase *for a game* modifies the adjective *ready*.]

Early **in the morning** our puppy awakens us. [The adverb phrase *in the morning* modifies the adverb *early*.]

● EXERCISE 7.   Each of the following sentences contains an adverb phrase. After the proper number on your paper, write the phrase and the verb, adjective, or adverb it modifies. Be sure not to select any adjective phrases.

EXAMPLE   1. Pecos Bill will live forever in the many legends about him.
            1. *in the many legends, will live*

1. When he was a baby, Pecos Bill was dropped from a covered wagon.
2. He fell into the Pecos River.
3. There were several other children in the wagon.
4. His parents did not miss him for a long time.
5. Pecos Bill was reared by coyotes.
6. He thought for many years that he was a coyote.
7. After a long argument a cowboy convinced him that he was not a coyote.
8. At last, Bill became a cowboy himself.
9. He was soon known throughout the West.
10. Hunting gold, he dug the Grand Canyon in a week's time.

4 d

11. During a drought he dug the bed of the Rio Grande.
12. On one occasion Bill rode a cyclone.
13. He rode the bucking wind without a saddle.
14. On another occasion, a ten-foot rattlesnake attacked him.
15. After that a mountain lion startled Bill.
16. The lion leaped from a ledge above Bill's head.
17. Bill had him tamed soon after the leap.
18. He even put a saddle on the lion and rode him.
19. You can see that Pecos Bill was always in difficulty.
20. Stories like these about Pecos Bill are common in the West.

Two or more adverb phrases may occur in succession.

> He drove **for hours through the storm.** [Both adverb phrases, *for hours* and *through the storm*, modify the verb *drove*.]

> The library opens **on weekdays at eight o'clock.** [Both adverb phrases, *on weekdays* and *at eight o'clock*, modify the verb *opens*.]

Sometimes an adverb phrase is followed by an adjective phrase modifying the object of the preposition in the adverb phrase.

> The boat landed **on an island** [adverb] **near the coast** [adjective].

Many adverb phrases may be moved from one part of the sentence to another. In this they are unlike adjective phrases, which usually follow the word they modify. Adverb phrases can often be placed in different parts of the sentence without changing the meaning.

> We planted spruce seedlings **along the driveway.**
>
> **Along the driveway** we planted spruce seedlings.
>
> **At our house** we have dinner early.
>
> We have dinner early **at our house.**

● EXERCISE 8. The following paragraph contains twenty adverb phrases. List the phrases in order on your paper, writing the number of the sentence before each phrase. After each phrase, write the word it modifies. Many sentences contain more than one adverb phrase. Be sure not to select any adjective phrases.

EXAMPLE 1. In the clearing I saw a white-tailed deer.
    1. *In the clearing, saw*

1. In the spring I hiked through a national park. 2. Around me were many kinds of animals. 3. On several occasions I spotted some deer. 4. I found a doe and her spotted fawn in a little glade. 5. When they saw me, they ran quickly into the forest. 6. I was glad that they were protected by law. 7. At one time the Key deer, approximately the size of large collies, were hunted without restrictions. 8. Almost all of them were killed by hunters. 9. Now the population of Key deer is increasing in the Big Pine Key of southern Florida. 10. During Colonial times game laws protected the white-tailed deer from hunters.

11. For many hours I wandered among the scores of animals. 12. At my approach, I could hear animals as they scurried through the trees in alarm. 13. Soon after sundown I returned to my car.

● EXERCISE 9. Write original sentences using the following word groups as adverb phrases. Underline the phrase and draw an arrow to the word or words that each phrase modifies.

EXAMPLE   1. to the tower

1. *They sent radio signals to the tower.*

1. under the stone	6. during the winter
2. near the seashore	7. without her cane
3. around 1:00 A.M.	8. by some coincidence
4. up the hill	9. in the meantime
5. on the chalkboard	10. toward the west

● REVIEW EXERCISE A. The following paragraph contains eight adjective phrases and twelve adverb phrases. List the phrases in order on your paper, writing the number of the sentence before each phrase. After each phrase, write *adj.* for an adjective phrase or *adv.* for an adverb phrase. Remember that adjective phrases modify nouns or pronouns and that adverb phrases modify verbs, adjectives, or adverbs.

EXAMPLE   1. To many people Spain is the most beautiful country in Europe.
            1. *To many people, adv.*
            1. *in Europe, adj.*

1. Spain is located in the southwest corner of Europe. 2. Several centuries ago it was a country with great power. 3. Columbus sailed under the Spanish flag, and Mexico was conquered by Cortes of Spain. 4. Spain was an empire in the days of the early explorers. 5. After the defeat of the Spanish Armada, Spain's power declined. 6. For a while Napoleon ruled the country. 7. Since Napoleon's time Spain has had many

forms of government. 8. In 1936 a revolt against the government was launched by Francisco Franco. 9. For three years a civil war raged in Spain. 10. Then, after much bloodshed, Franco was declared the *caudillo*, or leader, of the nation.

DIAGRAMING ADJECTIVE AND ADVERB PHRASES

To diagram a prepositional phrase—either adjective or adverb—place the preposition on a slanting line below the word modified. Then put the object of the preposition on a horizontal line connected with the slanting line. Let the slanting line extend slightly beyond the line for the object.

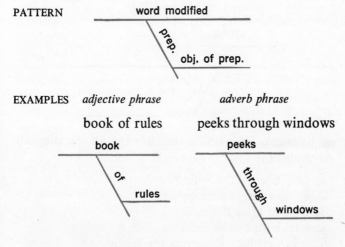

PATTERN

EXAMPLES   *adjective phrase*   *adverb phrase*

book of rules   peeks through windows

If the preposition has two objects, draw two horizontal lines and connect them with a dotted line on which you write the conjunction. Modifiers of the objects are diagramed in the usual way. They are placed on slanting lines below the words they modify.

EXAMPLES   *adjective phrase*

a plane with ten passengers and three crew-
men

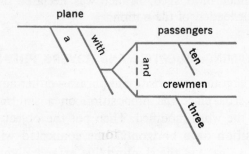

adverb phrase

landed in rain and fog

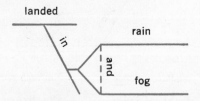

● EXERCISE 10.   Using the patterns above, diagram
the following groups of words.

1. rain against the window
2. some weeds in the garden
3. dashed after the ball
4. hats with bright feathers
5. was well hidden among the bushes
6. games for older boys
7. looked in the attic or the basement
8. cars for sale
9. lighted by a small candle and a very dim lamp
10. houses with green shutters and tile roofs

Here is a complete sentence containing adjective and adverb phrases. Study the diagram until you are sure that you understand the position of every word.

The family down the street is moving to Canada in the fall.

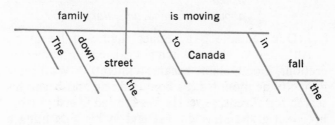

● EXERCISE 11. Diagram the following sentences. Each sentence contains an adjective phrase or an adverb phrase or both.

1. Our car is parked across the street.
2. Sit in the front row.
3. The visitor from Ireland has left.
4. A movie with my favorite actor is showing.
5. A dog with long ears trotted behind his master.
6. The old wagon was stuck in the mud.
7. A play about Napoleon will be given tonight.
8. Years of study and hard work were finally rewarded.
9. We painted with oils and water colors.
10. The plane with only one engine landed on a slippery runway.

● REVIEW EXERCISE B. The following paragraph contains eight adjective phrases and twelve adverb phrases. List the phrases in order on your paper, writing the number of the sentence before each phrase. After each phrase write adjective (*adj.*) or adverb (*adv.*). Then write the word or words the phrase modifies.

EXAMPLE 1. In the seventeenth century a famous story about knighthood was published.
1. *In the seventeenth century, adv., was published*
1. *about knighthood, adj., story*

1. Don Quixote is a comical figure of literature. 2. Although knighthood had not existed for many generations, Don Quixote became a knight. 3. With some difficulty he mounted his bony old nag and began his search for adventure. 4. He was dressed in armor from his great-grandfather's time, and at his side hung a very dull sword. 5. Soon he encountered his first adventure. 6. In his path stood twenty windmills. 7. But in Don Quixote's eyes the windmills were giants. 8. Like a knight in a tournament he charged at the windmills. 9. A vane in a windmill caught his armor. 10. It lifted him and threw him into the air. 11. Don Quixote had an explanation for the situation. 12. During his charge on the giants, a magician had changed them into windmills. 13. Adventures like the windmill fight occur often in *Don Quixote*.

● REVIEW EXERCISE C. For each of the following words, write one original sentence containing an adjective phrase and one containing an adverb phrase. Remember that an adjective phrase must modify a noun or pronoun and that an adverb phrase must modify a verb, adjective, or adverb.

EXAMPLE 1. snowman
1. *We made a snowman with a big hat.*
The snowman melted in the first thaw.

1. pie 2. turkey 3. climbed 4. appeared 5. parade

CHAPTER 5

Complements

Direct and Indirect Objects;
Predicate Nominatives,
Predicate Adjectives

Every sentence, long or short, is built upon a foundation called the *sentence base*. The sentence base always contains a subject and verb. For some sentences another element essential to the meaning of the sentence appears in the complete predicate with the verb. This word is a *complement* ("completer"). It completes the meaning begun by the subject and verb.

COMPLEMENTS WITH ACTION VERBS

Some verbs express action by themselves: *Children play; Work began.* Many verbs, however, call for another word to indicate the person or thing that the action of the subject is directed toward. A complement that indicates the receiver of an action is called an *object*. There are two kinds of objects: *direct objects* and *indirect objects.*

The Direct Object

The complements in the following sentences are direct objects of the verb. Notice that they are all nouns or pronouns.

> Achilles fought **Hector** outside Troy.
> Achilles killed **him.**
> The Greeks won the **war.**

5a. The *direct object* receives the action of the verb or shows the result of that action. It answers the questions "What?" or "Whom?" after an action verb.

EXAMPLES   Gorillas eat **berries.** [*Berries* receives the action of the verb *eats.*]

That shop manufactures small **parts** for jet engines. [*Parts* is the result of the action of the verb *manufactures.*]

A direct object can never follow a linking verb, since a linking verb does not express action. You should notice, also, that a direct object is never in a prepositional phrase.

EXAMPLES   John Jay was the first Chief Justice of the United States. [The verb *was* does not express action; therefore, it has no direct object.]

I learned a **lesson** in safety. [*Lesson* is the direct object of the verb; *safety* is the object of the preposition.]

Direct objects may be compound:

> We bought **ribbon, wrapping paper, and tape.** [The compound direct object of the verb *bought* is *ribbon, wrapping paper,* and *tape.*]

● EXERCISE 1. Each of the following sentences contains a direct object. Copy the direct object after the proper number. Remember that you can find a direct object by asking "What?" or "Whom?" after an action verb.

EXAMPLE   1. Clyde Beatty trained lions.
　　　　　 1. *lions*

1. Ellen redecorated her room.
2. We studied wildlife at camp.
3. Mrs. Gibson read a story to her class.
4. Bill recited a poem for the talent show.
5. Our neighbors drive me to school every day.
6. On his last fishing trip my father caught a marlin.
7. Mr. Thrasher raises Irish setters and boxers.
8. Suddenly Pete found himself alone in the museum.
9. During the winter we often attend concerts.
10. The Christmas parade delighted us.

● EXERCISE 2. There are twenty direct objects in the following sentences. Copy the direct objects after the proper numbers.

1. In the First Punic War Rome defeated the Carthaginian navy.
2. Later a Roman army invaded Africa and fought on land.
3. In the Second Punic War Hannibal crossed the Alps from Spain into Italy.
4. He used elephants against the Romans.
5. He had twenty thousand infantrymen and six thousand cavalrymen.
6. He won many battles, but Fabius, a Roman general, eventually caused his defeat.
7. Fabius fought no major battles against Hannibal.
8. He harassed Hannibal with minor skirmishes.

5 a

9. This tactic gradually weakened Hannibal's army.
10. Hannibal could neither capture Rome nor crush Rome's army.
11. Thus he wasted his strength.
12. Hannibal's defeat ended the war between Rome and Carthage.
13. Later Hannibal killed himself.
14. Carthage finally acknowledged Rome's power and served her former enemy.
15. She surrendered her fleet and paid huge sums of money to Rome.

● EXERCISE 3. There are ten direct objects in the following paragraph. Copy each one after the number of its sentence. Some sentences do not contain direct objects.

1. The ways of primitive man have always fascinated modern man. 2. Students of this subject are anthropologists. 3. Anthropologists have discovered many things about the life of early men. 4. Early men probably did not have ideas—rather, they received mental pictures. 5. They would see in their minds a picture of food, for example. 6. Perhaps they saw a new kind of shelter. 7. Primitive man drew pictures long before he learned to write. 8. Early man gave human characteristics to fire and to other natural phenomena. 9. Light, water, and fire were essential to his life. 10. He worshiped them, but he did not understand them.

The Indirect Object

The next kind of complement you will study is the *indirect object*. Some verbs have both direct and indirect objects. When they do, the sentence base consists of subject, verb, indirect object, and direct object. Like all complements, the indirect object helps to complete the meaning begun by the subject and verb.

You have learned that a direct object answers the questions "What?" or "Whom?" after an action verb. An indirect object answers the questions "To what?" or "To whom?" or "For what?" or "For whom?" after an action verb. The indirect object always comes before the direct object in the sentence.

> Dad left the **waiter** a tip. [*Waiter* is the indirect object of the verb *left*. It answers the question, "For whom did he leave a tip?"]
>
> Despite her nervousness, Lynn gave the **audience** a quick glance. [To what did she give a quick glance? *Audience* is the indirect object of the verb *gave*.]

5b. The *indirect object* of the verb precedes the direct object and tells to whom or what or for whom or what the action of the verb is done.

Linking verbs do not have indirect objects, of course, since they do not show action. Indirect objects have two characteristics in common with direct objects: (1) They are never in prepositional phrases, and (2) they may be compound.

EXAMPLES The travel bureau sent the necessary information to us. [*Information* is the direct object of the verb *sent*. *Us* is the object of the preposition *to*.]

The travel bureau sent **us** the necessary information. [*Us* is the indirect object of the verb *sent*. It precedes the direct object,

5 b

information, and answers the question "To whom?"]

Higgins threw **Gregory** and **Anderson** slow curve balls for the first pitch. [*Curve balls* is the direct object of the verb *threw; Gregory and Anderson* is the compound indirect object of the verb.]

● EXERCISE 4.   Each of the following sentences contains a direct object and an indirect object. After the sentence number, copy the indirect object and then the direct object on your paper. Underline the indirect objects.

EXAMPLE   1. Italy has given the Western world an incomparable heritage of art.
                1. *world, heritage*

1. My uncle gave me a special stamp.
2. Agnes sold me her rock collection.
3. The director told us the history of the museum.
4. Dad lent his younger brother a large sum of money.
5. The government buildings in Washington give the city an air of stately dignity.
6. The principal promised our class a trip to Washington.
7. A magician was showing the audience the secret of his rope trick.
8. Congress awarded the astronaut a medal for distinguished service to his country.
9. Hand me the book on the table.
10. Dan threw the birds some bread crumbs.

● EXERCISE 5.   All of the following sentences contain direct objects, and some contain indirect objects, too. Write the numbers 1–10 on your paper. After each number, write the object or objects in the sentence. Underline the indirect objects.

1. The inspector explained the case to his assistants.
2. Mrs. Griffin set a place for him at the table.
3. Evelyn is reading us a chapter from *David Copperfield.*
4. My pen pal sent me his picture.
5. Professor Cross presented a clear discussion of space travel to his listeners.
6. The costume shop lent our drama group some costumes of the 1870's.
7. Will Rogers left us many amusing stories.
8. I wrote Max a long letter about my discovery.
9. Mr. Short brought his family some camping equipment.
10. The blind poet Milton dictated his poetry to his daughters.

● EXERCISE 6. There are twenty objects of verbs, direct and indirect, in the following paragraph. List them on your paper, writing the number of the sentence before each one. Underline the indirect objects.

1. Tony's parents took him to an aquarium. 2. The guide at the entrance gave them some information about exhibits. 3. They walked around the main building and studied the fish in the glass tanks. 4. One large tank contained porpoises, sea turtles, sharks, and many small fish. 5. A man in diving equipment gave them a scare. 6. He entered the tank! 7. The fish swarmed around him and he fed them smaller fish from a basket on his arm. 8. Next Tony and his parents moved upstairs; there the porpoises performed for them, leaping high into the air. 9. They snatched fish from the attendant's hand. 10. At the sharks' pool, an attendant was giving the sharks their dinner. 11. He

tied a rope around a fish and lowered it to the surface of the water. 12. In a few seconds the sharks stripped the fish of its flesh. 13. Finally, around closing time, Tony and his parents left the aquarium.

SUBJECT COMPLEMENTS

In addition to direct objects and indirect objects, there are two other kinds of complements: the *predicate nominative* and the *predicate adjective*. These two complements are both called *subject complements*, since they refer to the subject of a sentence. The words in heavy type in the following sentences are subject complements. Notice that they all follow linking verbs.

> Claude has been **president** of his class for three years. [*President* refers to the subject *Claude*.]
> Tomorrow will be too **late**. [*Late* refers to the subject *tomorrow*.]
> Was it **you**? [*You* refers to the subject *it*.]
> Barbara looks **sleepy** this morning. [*Sleepy* refers to the subject *Barbara*.]

5c. A *subject complement* is a complement that refers to (describes or explains) the subject.

Subject complements always follow linking verbs, never action verbs. In order to recognize subject complements, you should review your knowledge of linking verbs.

COMMON LINKING VERBS

be (all forms)	smell	appear	grow
taste	sound	become	remain
feel	look	seem	stay

There are two kinds of subject complements: the predicate nominative and the predicate adjective. Both occur in the predicate of a sentence, and both refer to the subject.

The Predicate Nominative

The words in heavy type in the following sentences are predicate nominatives:

> This piece of stone may be an old **arrowhead.**
> By night the sleet had become **snow.**
> Porpoises are **members** of the whale family.

(1) A *predicate nominative* is one kind of subject complement. It is a noun or pronoun that explains or identifies the subject of the sentence. It follows a linking verb.

EXAMPLES   A good dictionary is a valuable **tool** for homework assignments. [*Tool* is a predicate nominative following the linking verb *is.* It refers to the subject *dictionary.*]

That unlucky swimmer might have been **you!** [*You* is a predicate nominative following the linking verb *might have been.* It identifies the subject *swimmer.*]

You must be careful not to confuse a predicate nominative with a direct object. Remember that a direct object must follow an action verb; a predicate nominative must follow a linking verb. Like other kinds of complements, predicate nominatives are never in prepositional phrases.

EXAMPLES   This slice is the **end** of the loaf. [*End* is a predicate nominative referring to the subject *slice. Of the loaf* is a prepositional phrase used as an adjective to modify *end.*]

5 c

Last year the delegates were **Joan Atkins and Marcia Philipo** from Carbondale School. [The compound predicate nominative is *Joan Atkins and Marcia Philipo*.]

● EXERCISE 7.   Each of the following sentences contains a predicate nominative. After the proper number on your paper, copy the linking verb and predicate nominative from each sentence.

EXAMPLE   1. Siam became modern Thailand.
            1. *became, Thailand*

1. Whales are mammals.
2. The real villain is the little boy down the street.
3. Roger will soon be a dentist.
4. Helene may become a good actress.
5. Rhode Island is the smallest state in the Union.
6. The old green convertible is theirs.
7. Can it be they at this hour?
8. He may be the most likely choice for the office.
9. Our present enemies were once our friends.
10. Dag Hammarskjöld was the Secretary General of the United Nations for over eight years.

● EXERCISE 8.   The sentences below contain predicate nominatives. After each number, write the verb and the predicate nominative.

1. Sea cows are the sirens of ancient legends.
2. They became mermaids in the sailors' stories.
3. Armadillos are our oddest animals.
4. Their outer covering is a series of bony plates.
5. Television is an important tool of education.
6. Space travel has become a subject for complex research.
7. Many stars are brighter objects than our sun.
8. The origin of comets has long been a mystery to us.

9. Halley's Comet should be the next bright comet to appear.
10. The Hebrides are a group of about five hundred islands off the coast of Scotland.

The Predicate Adjective

Like the predicate nominative, the *predicate adjective* is a subject complement that is found in the predicate and refers to the subject.

> The students were **hoarse** from cheering. [*Hoarse* is a predicate adjective modifying the subject *students*.]
>
> Watermelon tastes **good** on a hot day. [*Good* is a predicate adjective modifying the subject *watermelon*.]
>
> The cake was **light** and **delicious**. [*Light* and *delicious* are predicate adjectives modifying the subject *cake*.]

Like predicate nominatives, predicate adjectives always follow linking verbs.

(2) A *predicate adjective* is one kind of subject complement. It is an adjective that modifies the subject of the sentence. It follows a linking verb.

● EXERCISE 9. Each of the following sentences contains a predicate adjective. After the proper number on your paper, copy first the linking verb and then the predicate adjective.

EXAMPLE 1. Prairie dogs are very sociable.
  1. *are, sociable*

1. The homework was easy tonight.
2. That pitcher of lemonade tasted sour.
3. Our rug is too small for our living room.

4. After a cold shower she felt good.
5. The audience remained silent for a few seconds after the performance.
6. The water looked dark green because of the chemicals in it.
7. During the interrogation the detective became angry.
8. We grew tired of his complaints.
9. From my seat the drums sound too loud.
10. In the midst of the panic, Sam stayed calm.

● EXERCISE 10.   Think of an appropriate predicate adjective for each blank in the following sentences. Write the predicate adjective on your paper after the sentence number.

1. The pie at dinner tasted ——.
2. Even from a distance of five miles, the cannons sounded ——.
3. To the station attendant the lady seemed —— beyond belief.
4. The sword felt —— in his hand.
5. Emily was —— about the change in plans.
6. Most holidays seem —— to me.
7. My date for the prom is —— and ——.
8. Our football team looks ——, while the opposing team looks ——.
9. The last time I saw them they were ——.
10. The manager of the park becomes —— when people litter the park with paper and food.

● REVIEW EXERCISE A.   There are twenty complements of all kinds in the following paragraph. Copy each complement after the number of the sentence. Then identify it as a direct object (*d.o.*), an indirect object (*i.o.*), a predicate nominative (*p.n.*), or a predicate adjective (*p.a.*).

EXAMPLE 1. Shall I tell you the old story of Barbara Allen?

1. *you, i.o.*
   story, d.o.

1. A mountaineer sang us the ballad of Barbara Allen. 2. It is a beautiful ballad about a cruel girl. 3. Ballad hunters have found ninety-two versions of "Barbara Allen" in Virginia alone. 4. The stories of all versions are similar. 5. A young man was ill with a broken heart. 6. His servant brought the young man's sweetheart to his master's bed. 7. The sweetheart was Barbara Allen. 8. The young man told Barbara Allen his tale of love for her. 9. But the young man had once slighted her, and now she was cruel to him. 10. She left his house; soon after, she heard the death bell. 11. Every knell was terrible to her. 12. It warned her of doom, and she became repentant. 13. She had killed her lover this day, and she would be the victim of love tomorrow. 14. So fate punished the cruel Barbara Allen.

Diagraming Complements

Except for the indirect object, the parts of a sentence base always go on the main horizontal line. You have already learned how to diagram a sentence base consisting of a subject and verb. Now you will learn to diagram a sentence base which contains a complement also.

Direct Objects

The direct object is placed on the horizontal line with the subject and verb. A short vertical line separates it from the verb.

PATTERN

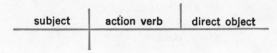

EXAMPLES   1.   We pulled taffy. [d.o.]

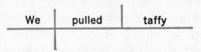

2.   Lizards eat flies and earthworms.
[compound d.o.]

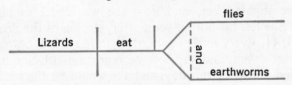

Notice that the vertical line between the verb and
the direct object stops at the horizontal line.

Predicate Nominatives and Predicate Adjectives

The diagram for a predicate nominative and a
predicate adjective is similar to the diagram for the
direct object. Instead of a vertical line separating the
complement from the verb, use a diagonal line slanting back toward the subject and verb.

PATTERN

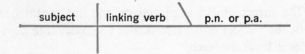

EXAMPLES 1. The sun is a star. [p.n.]

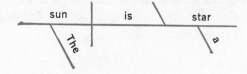

2. Peaches are delicious. [p.a.]

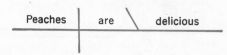

3. The Indigo snake is large and shiny.
[compound p.a.]

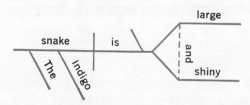

● EXERCISE 11. Diagram the following sentences.

1. Turtles are reptiles.
2. Turtles have no teeth.
3. Their horny bills tear their food.
4. Turtles may grow very old.
5. The alligator snapper is the largest freshwater turtle.
6. Its mouth is huge.
7. Its jaws are very powerful.
8. The snapper can maim a hand or foot.
9. Few turtles are dangerous.
10. Most are quiet and slow.

Indirect Objects

To diagram an indirect object, write it on a short horizontal line below the verb, with a slanting line joining it to the verb.

PATTERN

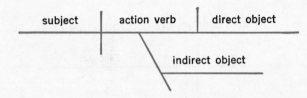

EXAMPLES 1. The veterinarian gave us a dog. [i.o.]

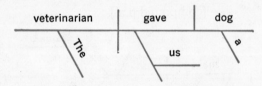

2. The guide showed my cousin and me the falls. [compound i.o.]

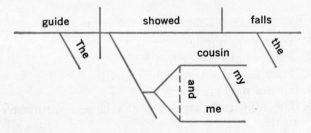

● EXERCISE 12. Diagram the following sentences.

1. I handed the clerk a dollar.
2. Several businessmen gave our school a check.
3. His uncle left him a fortune.

4. The teacher assigned us a project.
5. Send them your extra clothes.
6. My aunt knitted Violet and me sweaters.
7. The students gave him their attention.
8. The store offered Ann and Dottie good salaries.
9. The carpenter built himself a desk.
10. My neighbor lent me his camera.

● REVIEW EXERCISE B.   Each of the following sentences contains one or more complements. Copy the complements on your paper, putting the number of the sentence before each one. Then tell whether the complement is a direct object (*d.o.*), indirect object (*i.o.*), predicate nominative (*p.n.*), or predicate adjective (*p.a.*).

1. Rip Van Winkle was a lazy man.
2. He was also a henpecked husband.
3. He took his gun and his dog and climbed a mountain near his home.
4. On top of the mountain he met a strange little man.
5. The man offered him a drink from his jug.
6. The drink tasted good.
7. Rip became tired and lay down.
8. He was soon asleep.
9. Later he opened his eyes with a start.
10. His gun had become rusty, and his dog did not answer.
11. The people of the village looked strange.
12. He asked advice from the people around him.
13. Finally he located his home.
14. It was hardly recognizable.
15. Rip had been asleep for twenty years.
16. His wife was dead.
17. Rip had become an old man.
18. He told visitors his strange story.

PART TWO

Usage

CHAPTER 6

Agreement of Subject and Verb

Singular and Plural Number

Some of the most common mistakes in speaking and writing are made when verb and subject do not agree. Perhaps you have overheard a conversation like this one:

> Ken: How many is in your club?
> Tom: We was hoping for twenty, but there's only fifteen of us so far.

Do you see the three errors in agreement in that passage? The verbs and their subjects do not agree in number. This chapter will help you to avoid such errors.

NUMBER

All nouns and pronouns have number. They are singular in number if they refer to one thing. They are plural in number if they refer to more than one thing.

6a. When a word refers to one person or thing, it is *singular* in number. When a word refers to more than one, it is *plural* in number.

EXAMPLES   hat, I, sky, principle [singular]

hats, we, skies, principles [plural]

● EXERCISE 1.   Write the numbers 1–18 on your paper. If a word is singular, write *S* after its number. If it is plural, write *P*.

1. morning	7. they	13. cave
2. calves	8. heights	14. we
3. women	9. goose	15. leaves
4. she	10. it	16. chief
5. pencils	11. mosquitoes	17. mailmen
6. shelf	12. fellowmen	18. babies

6b. A verb agrees with its subject in number.

Two words *agree* when they have the same number. The number of the verb must always agree with the number of its subject.

EXAMPLES   He fights. [singular subject and singular verb]

Animals fight. [plural subject and plural verb]

(1) Singular subjects take singular verbs.

EXAMPLES   The **lightning fills** the sky. [The verb *fills* is singular to agree with the singular subject *lightning*.]

Linda begins her vacation today. [The verb *begins* is singular to agree with the singular subject *Linda*.]

(2) Plural subjects take plural verbs.

EXAMPLES   **Cheetahs run** faster than most other animals. [The verb *run* is plural to agree with the plural subject *cheetahs*.]

New **families move** into our neighborhood frequently. [The verb *move* is plural to agree with the plural subject *families*.]

Notice that an –*s* ending is often a sign of the singular in the verb and a sign of the plural in the subject.

◆ NOTE   When a sentence contains a verb phrase, it is the helping verb that agrees with the subject.

EXAMPLES   The **motor is** running. The **motors are** running.

The **train has** been delayed. The **trains have** been delayed.

● EXERCISE 2.   The subjects and verbs that follow are in agreement. If an item is singular, write *S* after its number. If it is plural, write *P*.

1. men work
2. wind howls
3. owls hoot
4. we practice
5. days pass
6. monkeys chatter
7. Paul writes
8. it seems
9. snakes hiss
10. glasses break
11. night arrives
12. gates open
13. she tries
14. actor rehearses
15. students study
16. leaf falls
17. thieves steal
18. girl giggles
19. they watch
20. lion lurks

● EXERCISE 3.   The subjects and verbs in the following sentences agree in number. Write each subject and verb on your paper, changing them to the opposite

6
a-b

number. If the verb consists of more than one word, write the whole verb phrase.

EXAMPLES   1. Many exhibits are housed in the Smithsonian Institution.
    1. *exhibit is housed*
    2. The museum is located in Washington, D.C.
    2. *museums are located*

1. The museum was built in 1846.
2. Several million persons visit the Smithsonian Institution each year.
3. They see there a 2,573-pound meteorite.
4. A two-story colonial farmhouse is also on exhibit.
5. Visitors always marvel at the Wright brothers' original plane.
6. Five halls have a magnificent collection of Indian material.
7. Tourists are taken through the various branches of the museum.
8. Many private citizens have donated gifts to the Smithsonian.
9. Women especially like the displays of dresses of the First Ladies.
10. Washington's uniform appeals to the children as well as the adults.

● EXERCISE 4.   In each of the following sentences, two verbs are written in parentheses. Choose the one which agrees with the subject. Write the subject and verb after the proper number.

EXAMPLE   1. Cherry trees (lines, line) the Potomac.
    1. *trees line*

1. An electric computer (solves, solve) difficult problems quickly.

2. Many colleges (has, have) computers.
3. Over one hundred thousand forest fires (is, are) reported each year.
4. Lightning sometimes (causes, cause) fires.
5. Careless people (is, are) often at fault.
6. Forest rangers (says, say) that we can prevent forest fires.
7. Some Polynesian divers (descends, descend) almost forty-five feet without special equipment.
8. The owl's eyes (makes, make) him look wise.
9. Actually, the owl (sees, see) poorly during the day.
10. Every year scientists (discovers, discover) new drugs to fight diseases.

PROBLEMS IN AGREEMENT

In the exercises so far, it has been easy to make the subjects and verbs agree because the verbs have followed their subjects closely and the number of the subject has been clear. However, a phrase may come between the subject and verb creating an agreement problem. Or, the subject may be a pronoun, the number of which is hard to determine.

Phrases Between Subject and Verb

Sometimes a prepositional phrase comes between the subject and verb in a sentence. If the object of the preposition is different in number from the subject of the sentence, you must be especially careful to make the verb agree with the subject in number. Notice the subject-verb relationships in the following sentences.

WRONG   The special effects in the movie was particularly original. [The verb should agree with the plural subject *effects*, not with the singular noun *movie*, which is the object of the preposition *in*.]

RIGHT   The special **effects** in the movie **were** particularly original.

WRONG   The lights in the stadium has been turned on. [The verb should agree with the plural subject *lights*, not with the singular noun *stadium*, the object of the preposition *in*.]

RIGHT   The **lights** in the stadium **have** been turned on.

6c. The number of a subject is not changed by a phrase following the subject.

EXAMPLES   **Seats** for the concert **are** reserved.
One of us **is** guilty.
The successful **candidate,** with two of his aides, **has** entered the auditorium.
Scientists from all over the world **have** gathered in Geneva.

● EXERCISE 5.   Copy the subject from each of the following sentences. Then choose the correct verb from the two in parentheses and write it after the subject.

EXAMPLE   1. No clue to the crimes (was, were) found.
1. *clue was*

1. A book about reptiles (was, were) published by the university.
2. The annual meeting of tribes (is, are) being held in Cherokee, North Carolina.
3. The dates for the school book fair (has, have) been set.

4. Remains of a prehistoric animal (shows, show) scientists some facts about life on our planet hundreds of centuries ago.
5. The search for the missing planes (continues, continue).
6. Members of the science club (takes, take) a field trip once a month.
7. Copies of the play (has, have) been ordered.
8. The teacher, along with her students, (enjoys, enjoy) a trip to the museum.
9. A lecture on good study habits (serves, serve) a useful purpose.
10. The girls in the orchestra (is, are) planning a party.

● EXERCISE 6. Choose the correct verbs from the following paragraph and write them on your paper. Before each verb, write the number of its sentence. Be prepared to identify the subjects.

1. *Moby Dick*, an exciting story about Captain Ahab and a great white whale, (interests, interest) readers of all ages. 2. The men on Ahab's ship, the *Pequod*, (fears, fear) him because of his desire to capture the great whale named Moby Dick. 3. Many signs of bad luck (occurs, occur) during the voyage. 4. But Ahab, with his crew, (continues, continue) to look for Moby Dick. 5. Finally, above the waves (appears, appear) a seeming mountain of white. 6. Then the sailors of the *Pequod* (knows, know) that they have found Moby Dick. 7. Ahab, together with some of his men, (gives, give) chase. 8. Two of the small boats (is, are) finally destroyed. 9. The whale, plunging through the waves, (throws, throw) Ahab's boat high in the air. 10. The *Pequod* picks up most of the men, but one of the sailors (is, are) not found.

6 c

Indefinite Pronouns

In Chapter 2 you saw that one kind of pronoun is the *indefinite* pronoun. It is so called because the person or thing to which it refers is not named. Like all pronouns, indefinite pronouns take the place of nouns. Unlike personal pronouns, however, indefinite pronouns replace or refer to nouns that are usually not named. Here are some examples of personal and indefinite pronouns:

PERSONAL	INDEFINITE
we	anybody
you	both
he	either
them	everyone

When indefinite pronouns are used as subjects of sentences, their verbs must agree with them.

6d. The following common words are singular: *each, either, neither, one, everyone, everybody, no one, nobody, anyone, anybody, someone, somebody.*

EXAMPLES   **Anyone** without tickets **is** asked to see Mr. Harris.

Each of the newcomers **was** welcomed to the city.

No one understands a person who mumbles.

● EXERCISE 7. Find the subject of each sentence below and write it on your paper after the number. Then choose the correct verb from the two in parentheses and write it after the subject. Remember that the number of the verb is not affected by a word in a prepositional phrase.

EXAMPLE   1. One of the dogs (is, are) mine.
      1. *One is*

1. Neither of the languages (is, are) widely spoken today.
2. Everybody in those classes (wants, want) to learn a foreign language.
3. Someone among the local distributors (supplies, supply) us with tapes.
4. Each of us (records, record) his voice each day.
5. No one in either of the two schools (was, were) ever in a language laboratory before.
6. Everyone with an interest in foreign languages (is, are) glad to have the chance to use the laboratory.
7. Anybody with earphones (feels, feel) rather important.
8. Everybody in Mr. Woodring's and Miss Oliver's classes (files, file) quietly down to the lab.
9. There one of the laboratory instructors (helps, help) us adjust our machines.
10. Of all those thirty-seven students, no one (likes, like) to miss a session in the lab.

6e. The following common words are plural: *both, few, many, several.*

EXAMPLES   **Few** of my neighbors **have** parakeets.
       Many of them **keep** dogs as pets.

● EXERCISE 8.   After the number of each sentence, copy the subject. Then choose the correct verb from the two in parentheses and write it after the subject.

6
d-e

1. Many of our group (has, have) had flu shots.
2. Everyone in the surrounding towns (was, were) warned about the epidemic.
3. Of the new cases, few (is, are) serious.
4. Neither of those paths (leads, lead) home.
5. Few (knows, know) how to write a good business letter.
6. Each of the stores (gives, give) gifts to our graduates.
7. Several of the tests for iron ore (has, have) been tried.
8. No one in that whole group of doctors (knows, know) an easy cure for the common cold.
9. Some in the group (doubts, doubt) the existence of intelligent life on other planets.
10. Many of them (suspects, suspect) that intelligent life exists somewhere else.
11. (Has, Have) either of you seen an ice hockey game?
12. In the corner (stands, stand) one of the suspects.
13. Some of the critics of America (thinks, think) we are too concerned with material goods.
14. Someone up in the trees (is, are) signaling us.
15. Several from the seventh grade (is, are) needed to form a debate team.
16. Many of the schools in our area (sends, send) delegates to the state convention.
17. Both of the coaches for the varsity team (works, work) with the boys every afternoon.
18. Several of the days last week (was, were) uncomfortably hot.
19. Many of the good players in the junior orchestra (hopes, hope) to be promoted to the senior orchestra.
20. (Has, Have) both of you seen the art exhibit?

6f. The words *all, any, most, none,* and *some* may be either singular or plural.

In order to know whether to use a singular or plural verb with the pronouns *all, any, most, none,* and *some,* you must observe the sense of the sentence. If the pronoun refers to one person or thing, it is singular and takes a singular verb. If it refers to more than one person or thing, it is plural and takes a plural verb. Study the following examples and note how the number of the pronoun changes as its meaning changes.

EXAMPLES   **All** of the nation's interest **centers** on politics during a political convention. [The subject *all* is singular because it refers to one thing—*interest.* The verb *centers* is singular to agree with it.]

All of the states **send** delegates to national political conventions. [The subject *all* is plural because it refers to more than one thing—fifty *states.* The verb *send* is plural to agree with it.]

Some of the excitement of such a convention **is** conveyed by television coverage. [The subject *some* is singular because it means "a part" of the excitement. The helping verb *is* is singular to agree with it.]

Some of the delegates **are** disappointed in the candidate who was chosen. [The subject *some* is plural because it refers to more than one delegate. The verb *are* is plural to agree with it.]

6f

● EXERCISE 9. Write ten original sentences using the words below as subjects. Make sure that the verbs agree with the subjects in number.

1. either
2. one
3. many
4. any
5. everybody
6. none
7. several
8. some
9. most
10. few

Compound Subjects

A compound subject, you will recall, consists of two or more connected subjects having the same verb. When two subjects are connected by *and*, even if they are both singular, they are followed by a plural verb.

6g. Subjects joined by *and* take a plural verb.

EXAMPLES   **A dictionary and** a one-volume **encyclopedia make** a good beginning for a reference library.

   Mr. Duffy and his son have gone fishing.

EXCEPTION   A compound subject that refers to a single person or to two or more things considered as a unit (one thing) takes a singular verb.

   A sweater and skirt makes a good outfit for school. [*Sweater and skirt* is considered one outfit.]

   A wife and mother has a challenging job. [One person is meant.]

● EXERCISE 10. Some of the following sentences have compound subjects and some do not. Copy each subject after the proper number, then choose the correct verb from the parentheses. If you choose a singular verb with a compound subject, be prepared to explain why.

1. (Is, Are) New York and Chicago the two largest cities in the United States?
2. Sleet with some snow (is, are) predicted for tomorrow.
3. My guide and companion for the tour (was, were) Dick.
4. New words and new meanings for old words (is, are) included in all modern dictionaries.
5. Your fingernail and a piece of glass (is, are) two means for testing hardness in minerals.
6. Both talc and gypsum (shows, show) a fingernail scratch.
7. The leader with his group (has, have) just left for the summit.
8. The opossum and the kangaroo (is, are) members of the same family of mammals.
9. Rattlesnakes, copperheads, coral snakes, and cottonmouths (is, are) four kinds of poisonous snakes found in the United States.
10. A horse and buggy (seems, seem) an unusual method of travel today.

6h. Singular subjects joined by *or* or *nor* take a singular verb.

EXAMPLES   The chief **geologist or** his **assistant is** due to arrive tonight.

A large **station wagon or** a small **truck has** enough room for the bicycles.

Neither a **rabbit nor** a **raccoon does** that kind of damage in a garden.

6
g-h

6i. When a singular subject and a plural subject are joined by *or* or *nor*, the verb agrees with the nearer subject.

EXAMPLES Neither the **air-conditioner nor** the **lights work.** [The verb *work* is plural to agree with *lights*, the part of the compound subject that is nearer to it.]

Flowers or a book usually **makes** an appropriate gift. [The verb *makes* is singular to agree with the part of the compound subject that is nearer to it, *book*.]

Compound subjects having both singular and plural parts often sound awkward even if they are correct. It is usually better to rephrase a sentence to avoid such constructions.

AWKWARD Two boys from Argentina or a girl from Chile is to speak to our class today.

BETTER Today our class will hear two boys from Argentina or a girl from Chile.

● EXERCISE 11. Choose the correct verb from the two in parentheses and write it on your paper. Be able to explain the reason for your choice.

1. Either a loan or a scholarship (is, are) available to selected applicants.
2. A desk or a bookcase (goes, go) into that corner.
3. Neither sheets nor towels (is, are) furnished at camp.
4. (Has, Have) the books or other supplies come?
5. A vocabulary notebook or vocabulary flashcards (is, are) helpful for review.
6. Either the clock on the town hall or my watch (is, are) wrong.

7. Another boy or girl (takes, take) the part of the narrator.
8. A map or a guidebook (has, have) been my constant companion in this city.
9. Enthusiasm for the proposal or excitement about it (is, are) not the same as solid support.
10. A course in ceramics or a course in woodworking (is, are) recommended.

Other Problems in Agreement

There are a few other constructions that may pose special problems in agreement of subject and verb. This section will cover some of these.

Some nouns that are singular in form name a group of people or things: *class, family, team, group, flock,* for example. These nouns are called *collective nouns.* They are singular when they are used to mean the group as one unit. They are plural when they are used to mean the individual members of the group.

6j. Collective nouns may be either singular or plural.

EXAMPLES   The **class were** divided in their opinions of the play. [Here *class* means several individuals; it is plural and takes a plural verb.]

The **class has** decided to have a science table in the room. [Here *class* is thought of as one unit; it is singular and takes a singular verb.]

The **family are** coming from all over the state for the reunion. [*Family* is plural because it suggests several members acting as individuals.]

6
i-j

The **family plans** to attend Bill's graduation. [*Family* is singular because it is acting
as one unit.]

6k. When the subject follows the verb, as in sentences beginning with *there* and *here*, be careful
to determine the subject and make sure that
the verb agrees with it.

In sentences that begin with *there* or *here*, you may
have difficulty in finding the subject. Until you are
sure what the subject is, you cannot make the verb
agree with it. In analyzing such sentences, you should
remember that the subject is the word about which
something is said. Look for the verb first, and then
find the word about which the verb makes a statement.

EXAMPLES   There **are** three sparrow's **eggs** in that
nest. [*Are* is the verb. What are? The subject must be *eggs*.]

Here **comes Karen** with her new bicycle.
[*Comes* is the verb. Who comes? *Karen*.
Karen must be the subject.]

In conversation as well as in writing be especially
careful not to use the contractions *here's* and *there's*
with plural subjects. They are singular and must have
singular subjects. If a plural verb is called for, you
must use *here are* or *there are*.

● EXERCISE 12.   Copy the subject from each of the
following sentences. Then choose the correct verb
from the two in parentheses and write it after the
subject.

1. There (is, are) at least two ways to find this answer.
2. The group (was, were) all going to different camps.
3. Here (is, are) fifteen members of the Little League, all hungry.
4. (Is, Are) both of the twins graduating this year?
5. Here (is, are) some sandwiches and milk.
6. Here (is, are) the shells from Old Orchard Beach.
7. (Here's, Here are) the answers to the test.
8. On the steps of the Capitol there (is, are) several senators and congressmen.
9. That flock of geese (makes, make) a beautiful pattern in the sky.
10. There (is, are) neither time nor money enough.

6l. Words stating amounts are usually singular.

Some words that are plural in form may be singular in meaning if they mean an amount of something.

EXAMPLES Thirty-five **cents is** enough for lunch today. [Although *thirty-five cents* is plural in form, it means a single amount of money. It takes a singular verb, *is*.]

Two **weeks** never **seems** long enough for vacation. [Although *two weeks* is plural, it is thought of here as a single unit of time. It takes a singular verb, *seems*.]

6m. The title of a book, organization, or country, even when plural in form, usually takes a singular verb.

EXAMPLE *Lost Pony Tracks* **is** a book about an Easterner who moved to a ranch in the West.

6
k-m

● Exercise 13. Write the numbers 1–10 on your paper. Choose the correct one of the two verbs in parentheses and write it after the number.

1. "The Hundred Dresses" (is, are) a story about a lonely girl.
2. Two cups of flour (seems, seem) too much for that recipe.
3. Three days (was, were) all the time I missed from school last year.
4. Morgan and Company (advertises, advertise) beach bags for a dollar.
5. The Veterans of Foreign Wars (is, are) holding its convention in Chicago this year.
6. Five pounds of sugar (is, are) a lot to carry with all the other groceries.
7. Two hours of homework in one subject (is, are) unfair.
8. *Children of the Sea* (was, were) written by Wilfrid S. Bronson.
9. Three weeks of rehearsal time usually (proves, prove) to be sufficient.
10. Fifty cents (is, are) all I have been able to save this month.

6n. *Don't* and *doesn't* must agree with their subjects.

The words *don't* and *doesn't* (contractions of *do not* and *does not*) must, like all other verbs, agree with their subjects. Mistakes are often made with these forms. Be careful, when you use them, to use *don't* with all plural subjects and the pronouns *I* and *you*. Use *doesn't* with all singular subjects except *I* and *you*.

WRONG   Ben don't exercise enough.
RIGHT   Ben **doesn't** exercise enough.
WRONG   That answer don't make sense.
RIGHT   That answer **doesn't** make sense.

If you are in doubt as to whether to use *don't* or *doesn't* in a sentence, substitute *do not* or *does not*. Your ear will usually tell you which is correct. In the sentences above, for example, if you substitute *do not* for *don't* in the first and third sentences, you realize at once that they are wrong.

● EXERCISE 14. *Oral Drill*. Read the following sentences aloud, supplying *don't* or *doesn't* as needed. Saying the correct form several times will help you to write the verb correctly.

1. The boy —— understand the problem.
2. —— he want the prize?
3. The lettuce —— look fresh.
4. That school —— have a stage.
5. It —— matter to him.
6. He —— see the rainbow.
7. The boxer and the poodle —— get along.
8. The curtains in the room —— match the color of the walls.
9. Mary —— need to go with me.
10. This bar of candy —— taste good.

● EXERCISE 15. Using the subjects below, write ten original sentences with *don't* or *doesn't* for verbs.

1. the senators from Oklahoma
2. an eclipse of the sun
3. algebra
4. our music teacher
5. watermelon
6. this typewriter
7. that old bicycle
8. your new idea
9. movie stars
10. piano lessons

6n

6o. **A few nouns, though plural in form, take a singular verb.**

EXAMPLES **Mathematics seems** easy this year.

Civics is being taught by Mr. Rodgers while Miss Emerson is away.

Mumps is certainly an uncomfortable disease.

The **news was** not encouraging.

● REVIEW EXERCISE A.   This exercise covers all the rules in this chapter. Write the numbers 1–20 on your paper. After each number, write the correct verb from the parentheses.

1. Unfortunately, my father (doesn't, don't) get a vacation this year.
2. Many of the men in his shop (gets, get) only a few days.
3. The safety commissioner or the radio announcer (suggests, suggest) that we drive especially carefully on holidays.
4. Each of us (knows, know) that many accidents are caused by carelessness.
5. Our car (doesn't, don't) have any antifreeze yet.
6. There (is, are) several islands in the state of Hawaii.
7. Several of the place names in our country (comes, come) from Indian words.
8. Five hours (is, are) all you need to fly across the Atlantic.
9. Anyone on the tennis courts today (is, are) liable to get a sunburn.
10. The architects (wasn't, weren't) sure what kind of building to plan for the new hotel.

11. Some of the many kinds of seaweed (is, are) edible.
12. One of the wheels (wasn't, weren't) functioning properly.
13. Both Janet and Hilda (hopes, hope) to get summer jobs.
14. The plane and its pilot (wasn't, weren't) hurt.
15. (Is, Are) there enough copies of the music to go around?
16. I hope it (doesn't, don't) rain tomorrow.
17. Economics (is, are) a complex but fascinating subject.
18. Either the leader or his followers (doesn't, don't) understand the instructions.
19. A herd of cattle (was, were) grazing on the hill.
20. Brown Brothers (has, have) a sale of sports clothes this week.

● REVIEW EXERCISE B. Write the numbers 1–20 on your paper. Choose the correct verb for each sentence and write it after the number. Be able to cite the rule for each choice that you make.

1. *Great Expectations* (is, are) the first novel by Charles Dickens that I have read.
2. Several of the novels of this author (is, are) interesting to young people.
3. A few of his titles (is, are) *Oliver Twist*, *David Copperfield*, and *A Tale of Two Cities*.
4. New readers in every generation (discovers, discover) Dickens' charm for themselves.
5. Every one of Dickens' novels (was, were) read eagerly in America.
6. A writer in England or a writer in America (knows, know) that his audience includes English-speaking people all over the world.

60

7. One of the advantages of learning a foreign language (is, are) the ability to read the literature of that language.
8. Translations of literature (is, are) generally inferior to the original works.
9. There (is, are) simple books for beginning students in all languages.
10. Two years (is, are) usually long enough to acquire a fairly good knowledge of a foreign tongue.
11. French and Spanish probably (is, are) the most popular languages to study.
12. Language class at any level (requires, require) repeated drill on pronunciation.
13. Accurate pronunciation (doesn't, don't) come easily to some students.
14. None of the sounds in English (is, are) quite like the sounds of some of the French vowels.
15. Everybody (is, are) quite likely to have some trouble with accents, too.
16. Knowledge of foreign languages (is, are) important for scientists.
17. Reports of research (is, are) published in many different languages.
18. Anyone in a certain field of knowledge (is, are) expected to keep informed in that field.
19. The exchange of ideas among scientists (is, are) a vital kind of communication.
20. Many (finds, find) German a useful language to know.

CHAPTER 7

Using Verbs Correctly

Principal Parts; Regular and Irregular Verbs

A single verb has many forms, which you must know if you are to speak and to write correctly. A verb has several different forms because it expresses different times (present, past, and future). The time expressed by a verb is called its *tense:* present tense, past tense, future tense.

PRINCIPAL PARTS

Every verb has four basic parts, which are called its principal parts. You must know all of these in order to form the different tenses correctly. Two of the principal parts are called *participles*.

The *present participle* of a verb always ends in *–ing:*

     calling hoping riding going

The *past participle* is the form used with *have, has,* or *had:*

     (have) called (has) hoped (had) ridden

143

7a. The four basic forms of a verb are the *infinitive*, the *present participle*, the *past*, and the *past participle*. These basic forms are called the *principal parts*.

INFINITIVE	PRESENT PARTICIPLE	PAST	PAST PARTICIPLE
talk	talking	talked	(have) talked
draw	drawing	drew	(have) drawn

The following sentences show how each form is used to express time.

1. They **draw** excellent pictures. [*present time*]
2. Susan **is drawing** one now. [*present time*]
3. Last week she **drew** two maps. [*past time*]
4. She **has** often **drawn** cartoons. [*past time*]
5. Perhaps she **will draw** one for you. [*future time*]

The following list gives the six tense (time) forms of a verb. A list of all the forms of a verb is called its *conjugation*.

CONJUGATION OF <u>SEE</u>

INFINITIVE	PRESENT PARTICIPLE	PAST	PAST PARTICIPLE
see	seeing	saw	(have) seen

PRESENT TENSE

Singular	*Plural*
I see	we see
you see	you see
he sees	they see

PAST TENSE

Singular	*Plural*
I saw	we saw
you saw	you saw
he saw	they saw

FUTURE TENSE

Singular	*Plural*
I will (shall) see	we will (shall) see
you will see	you will see
he will see	they will see

PRESENT PERFECT TENSE

Singular	*Plural*
I have seen	we have seen
you have seen	you have seen
he has seen	they have seen

PAST PERFECT TENSE

Singular	*Plural*
I had seen	we had seen
you had seen	you had seen
he had seen	they had seen

FUTURE PERFECT TENSE

Singular	*Plural*
I will (shall) have seen	we will (shall) have seen
you will have seen	you will have seen
he will have seen	they will have seen

Regular Verbs

7b. A *regular verb* forms its past and past participle by adding *–ed* or *–d* to the infinitive form.[1]

INFINITIVE	PRESENT PARTICIPLE	PAST	PAST PARTICIPLE
clean	cleaning	cleaned	(have) cleaned
inspect	inspecting	inspected	(have) inspected

[1] The addition of *–ed* sometimes means that the final consonant must be doubled, as in *hop, hopped* and *skip, skipped.*

7
a-b

Irregular Verbs

Many verbs, as you know, do not follow the regular way of forming principal parts. These *irregular verbs* are the troublesome ones. To avoid errors, you must learn the principal parts of common irregular verbs. You will find that you know many of them already.

7c. An *irregular verb* is one that forms its past and past participle in some other way than a regular verb.

Irregular verbs form their past and past participles in several ways:

(1) by changing a vowel

ring	rang	(have) rung
come	came	(have) come
shrink	shrank	(have) shrunk

(2) by changing a vowel and consonants

do	did	(have) done
go	went	(have) gone
see	saw	(have) seen

(3) by making no change

hurt	hurt	(have) hurt
put	put	(have) put
burst	burst	(have) burst

Memorize the principal parts of the following irregular verbs if you do not already know them. Study them ten at a time, until you have mastered them all. When you are practicing these verbs, always use *have* before the past participle. The past participle can never be used alone.

COMMON IRREGULAR VERBS

INFINITIVE	PRESENT PARTICIPLE	PAST	PAST PARTICIPLE
begin	beginning	began	(have) begun
blow	blowing	blew	(have) blown
break	breaking	broke	(have) broken
bring	bringing	brought	(have) brought
burst	bursting	burst	(have) burst
choose	choosing	chose	(have) chosen
come	coming	came	(have) come
do	doing	did	(have) done
drink	drinking	drank	(have) drunk
drive	driving	drove	(have) driven
eat	eating	ate	(have) eaten
fall	falling	fell	(have) fallen
freeze	freezing	froze	(have) frozen
give	giving	gave	(have) given
go	going	went	(have) gone
know	knowing	knew	(have) known
lose	losing	lost	(have) lost
ride	riding	rode	(have) ridden
ring	ringing	rang	(have) rung
run	running	ran	(have) run
see	seeing	saw	(have) seen
shrink	shrinking	shrank	(have) shrunk
sink	sinking	sank	(have) sunk
speak	speaking	spoke	(have) spoken
steal	stealing	stole	(have) stolen
swim	swimming	swam	(have) swum
take	taking	took	(have) taken
throw	throwing	threw	(have) thrown
wear	wearing	wore	(have) worn
write	writing	wrote	(have) written

7c

● EXERCISE 1. *Oral Drill.* Here is an exercise for the whole class to do together. Let one student choose a verb from the list of irregular verbs and begin a pattern like this: Today we *go* to the store. Then let another student give the other three sentences: Now we are *going* to the store. Yesterday we *went* to the store. Twice we have *gone* to the store. Do the same with the other irregular verbs in the list.

● EXERCISE 2. The following exercise covers the first ten irregular verbs on page 147. Write the numbers 1–20 on your paper. For the blank in each sentence, write the correct form of the verb given before the sentence.

1. *come* Porpoises have often —— to the rescue of shipwrecked sailors.
2. *burst* When the dike ——, the people fled to higher ground.
3. *break* The record for the four-minute mile has been —— many times.
4. *drive* After reading an article on Cape Hatteras, North Carolina, my parents —— there for a vacation.
5. *begin* I have —— my assignment for tomorrow.
6. *break* Because her glasses were ——, we had to go home.
7. *blow* Finally we —— air into the large balloons that we had bought at the fair.
8. *burst* When one ——, we were surprised at the loud noise it made.
9. *do* Do you remember what we —— then?
10. *come* Finally the time —— to go home.
11. *bring* What has your mother —— you from Mexico?

12. *choose* Mimi and Julia have —— to stay in the glee club.
13. *drink* Every morning fresh footprints showed that the moose had —— from the brook.
14. *bring* Paul —— a turtle egg to school today.
15. *begin* It —— to rain about an hour ago.
16. *choose* After days of indecision, Don —— to keep the smallest puppy in the litter.
17. *do* Shirley —— everything possible to make the patient comfortable.
18. *drive* Dad has —— our car almost fifty thousand miles.
19. *blow* The wind has —— down a large branch of the old oak.
20. *drink* Sam —— the milk at one gulp then put the glass down.

● EXERCISE 3. The following exercise covers the next ten verbs on page 147. Write the numbers 1–20 on your paper. For the blank in each sentence, write the correct form of the verb given before the sentence.

1. *eat* We have —— a bushel of peaches this summer.
2. *lose* My sister —— two pounds each week when she dieted.
3. *freeze* Parts of the body are sometimes —— during operations.
4. *give* I should have been —— a better grade in geography.
5. *ring* After the bell has —— today, let's go down to the beach.
6. *ride* The last time we were there we —— the Ferris wheel.
7. *know* We have —— for several centuries that the earth is round.

8. *go*   Last Sunday we —— with our parents on a picnic.

9. *eat*   After we had —— all the hot dogs that we could hold, we roasted marshmallows.

10. *fall*   The temperature has —— thirty degrees in the last twenty-four hours.

11. *freeze*   I am afraid that the tomato plants have ——.

12. *run*   In 1954 Roger Bannister —— a mile in less than four minutes.

13. *know*   Ann —— that she had lost some of her science notes.

14. *give*   Henry and Ernest —— their book reports yesterday.

15. *ride*   Molly has —— in two horse shows.

16. *fall*   That skier must have —— more than once.

17. *run*   While we waited in the bleachers, Joe —— down to the dugout.

18. *go*   Since Alan doesn't answer, I guess he has —— to the pool.

19. *ring*   The phone has —— at least ten times today.

20. *lose*   When Craig went to the board, he —— his place in the story.

● EXERCISE 4. The following exercise covers the last ten verbs on page 147. Write the numbers 1–20 on your paper. For the blank in each sentence, write the correct form of the verb given before the sentence.

1. *swim*   Florence Chadwick —— the English Channel in 1950.

2. *write*   A friend of my parents has —— a novel about our town.

3. *throw*   The fullback was —— for a loss.

4. *steal*   Dad's car was —— during the night!

5. *sink*　In the fourteenth century pirates —— many ships.

6. *speak*　Until the voyage of Columbus most men had —— of the earth as flat.

7. *take*　Man has always —— an interest in the unknown.

8. *write*　Have you —— your assignment for to-morrow?

9. *take*　I should have —— more time to find a book in the library.

10. *see*　When mother —— us, she brought us some cold lemonade.

11. *swim*　The children watched two ducks as they —— across a pond.

12. *sink*　They —— their heads in the water look-ing for food.

13. *shrink*　This sweater has —— to a baby's size!

14. *wear*　I had only —— it a few times.

15. *steal*　Two men have —— bases while you weren't paying attention.

16. *throw*　If you had —— the ball straight, I might have caught it.

17. *speak*　The visitors have —— a few words in Spanish to the delighted audience.

18. *write*　Helen has —— to her Congressman about the natural resources bill.

19. *shrink*　The time it takes to travel across the con-tinent has —— almost unbelievably in the last decade.

20. *wear*　This old jacket has certainly —— well.

● REVIEW EXERCISE A.　The following exercise covers several irregular verbs from the list on page 147. Write the numbers 1–20 on your paper. After each number, write the form of the verb that will fit cor-rectly in the blank.

1. *blow*   Last night the wind —— the garbage pail into the neighbor's yard.

2. *break*   Because she has —— so many promises, I no longer trust her.

3. *bring*   It was an open-book test, but I —— the wrong book.

4. *burst*   On Christmas Eve, the children almost —— with excitement.

5. *choose*   The coach has already —— the first-string players.

6. *come*   My father's boss —— to dinner last night.

7. *do*   Just because you have always —— it that way doesn't mean that it is right.

8. *drink*   At Nancy's party, six of us ate two chocolate cakes and —— four quarts of punch.

9. *fall*   He would have made another touchdown if he had not —— on the five-yard line.

10. *freeze*   The look she gave me would have —— water.

11. *go*   The whole troop wished they had not —— on the overnight hike.

12. *know*   Had I —— that, I would have refused the invitation.

13. *ring*   Who —— the fire alarm?

14. *run*   Even though he lost, he —— a good race.

15. *see*   Fortunately, Joe —— where the arrow landed.

16. *shrink*   Either John has grown, or his trousers have ——.

17. *speak*   He stopped suddenly after he had —— only a few words.

18. *throw*   The shortstop should have —— to first base.

19. *write*   I wish he had —— to me about it.

20. *swim*   Before we had lunch we —— out to the island.

SIX TROUBLESOME VERBS

There are three pairs of verbs that seem to be particularly troublesome for students. You should be especially careful not to misuse them. Study the following explanations of how to use *sit* and *set*, *rise* and *raise*, *lie* and *lay*.

Sit and Set

The verb *sit* means "to sit down" or "to rest," as in a chair. Its principal parts are *sit, sitting, sat,* (have) *sat*.

EXAMPLES   Bob **sits** in that seat.
Three girls **sat** on the platform.
I **had sat** there for a long time.

The verb *set* means "to place" or "to put." Its principal parts are *set, setting, set,* (have) *set*.

EXAMPLES   **Set** those tomato plants in a sunny place.
Paul **set** the toolbox on top of the motor.
Have you **set** a day for the meeting?
Hunters sometimes **set** traps for fur-bearing animals.

If you keep in mind the meaning of the sentence, you should be able to choose the correct verb. If the meaning is "to rest," use the verb *sit*. If the meaning is "to put" or "to place," use the verb *set*.

It may help you to know that *set* takes an object and that *sit* does not.

    I **will sit** here for a while. [no object]
    I **will set** your dinner on the table. [object: *dinner*]

If the verb has an object, you should use *set*.

● Exercise 5. *Oral Drill.* In the following sentences the verbs *sit* and *set* are correctly used. Read the sentences aloud several times to become familiar with the correct usage.

1. We *set* up the card table in the den.
2. Then we *sat* down to play a game of Monopoly.
3. We *set* our pieces on the board and began to play.
4. After we had been *sitting* there for an hour, we decided to make some fudge.
5. We *set* the pan on the stove.
6. After *setting* out all the ingredients, we mixed them and returned to our game.
7. We could not *sit* still for long.
8. We had to *set* the stove at the right temperature.
9. Once we almost *sat* too long.
10. The pan had been *set* on the wrong burner, and the fudge was beginning to burn.

● Exercise 6. Write the numbers 1–10 on your paper. For each blank, write the correct form of *sit* or *set*.

1. On the plane I —— next to a suspicious-looking man. 2. He —— a large briefcase down by his seat. 3. When the hostess asked him if he would like to —— it in the baggage rack, he refused. 4. He insisted that the briefcase must —— by his side. 5. As I —— beside him, I wondered about the contents of the briefcase. 6. His strange behavior —— my imagination working. 7. I thought that I might be —— next to a secret service man or a spy. 8. Perhaps the man had —— a time bomb to go off at a certain time. 9. As the pilot —— the plane down on the runway, I watched the briefcase carefully. 10. A sudden movement of the plane caused the briefcase to open, and there beside the man —— a small black and white puppy.

● EXERCISE 7. Write ten sentences. In five of them, use a form of the verb *sit*. In the other five, use a form of the verb *set*.

Rise and Raise

The verb *rise* means "to arise," "to get up," or "to go up." Its principal parts are *rise, rising, rose,* (have) *risen*.

EXAMPLES Like the sun, the stars **rise** in the east.
The chairman **rose** to speak.
He **had** already **risen** from the bench.

The verb *raise* means "to lift up" or "force up." Its principal parts are *raise, raising, raised,* (have) *raised*.

EXAMPLES **Raise** your arms above your head.
My mother **raised** the curtain.
We **raise** many of our own vegetables.

The verb *rise* never has an object; *raise* does.

Clouds of smoke **were rising** above the school. [no object]

Passing cars **were raising** clouds of dust. [object: *clouds*]

● EXERCISE 8. *Oral Drill.* Read the following sentences aloud. Note the uses of the verbs *rise* and *raise*, which are correct.

1. One of the peaks in the Alps *rises* over fifteen thousand feet in the air.
2. The American flag was *raised* on Iwo Jima in 1945.
3. The student *raised* an important question.
4. The speaker *rose* from his seat.

5. By midnight the Big Dipper had *risen* high in the heavens.
6. We have *raised* tulips for several years.
7. Look to see if the cake is *rising*.
8. When the starter *raises* his hand, the race is ready to begin.
9. Your voice *rises* at the end of a question.
10. In the movie a gigantic sea monster *rose* up out of the ocean.

● EXERCISE 9.   Choose the correct form of *raise* or *rise* to fill each blank below; then write it after the proper number on your paper.

1. The crowd had —— a great clamor to see a man fight a lion.
2. When the guards —— the gates, there stood Androcles, a small, meek tailor.
3. The lion —— to its feet when Androcles stepped into the arena.
4. When he saw that the lion had —— from the ground, Androcles swallowed hard.
5. He was afraid, but he —— to his full height.
6. The people in the Colosseum had —— to their feet in anticipation of the fight.
7. The tension —— as the lion poised for his attack.
8. Instead of attacking, the lion —— his paw for Androcles to see.
9. When he —— on his toes to see the paw, Androcles recognized it as the one from which he had removed a thorn.
10. He had come to the lion's aid once, and now the lion —— to the occasion and recognized his friend.

● EXERCISE 10. Write ten sentences, using each one of the following verb forms. Try for interest and variety in your sentences.

1. rising
2. raising
3. rose
4. have risen
5. raised
6. rises
7. had raised
8. had risen
9. will rise
10. raise

Lie and Lay

The verb *lie* means "to recline" or "to remain lying down."[1] Its principal parts are *lie, lying, lay,* (have) *lain.*

EXAMPLES   Rocky Ridge **lies** twenty miles east of here.

The dictionary **is lying** face down on the window seat.

Mrs. Miller **lay** down for a short nap.

Tom's bicycle **has lain** in the ditch all morning.

The verb *lay* means "to put down," "to place something." Its principal parts are *lay, laying, laid,* (have) *laid.*

EXAMPLES   **Lay** that puzzle aside and come help me, please.

Dad **is laying** linoleum in the kitchen.

Who **laid** the first telephone cable across the Atlantic?

Mother **has laid** your clean shirts and socks on the bed.

[1] The verb *lie* meaning to "tell a falsehood" is another word.

The verb *lie* never has an object; the verb *lay* may have an object. If the verb has an object, use a form of *lay*.

Errors in the use of *lie* and *lay* almost always occur because a form of *lay* has been used where a form of *lie* is required.

WRONG   Rose was laying down.
RIGHT   Rose **was lying** down.

WRONG   He laid in wait for us.
RIGHT   He **lay** in wait for us.

● EXERCISE 11.   *Oral Drill.*   Read the following sentences aloud. Pay attention to the use of the verbs *lie* and *lay*, which in these sentences are used correctly.

1. If you are tired, *lie* down for a while.
2. We *laid* our tools on the table an hour ago.
3. The two dogs *lay* down beside each other.
4. After *lying* there for a few minutes, they were ready to play again.
5. Vivian *laid* out her winter clothes.
6. Sometimes snow *lies* on the ground into late spring.
7. Do not *lay* the blame on someone else.
8. After Mr. Peterson had *lain* down for a few hours, he was ready to travel again.
9. The sheriff has *laid* a trap for the bank robber.
10. The animal is *lying* in wait for its prey.

● EXERCISE 12.   Write the numbers 1–10 on your paper. After each number, copy the correct verb from the parentheses. Remember that only a form of *lay* can have an object.

1. A book of stories by Edgar Allan Poe is (lying, laying) on the table.
2. Horror (lies, lays) in wait for the reader of Poe's stories.
3. Some of his characters (lay, laid) under the spell of strange diseases.
4. Few people have (lain, laid) down a story by Poe until it was finished.
5. Many have (lain, laid) awake at night after reading a Poe story.
6. In one of Poe's most lyrical poems, a lover grieves for Annabel Lee, who (lies, lays) "in a tomb by the sounding sea."
7. In "The Tell-Tale Heart" a man (lying, laying) in bed thinks the tick of a watch is a heartbeat.
8. The appeal of Poe's poem "The Bells" (lies, lays) in its musical sounds.
9. In "The Raven" a man's midnight encounter with a raven (lies, lays) a deep sorrow over his spirit.
10. "The Pit and the Pendulum" is a story of the tortures a man undergoes while he is (lying, laying) at the bottom of a dark pit.

● REVIEW EXERCISE B. Write the numbers 1–10 on your paper. In the parentheses, you will find various forms of *sit*, *set*, *rise*, *raise*, *lie* and *lay*. Choose the form that will make each sentence correct, and write it after the number.

1. Many minerals have (lain, laid) untouched in the earth for years.
2. Can't you (sit, set) still during class?
3. The old sailor (lay, laid) his hand on the tiller.
4. The cat was (lying, laying) peacefully on the arm of the couch.

5. The king and his advisers (sat, set) down at the table together.
6. After the celebration everyone (lay, laid) down to sleep.
7. A tiny cloud of black smoke (rose, raised) from a distant hill.
8. The painters (sat, set) their ladders against the walls of the barn.
9. Have you been (sitting, setting) in the library all day?
10. The sun had already (risen, raised) before we woke.

● REVIEW EXERCISE C. Write the numbers 1–20 on your paper. If a sentence contains a verb error, write the correct form of the verb on your paper after the number. If the sentence is correct, write *C* after its number.

1. Because I laid in bed too long, I was late getting to school.
2. Hughie threw the ball toward third base.
3. I have wore out my old green sweater.
4. The men set talking until early morning.
5. At the reception Diane chose to serve the cake.
6. Have you spoke to Miss Thatcher yet?
7. When I heard my name called late last night, I raised up to see what was happening.
8. After the car turned over, it busted into flames.
9. Ted knows a man who has wrote a play.
10. Have you saw *Hamlet* performed on the stage?
11. Our drama group raised enough money to build a small theater.
12. My bicycle was stole while I was in the library.
13. The police have went looking for it.

14. The pitcher and the catcher throwed the ball back and forth between them.
15. We went to the game and set in the bleachers.
16. After the flag was raised and the national anthem was sung, the game began.
17. The water in the pond had froze during the night.
18. Have we drunk a whole quart of milk?
19. The water level has continued to raise, even though the rain has stopped.
20. Halloween come on Friday last year.

● REVIEW EXERCISE D. Write the numbers 1–25 on your paper. For each sentence below, choose the correct form of the verb preceding it to fit into the blank. Then write that form on your paper after the sentence number.

1. *lie*   Deep-sea divers sometimes find treasure that has —— at the bottom of the ocean for centuries.
2. *eat*   Have you ever —— a pomegranate?
3. *lose*   After all his training, Danny —— the 1,000-meter race.
4. *drive*   My mother has —— me to school every day this week.
5. *give*   Who —— the main talk in assembly yesterday?
6. *run*   Some candidates have —— for President again and again.
7. *break*   This heat wave has —— all records.
8. *ring*   I think the doorbell —— a minute ago.
9. *swim*   Pete —— out to the raft before supper.
10. *rise*   If the oven isn't hot enough, the cake won't —— properly.
11. *sit*   Nine justices —— on the Supreme Court.

12. *sink* The big submarine —— beneath the surface with hardly a ripple.

13. *lay* Consulting his charts, the skipper —— a course to Barnegat Light.

14. *blow* The wind must have —— forty miles an hour last night.

15. *take* Jim has —— a course in electrical engineering.

16. *ride* The Robbinses have —— over in their pickup truck.

17. *know* Margie —— her answer wasn't right.

18. *do* Some of the early settlers —— their best to make friends with the Indians.

19. *fall* The barometer has —— during the day.

20. *choose* Would you have —— differently if you had known the consequences?

21. *bring* Marian and Ruth —— a new spirit of enthusiasm to the meeting.

22. *sit* Is it all right for those seedlings to be —— in the sun all this time?

23. *rise* A shout —— from the bleachers.

24. *shrink* Either I have grown or this shirt —— in the wash.

25. *go* The Pezzutis have —— to Mexico for a month.

CHAPTER 8

Using Pronouns Correctly

Nominative and Objective Case Forms

In the following sentences, notice the different forms of the pronouns:

> **He** and **I** work for the school newspaper. The editor assigns stories to **him** and **me**.

If you examine these sentences, you will notice that *he* and *I* are subjects of the first sentence, and that *him* and *me*, in the second sentence, are objects of a preposition. A pronoun may have one form when it is a subject and a different form when it is an object.

Some pronouns change their form according to the way they are used in sentences. This difference in forms is called *case*. There are three cases. Pronouns used as subjects and as predicate nominatives are in the *nominative* case. Pronouns used as objects are in the *objective* case. Pronouns that show ownership (*my, his, hers, their,* and so on) are in the *possessive* case. In this chapter, you will study the nominative and objective forms of pronouns.

163

Memorize the nominative and objective case forms of the following personal pronouns.

NOMINATIVE		OBJECTIVE	
I	we	me	us
you	you	you	you
he	they	him	them
she		her	
it		it	

Notice that the pronouns *you* and *it* are the same in the nominative and objective forms.

THE NOMINATIVE CASE

When you use a pronoun as a subject or after a linking verb, always use a nominative form of the pronoun.

8a. **The subject of a verb is in the nominative case.**

A pronoun used as the subject must always be one of these forms: *I, you, he, she, it, we, they.*

EXAMPLES   **They** made candles from antique molds. [*They* is the subject of the verb *made*.]

He and **I** mowed lawns on Saturday afternoon. [*He* and *I* are the subjects of the verb *mowed*.]

● EXERCISE 1. *Oral Drill.* Read aloud the following sentences to accustom your ear to the correct pronoun form.

1. Stephen and I are looking forward to a wonderful vacation.
2. He and I are sailing for Europe.

3. We students are taking a tour of several countries.
4. Stephen and I agree about most of the places we want to see.
5. He and I went on deck just before the ship sailed.
6. We and the other students crowded toward the railing.
7. He and I spotted our parents on the dock.
8. We on the boat and they on the shore waved and shouted.
9. Then he and I waved a final good-by.
10. As the ship was towed out into deep water, I suddenly felt very lonely.

Errors in the case of pronouns usually occur when the subject is compound, that is, when it consists of two subjects joined by *and* or *or*. For example, no one but a very small child would say, "*Me* had lunch." But many people make a similar mistake by saying something like, "*Helen* and *me* had lunch."

You can select the correct pronoun in a compound subject by trying each part of the subject alone with the verb.

WRONG   Her and me looked for tracks. [*Her looked for tracks* and *me looked for tracks* are clearly wrong.]

RIGHT   **She** and **I** looked for tracks. [*She looked for tracks* and *I looked for tracks* are correct.]

When a pronoun is immediately followed by a noun—*we girls, us girls*—you can determine the correct pronoun by dropping the noun.

EXAMPLE   (We, Us) girls voted together.
We [not us] voted together.
We girls voted together.

8a

● EXERCISE 2.   In the following sentences, choose the correct one of the two pronouns in parentheses, and write it after the proper number on your paper.

1. He and (me, I) pretended to be Tom Sawyer and Huck Finn.
2. (We, Us) boys have lively imaginations.
3. Once he and (I, me) were supposed to paint a fence.
4. Neither (he, him) nor I wanted to do it.
5. Jack and (I, me) decided to trick some friends.
6. When they came down the street, my friend and (I, me) pretended to be enjoying painting the fence.
7. (We, Us) two grudgingly agreed to let the other boys help us.
8. We and (they, them) were happy.
9. My friend and (me, I) enjoyed watching them work.
10. Later at the clubhouse (us, we) members had a good laugh.

● EXERCISE 3.   *Oral Drill.*   Use each of the groups of words below as the subject of a sentence, choosing the correct pronoun from the pair in parentheses.

EXAMPLE   1. My father and (I, me) ——
            1. *My father and I are going on a camping trip.*

1. The scientists and (them, they) ——
2. The coach and (us, we) ——
3. (Him, He) and (I, me) ——
4. My neighbors and (them, they) ——
5. You and (me, I) ——
6. (We, Us) players ——
7. Chris and (he, him) ——

 8. (Them, They) and (we, us) ——
 9. (Her, She) and I ——
10. The policeman and (he, him) ——
11. The James boys and (them, they) ——
12. Last night (him, he) and (they, them) ——
13. (We, Us) citizens ——
14. The fire fighters and (they, them) ——
15. Suddenly, you and (him, he) ——
16. For five years you and (me, I) ——
17. (Him, He) and his followers ——
18. (She, Her) and (I, me) ——
19. Both you and (him, he) ——
20. You spectators and (we, us) players ——

8b. **A predicate nominative is in the nominative case.**

A predicate nominative, as you learned on page 109, always refers to the subject. It follows a linking verb. A pronoun that is used as a predicate nominative must be in the nominative case: *I, you, he, she, it, we, they.*

EXAMPLES   The candidates for class president were **he** and **she.**

The members of the debating team are **we** three.

◆ NOTE   This rule is often ignored in the usage *It is me* or *It's me.* Although *me* is the objective form, it is usually acceptable as a predicate nominative. Careful writers prefer to follow the rule and use the nominative form in formal writing—*It is I.*

● EXERCISE 4.   After each number on your paper, write the correct pronoun from the parentheses.

8 b

1. See if it is (she, her).
2. Who are (they, them)?
3. The witness claimed that the thief was (him, he).
4. The next contestant will be (she, her).
5. The ones invited to the party are you and (them, they).
6. They were sure that it was (her, she) behind the mask.
7. The committee members are Jean, Andy, and (I, me).
8. Could the fortune-teller possibly be (her, she)?
9. The next batter should be (him, he).
10. Our closest neighbors are you and (them, they).

● EXERCISE 5. *Oral Drill.* Choosing the correct pronoun from the pair in the parentheses, use each word group as the predicate nominative in a sentence. Be sure to use a linking verb.

EXAMPLE   1. —— Mr. Lane and (he, him)
      1. *It could have been Mr. Lane and he.*

1. —— you and (they, them)
2. —— Angie and (her, she)
3. —— my mother and (she, her)
4. —— you and (us, we)
5. —— the neighbors and (them, they)
6. —— Cal, Pat, and (I, me)
7. —— her partner and (her, she)
8. —— the pilot and (he, him)
9. —— she and (them, they)
10. —— they and (us, we)

THE OBJECTIVE CASE

When you use a pronoun as an object of a verb or a preposition, always use the objective case form.

8c. **The direct and indirect objects of a verb are in the objective case.**

A pronoun used as the direct object or indirect object of a verb must always be one of these forms: *me, you, him, her, it, us, them.*

EXAMPLES   Mother called **me** to the phone. [*Me* is the direct object of the verb *called.*]

The hostess handed **her** a piece of cake. [*Her* is the indirect object of the verb *handed.*]

Difficulties in choosing the correct form of the pronoun usually arise when the object is compound. You can make sure the pronoun in a compound object is correct by trying it alone in the sentence. Study this example.

PROBLEM   The teacher chose (he, him) and (I, me)
WRONG   The teacher chose he.
            The teacher chose I.
RIGHT   The teacher chose **him.**
            The teacher chose **me.**
            The teacher chose **him** and **me.**

● EXERCISE 6.   *Oral Drill.*   The following sentences are all correct. Read them aloud, and explain the form and use of each italicized pronoun.

1. I took Jim and *her* to the rodeo with me.
2. The attendants gave *us* newcomers programs.
3. Then a guide showed *us* to our seats.
4. The bucking broncos frightened Jim and *her.*
5. But they delighted the crowd and *me.*
6. The wild bulls gave *us* all a real scare.
7. The cowboys rode *them* well.

8 c

8. The rope tricks pleased Alice and *me* most.
9. But the tricks did not impress *him* as much as the roping contest.
10. When the rodeo was over, I asked *him* and *her* if they were glad they went.

● EXERCISE 7. Write the numbers 1–18 on your paper. After each number, write a pronoun or pronouns that will correctly complete the sentence.

1. The man hired Fred and —— to run errands.
2. Lisa sent —— and —— Christmas presents.
3. We gave Bill and —— our old magazines and newspapers.
4. The lifeguard rescued —— and ——.
5. The magician showed my sister and —— his magic hat.
6. The storm frightened my sister and ——.
7. The host passed —— and —— generous helpings of chicken and dumplings.
8. The class chose —— and —— as its delegates to the convention.
9. The convention nominated Joe and —— on the first ballot.
10. The clerk charged Allen and —— ten dollars for the pants.
11. The ski lift carried —— and —— to the top.
12. The mayor gave —— and —— the keys to the city.
13. I handed Mr. Barnes and —— my resignation.
14. A neighbor drove —— and —— to the fair.
15. We raced —— and —— to the top of the hill.
16. The pitcher threw —— and —— a fast ball.
17. The police turned —— and —— over to the F.B.I.
18. Roger lent —— and —— some books about ships.

● REVIEW EXERCISE A. The following sentences require pronouns in either the nominative or objective case. Choose the correct pronoun for each sentence, and write it on your paper after the number.

1. My mother is giving Hazel and (I, me) a sewing lesson today.
2. (We, Us) girls have never even sewn on a button.
3. Mother's sister Julia and (she, her) say it is a disgrace.
4. They are determined to teach Hazel and (I, me) a few fundamentals.
5. In our family the expert needlewomen are (she, her) and Aunt Julia.
6. Hazel and (I, me) have pretty patchwork quilts from Aunt Julia.
7. She may teach (she, her) and (I, me) to embroider.
8. First Mother and (she, her) will emphasize mending.
9. We have given my father and (they, them) plenty of reason to complain.
10. When it comes to sewing, the lazy ones are Hazel and (I, me).
11. Sometimes Dad takes our brothers and (we, us) fishing.
12. (We, Us) girls don't enjoy that as much as the boys do.
13. Dad and (they, them) could spend hours on the lake.
14. Unfortunately, mosquitoes like Hazel and (I, me).
15. Mother and (we, us) always get restless after a few minutes.
16. The boys ignore Mother and (we, us).
17. Mother gives Dad and (they, them) a few threatening looks.
18. The captains of our boat are (he, him) and (she, her).

19. (They, Them) and the boys usually agree to compromise.
20. (We, Us) and our parents become a harmonious family again.

8d. The object of a preposition is in the objective case.

As you know, prepositions are always followed by objects. (If you need to review prepositions, see the list on page 74.) When a pronoun is used as the object of a preposition, it is in the objective case. The objective forms of pronouns, you recall, are *me, you, him, her, it, us, them.*

EXAMPLES   The secret is between **you** and **me.** [*You* and *me* are the objects of the preposition *between.*]

 We waited for Ed and **them** to arrive. [*Them* is one of the objects of the preposition *for.*]

● EXERCISE 8. *Oral Drill.* The pronouns in these sentences are all objects of prepositions and are in the objective case. Read the sentences aloud and identify the pronouns and the prepositions.

1. My father divided the money among the younger children and us.
2. We walked behind our parents and them.
3. I sat down beside him and her.
4. She turned her head toward Annie and me.
5. The boy walked between us girls.
6. I bought two hot dogs for Gwen and her.
7. The Allens will have a new house near the McHughs and them.

8. Look at him and me when you talk.
9. Vivian's mother is keeping the surprise party a secret from her and the twins.
10. Suddenly frogs were leaping around Herb and me.

● EXERCISE 9. Write the numbers 1–10 on your paper. Copy the correct one of the two pronouns in parentheses.

1. near Ken and (I, me)
2. for you and (she, her)
3. upon the firemen and (them, they)
4. with Dr. Thomas and (he, him)
5. behind Joe and (we, us)
6. by you and (they, them)
7. against Joyce and (me, I)
8. from his cousin and (he, him)
9. about Anita and (she, her)
10. except the Greens and (we, us)

● EXERCISE 10. Write ten short sentences, using each of the following prepositions. Follow the prepositions with compound objects. Make at least one of the objects in each sentence a pronoun.

EXAMPLE 1. toward
     1. *The dog ran toward Nina and her.*

1. before
2. for
3. between
4. to
5. from
6. around
7. beside
8. at
9. except
10. behind

● REVIEW EXERCISE B. The following sentences contain pronouns used as subjects, predicate nominatives, direct and indirect objects of verbs, and objects of prepositions. Write the numbers 1–10 on your paper.

8 d

After each number, write the correct pronoun from the parentheses. Be prepared to tell how the pronoun is used in the sentence.

1. A few generations ago people were prejudiced toward a woman doctor and regarded (she, her) and her patients with suspicion.
2. Her male colleagues and (she, her) had professional problems in common.
3. Yet many doctors were reluctant to associate with other professional women and (she, her).
4. Elizabeth Blackwell, the first woman doctor, thought of the public and (they, them) as old-fashioned.
5. The first woman to win a medical degree in the United States was (she, her).
6. Her parents had planned an unusual education for her sisters and (she, her).
7. Both of the other girls and (she, her) had more schooling than was usual for a woman in those days.
8. In a Paris hospital other medical students and (she, her) learned their profession.
9. Gradually, the public granted other hard-working women and (she, her) its recognition.
10. Florence Nightingale was a good friend and an inspiration to (she, her) and other women.

◆ NOTE Some students make serious errors by using *hisself* or *theirselfs* in the place of the correct objective case forms *himself* and *themselves*. You should remember that *hisself* and *theirselfs* are not acceptable words.

WRONG The batter hit hisself with the bat.
RIGHT The batter hit **himself** with the bat.

WRONG The cooks served theirselfs some of the cake.

RIGHT The cooks served **themselves** some of the cake.

● REVIEW EXERCISE C. Write the numbers 1–20 on your paper. Select the correct one of the two pronouns in parentheses, and write it after the proper number.

1. The cocaptains for this game will be Dick and (he, him).
2. We have heard many stories about you and (he, him).
3. We were told by (they, them).
4. They and (we, us) belong to the same club.
5. "Who are (they, them)?" he asked.
6. "Don't hide behind the coach and (they, them)," he said.
7. "What do you think about him and (I, me)?" he asked.
8. "You and (he, him) are both excellent players," we replied.
9. My parents gave their parents and (they, them) a farewell party.
10. They did not remember my brother and (I, me).
11. The panelists are Roger, Keith, and (I, me).
12. The moderator spoke to (we, us) before the meeting.
13. Are you and (he, him) ready?
14. The unexpected guests surprised my mother and (I, me).
15. When the door was opened, (he, him) and his wife were standing there.
16. Both (he, him) and (she, her) had written us, but we had not received their letters.
17. We had to serve (he, him) and (she, her) leftovers.

18. Luckily the group did not leave without (he, him) and (I, me).
19. (We, Us) hikers saw many beautiful scenes.
20. Will you call Karen and (I, me) in the morning?

● REVIEW EXERCISE D.   Use the following expressions correctly in sentences of your own.

1. my brother and me
2. us scouts
3. you and I
4. himself
5. he and she
6. the Jacksons and us
7. the principal and them
8. you and they
9. him and me
10. her husband and she

CHAPTER 9

Using Modifiers Correctly

Comparison of Adjectives and Adverbs; Double Negatives

If you had a peanut-butter sandwich for lunch on Monday, a hamburger on Tuesday, and roast chicken on Wednesday, you might say, "Monday's lunch was *good*, Tuesday's was *better*, and Wednesday's was *best* of all."

In comparing the meals, you used different forms of the adjective *good*. Each of the forms expresses a slightly different meaning. The contrast expressed by these different forms is called *comparison*.

COMPARING ADJECTIVES AND ADVERBS

9a. **The three degrees of comparison of modifiers are the** *positive*, **the** *comparative*, **and the** *superlative*.

Positive	San Francisco is a **large** city.
Comparative	Chicago is **larger** than San Francisco.
Superlative	New York is the **largest** of the three.

9a

(1) The positive degree is used when only one thing is being described.

> This suitcase is **heavy**.
>
> An **old** statue stood in the garden.
>
> Hattie began the job **cheerfully**.
>
> Bernie wrote **fast** when he came to the last question.

(2) The comparative degree is used when two things are being compared.

> My suitcase is **heavier** than yours.
>
> That statue is **older** than my grandmother.
>
> She began to talk **more cheerfully** about her plans.
>
> Hank wrote **faster**.

(3) The superlative degree is used when three or more things are being compared.

> Sylvia's suitcase is the **heaviest** of all.
>
> It is the **oldest** statue I have ever seen.
>
> Of all the girls, Hattie accepted the situation **most cheerfully**.
>
> Donald wrote the **fastest** of all.

◆ NOTE The superlative is often used for emphasis when it clearly refers to one of two: "Put your best foot forward." However, in your writing you will do well to observe rule (3).

Study the comparison of the following adjectives and adverbs.

POSITIVE	COMPARATIVE	SUPERLATIVE
happy	happier	happiest
short	shorter	shortest
anxious	more anxious	most anxious
slowly	more slowly	most slowly

You will observe that there are two ways of forming the comparative and superlative degrees. To form the comparative, the ending *-er* may be added to the end of the word itself (and sometimes the final letter is changed, as in *happy—happier*), or the word *more* may precede the word. To form the superlative degree, the ending *-est* is added to the end of the word, or the word *most* is put before it. These are the two regular methods of comparing adjectives and adverbs.

The rules telling you which method of comparing to use with a particular word are complicated and difficult to remember. Most of the time, you can tell which is correct by judging which sounds right. You can hear that *more quick* sounds wrong; therefore, you would say *quicker* or *more quickly*. Your ear tells you that *slowliest* is not a word; you would say *most slowly*. When you are in doubt about the correct comparative or superlative form of a modifier, look the word up in a dictionary or ask your teacher for help.

The comparative and superlative degrees of a few words are formed in irregular ways. You should memorize the ones given here.

POSITIVE	COMPARATIVE	SUPERLATIVE
good	better	best
well	better	best
bad	worse	worst

● EXERCISE 1. Write the numbers 1–10 on your paper. After each number, write the form of the italicized adjective or adverb that will correctly fill the blank in the sentence. If you are in doubt about the correct way to form the comparative or superlative degree of a modifier, look it up in your dictionary.

EXAMPLE   1. *good*   This is the —— show I have ever seen.

  1. *best*

1. *smart*   Is he —— than his brother?

2. *calm*   The lake was —— than usual after the storm.

3. *difficult* This is one of the —— tests I have ever taken.

4. *bright*   Many distant stars are actually —— than some that are closer to our planet.

5. *slow*   The closer she got to the dentist's office, the —— she walked.

6. *well*   The patient feels —— than he did last night.

7. *clear*   This is the —— night we have had in a long time.

8. *good*   Mary's is the —— of the two papers.

9. *early*   June's guests arrived —— than she expected.

10. *bad*   I played my —— game yesterday.

9b. Distinguish between *good* and *well* as modifiers.

Many errors with modifiers are made by students who confuse *good* and *well*. You should learn to use all the forms of these words correctly.

(1) Use *good* to modify nouns or pronouns.

The outcome was **good**.

We expect a **good** crop this fall.

She is **good** at badminton.

(2) Use *well* to modify verbs.

The game started **well.**

The trees are producing **well** this fall.

She plays badminton **well.**

EXCEPTION   When *well* means "in good health," it may be used after a linking verb to modify a noun or pronoun.

Mother feels quite **well** today.

9c. Use an adjective, not an adverb, after linking verbs.

Linking verbs (forms of *be*, and such words as *feel*, *taste*, *seem*, *appear*, etc.) are often followed by predicate adjectives modifying the subject. You must be careful not to use an adverb when an adjective is called for.

EXAMPLES   Ingrid looks **sleepy.** [The predicate adjective *sleepy* modifies the subject *Ingrid*. *Looks* is a linking verb.]

Ingrid looked **sleepily** at the clock. [The adverb *sleepily* modifies the action verb *looked*.]

Bill feels **uncertain** about the race. [The predicate adjective *uncertain* modifies the subject *Bill*. *Feels* is a linking verb.]

Bill felt his way **uncertainly** along the hall. [The adverb *uncertainly* modifies the action verb *felt*.]

9
b-c

● EXERCISE 2. Write the numbers 1–10 on your paper. After each number, write the one of the two words in parentheses that will make the sentence correct.

1. The fire feels (good, well) on this cold wintry day.
2. The wind is howling so (fierce, fiercely) I can hardly hear you.
3. At camp we always eat (good, well).
4. We moved as (slow, slowly) as a horse and buggy.
5. The stars look (beautiful, beautifully) on a clear night.
6. She did her work (good, well).
7. We (sure, surely) enjoyed our visit to San Diego.
8. We examined the bookbag (careful, carefully) before we bought it.
9. Hot chocolate tastes (good, well) on a winter evening.
10. The ball dropped (easy, easily) into the basket.

9d. Avoid double comparisons.

Comparison is expressed in either of two ways: by changing the form of the modifier (as with *pretty, prettier; small, smallest*) or by adding *more* or *most* to the modifier. Using both ways at once is not correct.

WRONG   This is the most finest performance he has given.

RIGHT   This is the **finest** performance he has given.

WRONG   Her hair is more curlier than her sister's.

RIGHT   Her hair is **curlier** than her sister's.

DOUBLE NEGATIVES

A common mistake with modifiers is using more than one negative word where only one is required. Words like the following are called negatives: *no, not, none, never, no one, nothing, hardly.* (Notice that many negatives begin with the letter *n.*) When such a word is used in a sentence it makes an important change in the meaning.

> I have been to Denver.
> I have **never** been to Denver.

Notice that one negative is enough to make the meaning clear. Using two negatives together is incorrect.

Positive	He said something.
Negative	He said nothing.
Double negative	He did*n't* say *nothing*.

9e. Avoid the use of double negatives.

Study the following examples until you are sure that you will not make mistakes in the use of negatives. (The word *not* when it is contracted to *n't* and attached to a verb is, of course, still a negative.)

WRONG   We can't hardly wait for the opening of the fair.

RIGHT   We can **hardly** wait for the opening of the fair.

WRONG   I never told no one about our secret hideout.

RIGHT   I told **no one** about our secret hideout.

RIGHT   I **never** told anyone about our secret hideout.

9
d-e

● EXERCISE 3.   Each of the following sentences contains a double negative or an error in comparison. Rewrite each sentence correctly.

1. There wasn't no ball game played today.
2. I can't hardly understand the speaker.
3. These olives are more saltier than the others.
4. When I looked for the cookies, I found that there weren't none left.
5. During intermission I couldn't find no one that I knew.
6. Marie is more gayer since she came back from Puerto Rico.
7. The football team didn't try nothing new in this game.
8. The book was more sadder than the movie.
9. We searched for hours for hidden caves, but we didn't find none.
10. Double negatives don't have no place in good English.

● REVIEW EXERCISE A.   Some of the following sentences are correct. Others contain double negatives or errors in adjective or adverb usage. If the sentence is correct, write a *C* after its number on your paper. If the sentence contains an error, rewrite it correctly.

1. He is the more intelligent of the two men.
2. The hare ran more faster than the tortoise.
3. The tortoise was more persistent.
4. No one plays center as good as George.
5. Time goes too slow when there's nothing to do.
6. You can't hardly find leather-bound books any more.
7. Dan reported that the fish are biting good today.
8. With the May Day Pageant approaching, we are more busier than ever.

9. After a swim in the cold water, she felt fine.
10. I wasn't hardly able to hear him.
11. We can't decide which of the Adams twins is the best looking.
12. Mr. Hyde didn't have no control over himself.
13. Killing didn't mean nothing to him.
14. He hardly considered his victims.
15. He was sure troubled when he changed into his normal self, Dr. Jekyll.
16. Dr. Jekyll wanted to be more wiser than he was.
17. He wanted to experiment with the most strangest of all formulas.
18. The formula was one which would quite easy change him from one personality to another.

● REVIEW EXERCISE B.   Write ten original sentences, using the constructions described below.

1. the superlative of *bright*
2. a single negative
3. the comparative of *useful*
4. the comparative of *good*
5. a linking verb and a predicate adjective
6. the superlative of *often*
7. the positive of *well*
8. the comparative of *joyful*
9. the superlative of *angry*
10. the comparative of *sharp*

PART THREE

Mechanics

CHAPTER 10

Capital Letters

Rules for Capitalization

You already know a great deal about the use of capital letters. For example, you have learned that proper nouns and proper adjectives are capitalized. You are accustomed to beginning sentences with capital letters. In this chapter you will review what you know and learn some more rules for using capitals.

10a. Capitalize the first word in every sentence.

If you have difficulty recognizing the beginning of sentences, the section on run-on sentences (pages 292–96) will help you.

WRONG   my dog knows several tricks. he will shake hands or play dead when I tell him to.

RIGHT   My dog knows several tricks. He will shake hands or play dead when I tell him to.

The first word of a direct quotation should begin with a capital whether or not it starts the sentence. For more on writing quotations, see pages 229–37.

◆ NOTE   Traditionally, the first word of every line of poetry begins with a capital letter. Some modern

10a

poets do not follow this style. If you are copying a poem, be sure to follow the capitalization that the poet used.

10b. Capitalize the pronoun *I*.

EXAMPLE   This week **I** have to write two papers and give a book report.

10c. Capitalize proper nouns.

A proper noun, as you learned on page 39, names a particular person, place, or thing. Such a word is always capitalized. A common noun names a kind or type of person, place, or thing. The common noun is not capitalized unless it begins a sentence or is part of a title.

PROPER NOUNS	COMMON NOUNS
Central High School	high school
Saturday	day
Albert Einstein	man
Sweden	country
Lassie	collie

Memorize the following rules about proper nouns, and study the examples that are given.

(1) Capitalize the names of persons.

EXAMPLES   Hello, **Aunt Celia.**
Here are **Pete** and **Nina.**
Mike's broken leg was set by **Dr. Buxton.**
Frank B. Gilbreth, Jr., is one of the authors of *Cheaper by the Dozen.*

(2) Capitalize geographical names.

Cities, Towns	Miami, Jackson, Indianapolis
States	Tennessee, Wyoming, Delaware
Countries	Australia, Finland, Egypt
Islands	Aleutian Islands, Long Island, Crete
Bodies of Water	Mississippi River, Lake Ontario, Chesapeake Bay, Jackson's Pond, Suez Canal, Indian Ocean
Streets, Highways	Main Street, White Avenue, Kingsbridge Road, Daniel Drive, Highway 14, Route 66, Sunset Boulevard, Park Plaza, Forty-eighth Street [In a hyphenated number, the second word begins with a small letter.]
Parks	Yosemite Park, Grand Canyon, Carlsbad Caverns
Mountains	Catskills, Alps, Mount Everest
Continents	Europe, Asia, South America, Antarctica
Sections of the country	the West, the Southeast

◆ NOTE Do *not* capitalize *east*, *west*, *north*, *south*, or any combinations of these, such as *northeast*, when the words merely indicate *direction*, as in these examples: two blocks *south*, headed *east*, a *north* wind.

EXAMPLES A green truck was going south on Oak Street. [direction]
The South has produced some of America's great writers. [section of the country]

10
b-c

(3) Capitalize names of organizations, business firms, institutions, and government bodies.

EXAMPLES   Dramatic Club
Harry's Sporting Goods
Community Chest Fund
Boy Scouts
Rice University
Carnegie Foundation
Federal Bureau of Investigation
City Planning Commission
the Senate

♦ NOTE Do not capitalize such words as *hotel*, *theater*, or *high school* unless they are part of the name of a particular building or institution.

EXAMPLES   Bijou Theater   a theater
Lane Hotel   the hotel
Taft High School   this high school

(4) Capitalize special events and calendar items.

EXAMPLES   Dogwood Festival   February
Easter   Independence Day
Monday

♦ NOTE Do *not* capitalize the names of seasons: spring, summer, fall, winter.

(5) Capitalize historical events and periods.

EXAMPLES   Revolutionary War
Battle of Salamis
Bronze Age

(6) Capitalize the names of nationalities, races, and religions.

EXAMPLES   Mexican, English, Iroquois, Negro, Indian, Presbyterian

(7) Capitalize the brand names of business products.

EXAMPLES Lux soap, General Electric stove, Pepsi Cola bottle [Notice that only the brand name of a product is capitalized; the common noun following it is not.]

(8) Capitalize the names of ships, planets, monuments, awards, and any other particular places, things, or events.

EXAMPLES Jefferson Memorial the *Crescent Limited*
Golden Gate Bridge Telstar
Merchandise Mart the Bill of Rights
the *Mayflower* Junior Achievement
Mars Award

● EXERCISE 1. Write the numbers 1–10 on your paper. In each of the following items, you are to choose the correct one of the two forms given. After each number on your paper, write the letter of the correct form (*a* or *b*). Be prepared to explain your answer.

1. a. My brother attends Columbia university.
   b. My brother attends Columbia University.
2. a. The fishing is good at Oconee Lake.
   b. The fishing is good at Oconee lake.
3. a. The House of Representatives passed the bill, but the senate did not.
   b. The House of Representatives passed the bill, but the Senate did not.
4. a. We drove through the Pocono mountains last Spring.
   b. We drove through the Pocono Mountains last spring.
5. a. Have you bought your Halloween costume?
   b. Have you bought your halloween costume?

6. a. My cousin from the south is visiting me.
   b. My cousin from the South is visiting me.
7. a. On his return from Africa, Mr. James had a number of stories to tell.
   b. On his return from africa, Mr. James had a number of stories to tell.
8. a. The Delo Gum Commercial uses cartoons.
   b. The Delo gum commercial uses cartoons.
9. a. Near the Washington Monument is a long reflecting pool.
   b. Near the Washington monument is a long reflecting pool.
10. a. We have some reproductions from the museum of Modern Art.
    b. We have some reproductions from the Museum of Modern Art.

● EXERCISE 2.   Each of the following sentences contains at least one uncapitalized proper noun. Copy all the proper nouns after the number of the sentence, beginning each with a capital letter.

EXAMPLE   1. On may day the seniors at anderson high school present a pageant.
                  1. *May Day, Anderson High School*

1. The George Washington bridge, which spans the Hudson river, is one of the largest suspension bridges in the world.
2. Glacier national park, in montana, is noted for its sixty glaciers.
3. Before the building of dams by the tennessee valley authority, much of the land in the south was flooded during heavy rains.
4. Thousands of cherokee indians live in the smoky mountains in and around cherokee, north carolina.

5. In 1961 the peace corps became an agency of the government by an act of congress.
6. On november 29, 1961, a chimpanzee named enos was safely recovered from the atlantic ocean after the completion of two orbits around the earth.
7. The last two states to be admitted to the united states were alaska and hawaii.
8. On new year's day many fans crowd into football stadiums for the annual bowl games.
9. The rose bowl is the oldest of the bowls.
10. The oldest institution of higher learning in america is harvard college.

● EXERCISE 3. In the following paragraph all capital letters have been omitted. Copy the paragraph, using capitals wherever they are needed.

last christmas my parents and i went to new york city for our vacation. as we stood on the corner of broadway and forty-second street, we marveled at the many signs. a camel cigarette sign particularly amazed me because every so often big puffs of smoke would come out of the sign. i was also intrigued by the sign on the times building, which spelled out the latest news. as far as we could see in all directions, there were crowds of people doing their holiday shopping. since we had decided to see a movie, we walked over to the radio city music hall, where we saw a movie and a stage show which featured the rockettes, a famous group of dancers. after the show was over, we strolled to rockefeller plaza. while we were watching the changing colors of the large fountain there, some friends of ours—mr. lester, his wife, and their son tom—came up to us. you can imagine how surprised we were to see people from our own hometown!

10d. Capitalize proper adjectives.

A proper adjective, which is formed from a proper noun, is always capitalized.

PROPER NOUN	PROPER ADJECTIVE
Greece	Greek theater
Hercules	Herculean task
Congress	Congressional hearing
England	English literature
Orient	Oriental custom

10e. Do *not* capitalize the names of school subjects, except languages and course names followed by a number.

EXAMPLES history, typing, mathematics, English, German, Latin, History 101, Music III, Art Appreciation I

● EXERCISE 4. Write the numbers 1–10 on your paper. In each of the following sentences, find the words that should be capitalized but are not. Write those words correctly after the sentence numbers.

EXAMPLE 1. Helga assured us that we were eating real german cooking.
　　　　1. *German*

1. The european Common Market has been one of the major developments of the 1960's.
2. We ordered swiss cheese and ham sandwiches on rye bread.
3. There are many students of french and spanish in this country, but few are learning russian or chinese.

4. The scandinavian countries have a high standard of living.
5. Greg said that he enjoyed listening to someone with an australian accent.
6. During the elizabethan age there were many great dramatists in England.
7. As one of her electives, Marge chose typing II.
8. I got my first notion of southern hospitality from visiting in Alabama.
9. One encounters England, France, Scotland, Russia, and the United States in studying canadian history.
10. The profile shot called attention to the actor's roman nose.

10f. Capitalize titles.

(1) Capitalize the title of a person when it comes before a name.

EXAMPLES   President Coolidge   Miss Wendell
              Mayor Lyons   Commissioner Jones

(2) Capitalize a title used alone or following a person's name if it refers to a high official or to someone to whom you wish to show special respect.

EXAMPLES   The Mayor is conferring with the City Council.
            Mr. Brabston is our new mayor.

            The Senator from South Dakota has the floor.
            He is one of the senators who were elected this year.

10
d-f

In a few hours we will know who has been elected President of the United States.

That is Mr. Hendricks, president of the Rotary Club.

The Superintendent is visiting classes today.

Cordell Hull, Secretary of State under Roosevelt, died in 1944.

When a title is used instead of a name in direct address, it should be capitalized.

EXAMPLES   Is it very serious, Doctor?
Good morning, Judge.

(3) Capitalize words showing family relationship when used with a person's name but *not* when preceded by a possessive.

EXAMPLES   We expect Uncle Fred and Aunt Helen to arrive tonight.
We always go to Grandpa Lowery's for a few weeks in the summer.
Jim's father is a miner.
That mitt belongs to his brother Bruce.
Angela's mother made some delicious brownies.

Words showing family relationship followed by a name and preceded by a possessive may be capitalized if they are considered part of the name.

EXAMPLES   Helen, this is my Aunt Liz.
We'll stay overnight with our cousin Ralph.

Words of family relationship may be capitalized or not when they are used without a name. Either way is acceptable.

Let's go with **Dad**. *or* Let's go with dad.

(4) Capitalize the first word and all important words in titles of books, periodicals, poems, stories, movies, paintings and other works of art, and so on.

Unimportant words in a title are *a, an, the,* and prepositions and conjunctions of fewer than five letters. Do not capitalize the word *the* before the title of a magazine or newspaper unless it begins a sentence.

Book	*The Adventures of Tom Sawyer*
Magazine	*Popular Mechanics*
Newspaper	the *Miami Herald*
Poem	"The Wreck of the Hesperus"
Story	"The Great Stone Face"
Movie	*How the West Was Won*
Painting	the *Mona Lisa*
Musical piece	"Rhapsody in Blue"

(5) Capitalize words referring to the Deity.

EXAMPLES God, the Creator, the Almighty

♦ NOTE The word *god,* when referring to pagan deities, is not capitalized.

EXAMPLE The Vikings had many gods.

● EXERCISE 5. Copy the following sentences, inserting capitals wherever they are needed.

1. Have you read e. a. robinson's poem "the man against the sky"?
2. While waiting to see dr. hoskins, I read the *chattanooga times* and *newsweek.*

3. *The thinker* is one of rodin's best-known pieces of sculpture.
4. We watched an old movie called *bad day at black rock* on television last night.
5. Today the voters will elect a new president and new congressman.
6. Uncle nick bought me a copy of *a tale of two cities*, a novel by charles dickens.
7. At our last meeting we elected a new secretary and listened to a speech by senator wayne doakes.
8. The principal speaker is dr. andrew holt, the president of the university of tennessee.
9. Besides uncle ted, there are aunt ella and aunt sara, my grandmother, and my great-grandfather.
10. Before the president's broadcast begins, an announcer always says, "Ladies and gentlemen, the president of the united states."

● REVIEW EXERCISE A.   Some of the following sentences are correct as they are; some are not. Write the numbers 1–20 on your paper. For correct sentences, write *C* after the proper number. For the others, copy the words that require capitals.

EXAMPLE   1. everyone was cheered on that gloomy monday by the thought that tuesday, columbus day, was a holiday.
　　　　　　1. *Everyone, Monday, Tuesday, Columbus Day*

1. In the fall everyone looks forward to the football season.
2. The football fan can see his favorite high school or college team play on saturday and his favorite professional team on sunday.
3. Last weekend i saw ohio state play michigan.

4. Ken's uncle introduced him to the captain of one of the world's largest passenger ships, the *queen elizabeth*.

5. The greeks believed that their various deities met on mount olympus to listen to zeus, the king of the gods.

6. Ann likes geography and history, but she makes her best grades in english and french.

7. The chief justice explained the ruling of the supreme court.

8. On july 4 miller's department store puts on a spectacular display of fireworks.

9. The *titanic* sank after hitting an iceberg off the coast of newfoundland.

10. My uncle went to amsterdam to see rembrandt's *the night watch*.

11. Fresh water is now being produced from salt water at a plant in freeport, texas.

12. Tod has registered for astronomy 212, which is taught by professor streifus.

13. Nan's brother has won several medals since he became a volunteer fireman.

14. At the world's fair we saw the fords and chevrolets of the future.

15. The first american to make a flight into space was commander alan b. shepard, jr.

16. In the *republic*, plato, a famous greek philosopher, describes what he considers to be an ideal society.

17. The President is expected to veto the bill passed by Congress.

18. The city planning commission has several proposals for improving tourist trade in our town.

19. Mr. McCloud, our mayor, has set aside the month of april for the arts festival.

20. Iceland is an island of volcanic origin located in the atlantic ocean near the arctic circle.

● REVIEW EXERCISE B.   Copy the following sentences, inserting capitals wherever needed.

1. Mail the letter to the union of south africa and the package to genoa, italy.
2. This year palm sunday is the last sunday in march.
3. Among the early settlers were roman catholics and congregationalists.
4. Like other north american indians, the ancient iroquois believed in many gods.
5. The department of agriculture publishes many pamphlets that are useful to the home gardener.
6. Did aunt josie send you that mexican straw hat?
7. The *windy jane* is a small white sailboat.
8. Last winter Jack had an iceboat at greenwood lake.
9. In history and in spanish, we are studying the same historical period.
10. One man is an armenian, the other a greek.

● REVIEW EXERCISE C.   Of the following sentences, some are correct as they stand. In the others certain words need capitals. For correct sentences, write *C* after the proper number. For the others, write in order the words that require capitals.

1. ned and I are spending the summer at camp medomak in washington, maine.
2. Tommy has a new English bicycle, a gift from his uncle.
3. Suddenly i saw the boeing 707 streaking across the sky.
4. Here is a new series of Norwegian airmail stamps.
5. The waters of the Mediterranean are very blue.
6. The table is made of asian teakwood.
7. The Ohio Tractor Company is looking for a qualified treasurer.

8. Have you ever seen a Mexican jumping bean?
9. We heard a performance of Verdi's *Aida*.
10. My brother is taking english, math II, social studies, biology, and french.
11. Just then i noticed her new persian rug.
12. Is the altoona bus company on strike?
13. Silk is an important Japanese export.
14. Jerry lives on the west side of oak street.
15. sometimes the boys went fishing at Lake Sunapee.
16. At Aspen, Colorado, I learned to ride a horse.
17. She is traveling by northeast airlines.
18. My favorite program is sponsored by gold crisp cereal.
19. Lever brothers has introduced a new soap.
20. Octopuses lurk in the mediterranean sea.

Summary Style Sheet

The following list may be used as a style sheet for quick reference. Be sure that you know and understand all of the rules represented.

10a. Cumulus clouds are often seen before a storm.

10b. Next month I will be thirteen years old.

10c. (1) Bert and Alice once heard Robert Frost reading his poems.
   (2) We moved from Ames, Iowa, in the Middle West, to New England that year.
   (3) The new president of the Chamber of Commerce is Wallace Gates, who owns Gates Auto Supply Center.
   (4) The Presque Isle Fair, which used to be held in the fall, opens on August 10 this year.
   (5) The effects of the Industrial Revolution in England were felt throughout the British Empire.
   (6) Many Indians, Chinese, and Japanese are Buddhists.

(7) Try this new **P**epperidge **F**arm bread.

(8) The **G**olden **G**ate **B**ridge and **F**ishermen's **W**harf are two of the attractions of San Francisco.

10d. My brother is the family's champion in playing **Ch**inese checkers.

10e. Next year we will have **M**r. **T**all for math and **M**iss **H**uddersfield for **E**nglish.

10f. (1) **M**rs. **C**ook, may **I** present the **R**everend **M**r. **P**erkins?

(2) Do you plan to run for reelection next year, **G**overnor?
Dave Dugan, who is the secretary of our class, likes to compare his duties with those of the **S**ecretary of **S**tate.

(3) My **c**ousin **E**mily is **U**ncle **F**rank's oldest daughter.

(4) There were some superb shots of sailing ships in **M**utiny on the **B**ounty.

(5) May the **L**ord bless us and keep us.

CHAPTER 11

Punctuation

End Marks, Commas, and Semicolons

In spoken language, your voice tells where thoughts are interrupted or completed, but in written language you must depend upon punctuation to indicate pauses and to make your meaning clear. To punctuate written papers so that your reader will readily understand what you are trying to say, learn the rules for punctuation in this chapter and in Chapter 12. Follow them whenever you write.

END MARKS

The term *end marks* refers to punctuation which appears at the end of sentences. Periods, question marks, and exclamation points are end marks.

11a. A statement is followed by a period.

EXAMPLES   The chess player considered his next move.
Tea is grown in Ceylon.

11a

11b. A question is followed by a question mark.

EXAMPLES Who has lost his book?
What time is it?

11c. An exclamation is followed by an exclamation point.

EXAMPLES What a high bridge!
How big the moon is!

11d. A request or an order is followed by either a period or an exclamation point.

EXAMPLES Please call the dog. [a request—no strong feeling is expressed]
Stay where you are! [The exclamation point shows strong feeling.]

To determine which end mark to use, consider whether the sentence expresses excitement or strong feeling. If it does, use an exclamation point; if it does not, use a period.

● EXERCISE 1. Read the following sentences and decide which end mark is needed for each one. Then write the last word of the sentence and the correct end mark. (Do not write in this book.)

1. Can you name a play by William Shakespeare
2. Look for a copy of *Romeo and Juliet* in your library
3. Shakespeare wrote many comedies, tragedies, and histories
4. Do you know how much formal schooling he had

5. Shakespeare had only an elementary school education, but he studied all his life
6. Of course, few people in Shakespeare's time went to college
7. Even in elementary school the students learned Latin and Greek
8. How strange Shakespeare's school would seem to us

● EXERCISE 2. In the following paragraph, all initial capital letters and end marks of punctuation have been omitted. You must decide where the sentences begin and end. Copy the paragraph, providing capital letters and marks of punctuation as needed.

have you read the Old English epic *Beowulf* it is an exciting poem about the adventures of a great hero perhaps the most exciting episode is Beowulf's fight with the fire dragon what a gory battle that was Beowulf was then an old man, and the fight with the fire dragon turned out to be his last adventure the flames from the dragon's nostrils killed him don't think, though, that Beowulf died without accomplishing his aim he managed to slay the dragon then he asked one of his warriors, Wiglaf, to look into the dragon's lair what do you think Wiglaf found the dragon had been guarding a great treasure of gold and jewels the treasure was later buried in the mound which was built over Beowulf's ashes what an appropriate tribute for the people to pay to their great king

11e. An abbreviation is followed by a period.

EXAMPLES   Ave.   Oct.
           Calif.   lb.
           Fri.   P.M.

11
b-e

Make it a practice to look up abbreviations in a dictionary if you are not sure of their spelling.

COMMAS

An end mark calls for a full stop, but a comma means a pause. It is like a traffic sign that tells a motorist to slow down and proceed with caution. A comma makes writing easier to understand, since it helps to convey the writer's meaning. You already know some uses for the comma; for example, you put a comma after your last name when you write it before your first name. You use a comma in writing a number of more than three digits (4,500). To make your writing clear, you ought to be familiar with several other important uses of the comma.

11f. Use commas to separate items in a series.

A series is three or more items written one after another. The items may be single words or groups of words.

EXAMPLES   December, January, and February are summer months in the Southern Hemisphere. [single words in a series]

For my lunch I had a sandwich, some milk, and an orange. [groups of words in a series]

The delegates nominated one candidate, voted, and installed him in office. [verbs in a series]

There were spots at the top, at the sides, and on the bottom. [phrases in a series]

◆ NOTE Some writers omit the comma before the *and* between the last two items of a series. Nevertheless, you should form the habit of including this comma, since it is sometimes necessary to make your meaning clear. Notice how the comma affects the meaning in the following example.

EXAMPLE   The samples of soil in the exhibit included clay, loam, coarse sand and gravel. [No comma is used. Is "coarse sand and gravel" one sample or two?]

The samples of soil in the exhibit included clay, loam, coarse sand, and gravel. [Comma is used. It is clear that ". . . coarse sand, and gravel" are two samples.]

Always be sure that there are at least three items in the series before you insert commas. Two items do not need a comma between them.

WRONG   You will need a pencil, and plenty of paper.

RIGHT   You will need a pencil and plenty of paper.

When the items in the series are separated by conjunctions, there is no need for commas.

WRONG   Take water, and food, and matches with you.

RIGHT   Take water and food and matches with you.

● EXERCISE 3. Some of the sentences below need commas; others do not. If a sentence is correct, write *C* after the proper number. If a sentence needs commas, copy the word preceding the comma, and write the comma after it.

11f

EXAMPLE   1. Open the window look up the street tell
me what you see.
   1. *window, street,*

1. Crabs and lobsters are both shellfish.
2. Man o' War Citation and War Admiral were three famous racehorses.
3. The pilot boarded the plane checked his instruments and prepared for takeoff.
4. Denise has guppies and goldfish and mollies in her home aquarium.
5. The writer opened his book and began to read one of his short stories to the audience.
6. Our dog will play dead roll over and stand on his hind feet for a piece of meat.
7. The police shone their spotlights down the street along the walls and into the yards.
8. Abraham Lincoln was a rail-splitter an attorney and finally the President of the United States.
9. Lincoln's wit his humanity and his service to his country will always be remembered.
10. The tornado took a heavy toll in lives and property.

11g. Use a comma to separate two or more adjectives preceding a noun.

EXAMPLES   The porcupine is a large, clumsy rodent.
Most medieval castles had thick, stone walls.

Do not place a comma between an adjective and the noun immediately following it.

WRONG   Pyrite is a pale, golden-colored, mineral.
[The last comma is incorrect.]
RIGHT   Pyrite is a pale, golden-colored mineral.

♦ NOTE Some adjectives are so closely connected in meaning to the nouns they modify that no comma is needed to separate them from another adjective. *Horned owl, oak chest,* and *electric light* are examples of such pairs of adjectives and nouns. Notice how the following sentences are punctuated:

> A huge horned owl lives in those woods. [not huge, horned owl]

> The boys are refinishing an old oak chest. [not old, oak chest]

> An unshaded electric light hung from the ceiling. [not unshaded, electric light]

You can test to see whether or not a comma is needed by inserting an *and* between the adjectives (*unshaded and electric,* for example). If the *and* sounds awkward, the comma is unnecessary.

● EXERCISE 4. Some of the following sentences need commas; others do not. If a sentence does not need additional punctuation, write *C* after its number. If it needs punctuation, copy the word preceding the needed comma, and write the comma after it.

1. Hundreds of years ago, sailors heard the singing of what they thought were beautiful alluring sirens.
2. Today we know that the sailors heard manatees, or sea cows, which are large slow bald-headed mammals.
3. The woman looked under the table the bed and the chairs for a mouse that she had seen.
4. Meanwhile, the frightened shivering mouse was scurrying into a hole in the wall.
5. The bright blue lights on the giant Christmas tree fascinated the children.

11g

6. According to Greek mythology, three Fates spin the thread of life measure it and finally cut it.
7. Shakespeare created such famous characters as Brutus Juliet and Falstaff.
8. Falstaff was a fat jolly fellow who liked to brag.
9. He pretended to be wise loyal and brave.
10. When he faced two men in battle, he begged for mercy ran away from the fight and later bragged about his bravery in the face of eleven men.

11h. Use a comma before *and, but, or, nor, for,* and *yet* when they join the parts of a compound sentence.

If you are not sure that you can recognize a compound sentence, you should review pages 28–29.

EXAMPLES   Betty offered to get the tickets, and I accepted gratefully.

They had been working very hard, but they didn't seem especially tired.

The twins will see their favorite baby-sitter, for their parents are going out.

A very short compound sentence is sometimes written without a comma.

EXAMPLE   It rained and it rained.

◆ NOTE   Do not confuse a compound sentence and a compound verb; do not place a comma between the parts of a compound verb.

COMPOUND SENTENCE   Usually we study in the morning, and we play baseball in the afternoon.

COMPOUND VERB   Usually we **study** in the morning and **play** baseball in the afternoon.

● EXERCISE 5. Among the following sentences are compound sentences, simple sentences with single verbs, and simple sentences with compound verbs. If the sentence is correctly punctuated, write *C* after the number. If it needs additional punctuation, copy the word preceding the needed comma, and write the comma after it.

1. According to Greek mythology, Paris, a young Trojan, was chosen to settle an argument among three of the goddesses.
2. Each of the goddesses wanted to be chosen the most beautiful and each of them offered Paris a gift.
3. Paris considered the three gifts and finally chose Venus, the goddess of love, as the most beautiful of the three.
4. Venus had promised Paris that he could have the most beautiful woman in the world as his wife and she did not forget her promise.
5. Helen was the most beautiful woman in the world but she was already married to Menelaus, a Greek king.
6. Nevertheless, Helen was taken from Menelaus and was given to Paris.
7. Menelaus called together all the Greek kings and warriors and they set sail for Troy to reclaim Helen.
8. The Greeks besieged Troy for ten years but the Trojans did not yield.
9. Finally, the Greeks built the famous Trojan horse and presented it to the Trojans.
10. In accepting the gift, the Trojans sealed their doom for hidden within the wooden horse were several Greek warriors.

11h

11i. Use commas to set off expressions that interrupt the sentence.

Two commas are needed if the expression to be set off comes in the middle of the sentence. One comma is needed if the expression comes first or last.

EXAMPLES   Our neighbor, Bill Foley, is a fine golfer.
Naturally, we expect to win.
My answer is correct, I think.

There are several kinds of expressions that may interrupt a sentence. One kind of interrupter is the *appositive,* a word that means the same thing as the word it follows. An appositive phrase is an appositive with its modifiers.

(1) Appositives and appositive phrases are usually set off by commas.

EXAMPLES   Jack, the newsboy, is late today. [*Newsboy* is an appositive, meaning the same person as Jack.]

Miss French, the secretary of our school, is in Florida. [*The secretary of our school* is an appositive phrase meaning the same person as Miss French.]

Occasionally when the appositive is a single word closely related to the preceding word, the comma is not needed.

EXAMPLES   our friend Howard
William the Conqueror

● EXERCISE 6.   Copy each appositive or appositive phrase and the word which precedes it. Supply commas where needed. Not all of the appositives require commas.

EXAMPLE 1. Mars one of the closest planets can be seen without a telescope.
1. *Mars, one of the closest planets,*

1. Norman Cousins editor of the *Saturday Review* was the main speaker.
2. We have a figurine made of clay from Kilimanjaro the highest mountain in Africa.
3. The whole class read the book *Kidnapped*.
4. Saint Augustine the oldest city in the United States has many very narrow streets.
5. Sugar cane an important Florida crop may be shipped raw or refined.
6. Do you own a thesaurus a dictionary of synonyms and antonyms?
7. At North Cape the northernmost point of Europe the sun does not set from the middle of May until the end of July.
8. The American mastodon an extinct, elephantlike animal was hunted by primitive man.
9. Stan's brother Paul entered the toboggan race.
10. At Thermopylae a narrow pass in eastern Greece a band of three hundred Spartans faced an army of thousands from Persia.

● EXERCISE 7. Write ten sentences containing the following groups of words as appositives. Insert commas wherever needed.

EXAMPLE 1. her twelfth birthday
1. *She is having a party on Tuesday, her twelfth birthday.*

1. an Eagle Scout
2. the club's president
3. Al
4. the Big Dipper
5. his best friend
6. a popular game
7. the umpire
8. the day of the picnic
9. a famous author
10. Mrs. Kimball

11i

(2) Words used in direct address are set off by commas.

A person often addresses by name someone to whom he is talking. In written conversation, a name used in *direct address* is set off by commas.[1]

EXAMPLES   Ben, please answer the doorbell.

Your tickets, Miss Blake, are in this envelope.

Mother needs you, Henry.

Stop, you fool!

● EXERCISE 8.   Copy the words in direct address from the following sentences. Insert commas either before or after the words, as needed.

1. Bill why did you name your dog Achilles?
2. Stop this incessant chatter class.
3. We my fellow students are going to win the game tomorrow.
4. Professor Adams when was the Battle of Marathon?
5. What is your opinion of the candidates Mark?
6. Please Dad may I use your hatchet?
7. Where my dear sir do you think you are going?
8. Senator Smith I have a proposal for improving our state.
9. Lisa if you apologize, I'm sure that Arlene will forget the incident.
10. You know that you shouldn't be on the couch Snoopy.

(3) Parenthetical expressions are set off by commas.

Words and phrases such as *however, for example, of course, in fact* often occur in sentences. They are called

[1] For rules governing the use of commas in quotations, see pages 230–31.

parenthetical expressions and are usually set off by commas.

COMMON PARENTHETICAL EXPRESSIONS

of course	on the other hand	in my opinion
however	I suppose	to tell the truth
for example	in fact	nevertheless
on the contrary	by the way	I believe

EXAMPLES The weather, in fact, was perfect.

Carl, on the contrary, prefers football to baseball.

To tell the truth, history is my worst subject.

◆ NOTE Such expressions may not be parenthetical.

Of course it is true.

I suppose we ought to go home now.

(4) Words such as *well, yes, no, why* **are followed by a comma when they are used at the beginning of a sentence or remark.**

EXAMPLES Yes, you may borrow my bicycle.
Why, it's Leo!
Well, I think you are wrong.

● EXERCISE 9. The following sentences contain parenthetical expressions and introductory words that require commas. Copy the parenthetical expressions and introductory words, inserting commas as needed.

1. Yes there are many constellations visible in the summer.
2. For instance on a summer night you can view the Scorpion, the Serpent, and the Serpent-Bearer.
3. To be sure we should not overlook the Milky Way.

4. The Milky Way in fact is more impressive in the summer than at any other time of year.
5. Of course Hercules is an interesting constellation.
6. Studying the constellations is in my opinion a most interesting hobby.
7. It does take some imagination however to pick out some of the constellations.
8. The Archer for example is hard to perceive.
9. The Scorpion on the other hand is quite clearly outlined.
10. Astronomy I think is a fascinating science.

11j. Use a comma in certain conventional situations.

(1) Use commas to separate items in dates and addresses.

EXAMPLES   She was born on January 26, 1952, in Cheshire, Connecticut.

A letter dated November 23, 1888, was found in the old house at 980 West Street, Davenport, Iowa.

Saturday, November 25, is the day of the party.

◆ NOTE   If a postal zone number is used in an address, the comma follows it. If a ZIP code number is used, no comma is used with it.

EXAMPLES   Chicago 16, Illinois
Fargo, North Dakota 58101

● EXERCISE 10. Most of the following sentences need commas; a few do not. If a sentence is correctly punctuated, write *C* after its number. Copy the other sentences, inserting commas wherever they are needed.

1. Mark Twain was born on November 30 1835 in Florida Missouri.
2. My new address is 3365 Clinch Avenue Lubbock Texas 79408.
3. Thomas Edison was born in Milan Ohio on February 11 1847.
4. Napoleon was defeated at Waterloo Belgium on June 18 1815.
5. In 1955 we moved from Ohio to Indiana.
6. On June 15 1752 Benjamin Franklin proved that lightning is electricity.
7. Between 1484 and 1782 approximately three hundred thousand women in Europe were executed for witchcraft.
8. In the United States the most famous witchcraft trials were held in Salem Massachusetts.
9. The scene of the robbery was a grocery store at 650 Gay Street.
10. My sister's college address is P.O. Box 76 Iowa State University Ames Iowa 52240.

(2) Use a comma after the salutation of a friendly letter and after the closing of any letter.

EXAMPLES   Dear Dad,   Dear Sharon,
           With love,   Yours truly,

● REVIEW EXERCISE A. Copy the following sentences, inserting commas wherever they are needed.

1. What did you tell the interviewer Keith?
2. Kate said to forward her mail to 5525 Dogwood Road Knoxville 2 Tennessee.
3. Boris Pasternak a well-known Russian novelist died in 1960.
4. The Hodges sent us a card from Lucerne Switzerland.

11 j

5. Quick violent flashes of lightning cause approximately 27,500 forest fires a year in the United States alone.
6. On the other hand lightning is beneficial because it changes the insoluble nitrogen in the air into nitrogen that plants can use.
7. Lightning does a great deal of damage but it also does man a great service.
8. A single flash of lightning strange as it seems could supply a home with electric power for thirty-five years.
9. Lightning strikes such tall objects as trees steeples and skyscrapers.
10. Electrical storms expected during the summer sometimes occur in the winter, too.

● REVIEW EXERCISE B. Copy the following sentences, inserting commas wherever they are needed.

1. Greece a country with a glorious past is one of the most beautiful countries in the world.
2. Greece is chiefly an agricultural nation but her industry is increasing rapidly.
3. Greece exports olives wine figs and tobacco.
4. Much of Greece is covered by mountains lakes and rivers.
5. In fact only one fourth of the land is arable.
6. The capital of Greece is Athens a city famous for its great philosophers.
7. Athens produced such great thinkers as Socrates Plato and Aristotle.
8. Everyone to be sure is familiar with the architecture and sculpture of ancient Greece.
9. The ruins of the Parthenon the temple of Athena testify to the artistry of the Greeks.

10. The Parthenon was completed in 432 B.C. and much of it still stands in Athens.

● REVIEW EXERCISE C. Copy the following sentences, inserting commas wherever they are needed.

1. Lincoln was shot by John Wilkes Booth on April 14 1865 in Washington D.C.
2. Booth a neurotic actor shot the President during a play.
3. Lincoln was carried to a nearby home for treatment but he died the next morning.
4. Booth fled the city but was later trapped in a barn near Port Royal Virginia.
5. Booth was shot by his pursuers or he took his own life.
6. Four of those associated with him in the plot were tried convicted and hanged.
7. The assassination of Lincoln has been called one of the most brutal shocking crimes in history.
8. Booth of course was a fanatic who thought he was doing humanity a service.
9. Recent scholarship has suggested that certain ambitious conniving members of Lincoln's government may have been involved in the plot.
10. Lincoln was succeeded by his Vice-President Andrew Johnson.

SEMICOLONS

The semicolon is an effective mark of punctuation if it is used sparingly. Part period and part comma, it says to the reader, "Pause here a little longer than you would for a comma, but do not come to a full stop as you would for a period." You should learn two uses for semicolons.

11k. Use a semicolon between the parts of a compound sentence if they are not joined by *and, but, or, nor, for, yet.*

EXAMPLES　　Take Mother's suitcase upstairs; leave Dad's in the car.

After school I went to the play rehearsal; then I studied in the library for an hour.

11l. A semicolon (rather than a comma) may be needed to separate the parts of a compound sentence if there are commas within the parts.

CONFUSING　　I wrote to Ann, Beth, and Meg, and Jean notified Terry and Sue.

CLEAR　　I wrote to Ann, Beth, and Meg; and Jean notified Terry and Sue.

Sometimes, instead of using a semicolon, it is better to separate a compound sentence or a heavily punctuated sentence into two sentences.

ACCEPTABLE　　In the tropical jungles of South America it rains every day; the vegetation is lush and fast-growing.

BETTER　　In the tropical jungles of South America it rains every day. The vegetation is lush and fast-growing.

ACCEPTABLE　　Although the rest of the state has had heavy rain, Aroostook County is very dry; the danger of forest fires is acute.

BETTER　　Although the rest of the state has had heavy rain, Aroostook County is very dry. The danger of forest fires is acute.

● REVIEW EXERCISE D. Copy the following paragraph, inserting end marks, commas, and semicolons wherever needed. Be sure to capitalize the first word in each sentence.

Tracy went to the sideshow at the circus in Jacksonville Florida he watched a man swallow a sword another man eat fire and a woman tell fortunes these acts amazed him but the magician pleased him more than anything else the magician was a distinguished-looking man who was dressed entirely in black his quick nimble hands performed strange acts he pulled rabbits out of his hat made cards disappear and suspended a woman in midair the audience was awed by the magician's skill who would not be the magician's final act was of course his best he placed a woman in a box and proceeded to saw the box in half how the audience gasped the woman on the other hand seemed unconcerned in fact she was smiling the magician finally put the two parts of the box back together opened the top of the box and lifted the woman out yes she was just as whole as she had been at the beginning of the act Tracy's father a former magician himself explained the trick but Tracy could not believe that anyone could be as quick with his hands as the magician was after the show he went backstage to interview the magician he wanted to submit the interview to his school paper.

● REVIEW EXERCISE E. If a sentence below is correct, write *C* after its number on your paper. Copy the sentences that are not correct, inserting punctuation or omitting it as needed.

1. On June 25, 1964 we left by plane for Montreal, Canada.

11
k-l

2. There we boarded the *Homeric* and sailed for Europe.
3. In England we visited Westminster Abbey, the burial place of many famous Englishmen.
4. We also went to see Scotland Yard the Thames River and Windsor Castle.
5. The beautiful stately Windsor Castle has been a residence of English sovereigns since the time of William the Conqueror.
6. Yes, England is a country with a rich heritage.
7. It is in fact a country in which the past and the present merge.
8. The Stone of Scone, for example, was used in ancient Scottish coronations today it lies beneath the coronation chair in Westminster Abbey.
9. London is large, and modern, it is also quaint, historic, and peaceful.
10. We found the English people hospitable, and interesting.

CHAPTER 12

Punctuation

Colons, Italics, Quotation Marks, Apostrophes, Hyphens

This chapter will help you to use correctly five more marks of punctuation. Together with end marks, the comma, and the semicolon, these five are the chief marks of punctuation that you will need in your writing.

COLONS

A colon is a punctuation mark that usually signals that something is to follow.

12a. Use a colon before a list of items, especially after expressions like *as follows* and *the following.*

EXAMPLES   A search showed that Jack's pocket contained the following: a knife, half an apple, a piece of gum, a dime and a nickel, and two rusty nails.

The question is as follows: if the plane leaves San Francisco at 2 P.M., at what

12a

225

time will it reach Chicago if it averages 500 miles per hour?

You will need these things for map work: a ruler, a box of colored pencils, and some tracing paper.

The colon is never used directly after a verb or a preposition. Omit the colon or reword the sentence.

WRONG   My favorite sports are: basketball, tennis, swimming, and bowling.

RIGHT   My favorite sports are the following: basketball, tennis, swimming, and bowling.

RIGHT   My favorite sports are basketball, tennis, swimming, and bowling.

WRONG   These cookies are made of: flour, brown sugar, butter, eggs, and nuts.

RIGHT   These cookies contain the following ingredients: flour, brown sugar, butter, eggs, and nuts.

RIGHT   These cookies are made of flour, brown sugar, butter, eggs, and nuts.

12b. Use a colon between the hour and the minute when you write the time.

EXAMPLES   8:30 A.M., 10:00 P.M., 9:04 this morning

12c. Use a colon after the salutation of a business letter.

EXAMPLES   Dear Sir: Dear Mr. Foster:
                Gentlemen: Dear Dr. Christiano:

● EXERCISE 1. Copy the following expressions and complete them with a list. Insert colons and commas where they are needed.

1. The following students will assemble on stage
2. The eight parts of speech are as follows
3. I am taking the following subjects this year
4. At the five-and-ten I bought
5. The mechanic listed the following damages to the car
6. You need these supplies for a picnic
7. We have studied the following kinds of punctuation marks
8. The performances will begin at
9. To succeed in sports, one should be
10. I have lived in three places

ITALICS OR UNDERLINING

In printed material, italics are letters that lean to the right—*like this*. When you write, you show that a word should be *italicized* by underlining it.

12d. Use italics (underlining) for titles of books, periodicals, works of art, ships, and so on.[1]

EXAMPLES *Dr. Jekyll and Mr. Hyde* is one of my favorite novels.

One of the most famous movies ever made is *Gone with the Wind*.

On board the *Queen Mary*, we found an old copy of the *Baltimore Herald*.

Have you heard the opera *Madame Butterfly*?

[1] For titles that are not italicized but enclosed in quotation marks, see rule 12n on page 235.

12
b-d

● EXERCISE 2. From the following sentences, copy the words that should be printed in italics and underline them.

1. In Under the Sea-Wind Rachel Carson writes about the life of a young mackerel.
2. One of the books Ralph Moody has written about his childhood is called Little Britches.
3. In a recent edition of Look, there is an article on our progress in space.
4. Our school newspaper, the Jackson Chronicle, received an award at the state convention.
5. Bert lent me a mystery called The Secret of the Haunted Cave.
6. The Queen Elizabeth is one of the world's largest passenger ships.
7. Lawrence of Arabia had some of the most beautiful photography I have ever seen in a movie.
8. Sprayberry High School is presenting Our Town, a play by Thornton Wilder.
9. In 1927 Charles Lindbergh flew his Spirit of St. Louis nonstop from New York to Paris.
10. The first novel that I read was Treasure Island.

QUOTATION MARKS

When a person's exact words are used in writing, it is customary to use quotation marks to show where the quotation begins and ends. It is easy enough to put quotation marks before and after a quotation, but problems sometimes arise when other marks of punctuation are used in combination with them. The rules in this section will help you to solve most of your problems in punctuating quotations.

12e. Use quotation marks to enclose a direct quotation—a person's exact words.

EXAMPLES   It was Shakespeare who wrote, "To thine own self be true."

"When the bell rings," said the teacher, "leave the room quietly."

If a person's words are not quoted exactly, no quotation marks are needed. Such a use is an *indirect* quotation.

INDIRECT QUOTATION   The reporter predicted that it would be a close game. [not the reporter's exact words]

DIRECT QUOTATION   The reporter predicted, "It will be a close game." [the reporter's exact words]

In order to write words spoken by other people, you must know more than how to use quotation marks correctly. You must learn where to use capital letters, whether to put commas and end marks inside or outside quotation marks, and when to begin a new paragraph. Study the following rules and examples until you are sure you can write conversation accurately.

12f. A direct quotation begins with a capital letter.

EXAMPLES   Harold said, "The icing isn't thick enough."

Richard Lovelace wrote, "Stone walls do not a prison make."

12
e-f

12g. **When a quoted sentence is divided into two parts by an interrupting expression such as** *he said* **or** *Mother asked,* **the second part begins with a small letter.**

EXAMPLES   "Lightning has always awed mankind," explained Mrs. Belmont, "and many people are still frightened by it."

"The time has come," insisted the speaker, "to improve our educational program."

A quoted sentence which is divided in this way is called a broken quotation. Notice that in broken quotations, quotation marks appear before the interrupting expression and after it also.

12h. **A direct quotation is set off from the rest of the sentence by commas.**

To set off means to separate from the rest of the sentence. If a quotation comes at the beginning of a sentence, a comma follows it. If a quotation comes at the end of a sentence, a comma precedes it. If a quoted sentence is interrupted, a comma follows the first part and precedes the second part.

EXAMPLES   "Science is more interesting than history," said Bernie. [quotation at beginning of sentence, followed by comma]

I asked, "Who is your science teacher?" [quotation at end, preceded by comma]

"It was Mr. Murphy," answered Bernie, "but now we have Mrs. Parkhurst." [quotation interrupted, with comma after the first part and before the second part]

◆ NOTE No comma is needed if an end mark is used instead.

EXAMPLES "Does she let you do experiments?" Glen wanted to know.
"I'll say she does!" Bernie exclaimed.

● EXERCISE 3. Copy the following sentences, inserting commas, quotation marks, and capitals where needed. Write *C* after the number of sentences that are correct as they stand.

1. The librarian politely told me to be quiet.
2. At the same time Mike whispered shut up!
3. He asked can't you see that people are studying?
4. I replied in a whisper I'm sorry that I disturbed you.
5. I should have known better, I said to myself, than to raise my voice.
6. Next time I quietly asked the boy across from me for his science book.
7. He whispered I'll give it to you in a minute.
8. But I need it now I explained.
9. He muttered something about people who forget their own books.
10. About that time the bell rang, and the librarian said it's time to go.

12i. A period or a comma following a quotation should be placed inside the closing quotation marks.

EXAMPLES "It's time to go," said the guide.
The man replied, "I'm ready."

12
g-i

12j. A question mark or an exclamation point should be placed inside the closing quotation marks if the quotation is a question or an exclamation. Otherwise it should be placed outside.

EXAMPLES   "How far have we come?" asked the exhausted man. [The question mark is inside the closing quotation marks because the quotation itself is a question.]

Who said, "Give me liberty or give me death"? [The question mark is outside the closing quotation marks because the quotation is not a question.]

"Jump!" screamed the woman. [The exclamation point is inside the closing quotation marks because the quotation itself is an exclamation.]

I couldn't believe it when he said, "No, thank you"! [The exclamation point is outside the closing quotation marks because the quotation itself is not an exclamation.]

● EXERCISE 4.   Copy these sentences. Insert the proper punctuation and capitalization.

1. What do you know about the life of Lewis Carroll Miss Luce asked Lydia
2. His real name was Charles Dodgson Lydia answered
3. He was a professor of mathematics at Oxford for many years added Lance
4. I'm sure that you've all read *Alice in Wonderland* and *Through the Looking Glass* continued Miss Luce
5. Yes the class chorused

6. Do you remember asked our teacher the Mad Hatter and the March Hare
7. What a wild time Alice spent with those two characters Lydia burst out
8. Yes Lance interrupted the March Hare offered Alice wine, and then told her that there was none
9. And they both asked her foolish riddles added Lydia
10. Are you surprised asked Miss Luce that a professor of mathematics could write children's literature

● EXERCISE 5. Rewrite each of the following sentences, changing the indirect quotation to a direct quotation. Be sure to use capital letters and punctuation wherever necessary.

EXAMPLE 1. We asked our parents if we could go on the sight-seeing tour.
       1. *We asked our parents,* "*May we go on the sight-seeing tour?*"

1. The principal announced that the annual talent parade would be held next week.
2. Our teacher asked us if we were going to enter the talent contest.
3. Jaylene said that she was going to do a modern ballet.
4. Ken suggested that he might do some rope tricks.
5. The teacher asked me what I was going to do.
6. I replied that I did not have any talent.
7. The teacher exclaimed that she was sure I was wrong.
8. Finally, I said that I would do a dramatic reading.
9. Then the teacher said that she was proud of us all.
10. We told her that we would do our best.

12j

12k. When you write dialogue (two or more persons having a conversation), begin a new paragraph every time the speaker changes.

EXAMPLE   "Let's get going," Bill said.

"What's your hurry, Bill?" Andy didn't seem at all worried.

"Well, I promised we'd be there by seven thirty. It's a half-hour ride, and it's nearly seven now," Bill explained.

12l. When a quotation consists of several sentences, put quotation marks only at the beginning and end of the whole quotation, not around each sentence in the quotation.

WRONG   "I'll wait for you at Burke's Drug Store." "Get there as soon as you can." "We don't want to be late," he said and rushed off down the hall.

RIGHT   "I'll wait for you at Burke's Drug Store. Get there as soon as you can. We don't want to be late," he said and rushed off down the hall.

12m. Use single quotation marks to enclose a quotation within a quotation.

EXAMPLES   "Let's sing 'Home on the Range,'" suggested Lefty.

"Did Mr. Numan really say, 'It's all right to use your books during the test'?" asked Sally.

12n. Use quotation marks to enclose the titles of chapters, articles, short stories, poems, songs, and other parts of books or periodicals.

EXAMPLES   Edgar Allan Poe wrote "The Raven."

Have you read Poe's short story "The Pit and the Pendulum"?

My article, "Sportsmanship at Forest Park Junior High School," was printed in the school newspaper.

Francis Scott Key wrote "The Star-Spangled Banner."

The assignment for tomorrow is Chapter 12, "Deserts and Other Hot, Dry Lands."

● EXERCISE 6.   Copy the following sentences, inserting quotation marks where they are needed.

1. Mother, have you seen my catcher's mitt? asked Bob. It's been missing since Monday. I need it for practice this afternoon.
2. The Long Search was the most exciting chapter in the story of the lion cubs.
3. In what poem did Longfellow write, The thoughts of youth are long, long thoughts? asked Isabel.
4. I think it was My Lost Youth, replied her father.
5. Mr. Evans said, one of the greatest changes in architecture has been in the design of churches. They no longer follow the traditional forms. Churches have been built that are shaped like stars, fish, and ships, among other things.
6. The latest issue of *Life* has some wonderful pictures of migrating birds.
7. Do you know the speech beginning What's in a name? from *Romeo and Juliet?* I asked her.

12
k-n

8. Yes, answered Emily. My mother used to say that to me when I was little. That was how I first heard of Shakespeare.
9. A human hand has more than twenty-five bones and twenty-five muscles, exclaimed Mark. No wonder a hand can do so many things!
10. There is an article called Tools for the Home Handyman in the Sunday paper.

● REVIEW EXERCISE A. Copy the following paragraphs, using quotation marks and other marks of punctuation wherever necessary. Remember to begin a new paragraph each time the speaker changes. Those punctuation marks which are already included in the exercise are correct.

Halloween finally arrived. Connie and Judy asked their mothers if they could go out for tricks or treats. When their mothers agreed, the two girls began planning their evening. We'll dress like witches and carry black cats said Connie. And we'll scare everyone in the neighborhood with our horrible masks Judy added. Oh, I can hardly wait to see the people's faces exclaimed Connie. I bet they'll be scared stiff.

Night came, and the two witches approached their first victim's house. It doesn't look as though anyone is home here said Connie, as she eyed the almost dark house. No, there's a faint light in the window argued Judy. Anyway we'll just scare them more if they're in the dark.

The girls approached the door and rang the doorbell. As the door slowly opened, a cold, moist smoke poured out. Then they heard the sounds of rattling chains and groaning voices. Suddenly, a hideous-sounding voice cackled Heh! Heh! Heh! Come in, children.

The two witches stood frozen in their tracks. Finally, Judy cried I'm leaving. I feel like a character in the story Hansel and Gretel. You can stay if you want to. I'm right behind you Connie gasped.

As the girls fled, a shape appeared through the smoke. A voice called after them trick or treat.

● REVIEW EXERCISE B. To show that you understand quotation marks, write a one-page narration which uses a great deal of dialogue. Put your characters—two will be enough—into an unusual situation, or have them discussing an assignment, a ball game, or a party. Make your conversation sound real and be sure it is punctuated correctly.

APOSTROPHES

The apostrophe is used (1) to show ownership or relationship, (2) to show where letters have been omitted in a contraction, and (3) to form the plurals of numbers and letters.

The Possessive Case

The possessive case of a word shows ownership or relationship.

EXAMPLES   Kathleen's desk   anybody's guess
             his bat   an hour's time
             horse's mane   a nickel's worth
             student's notebook   their car

Personal pronouns in the possessive case do not require an apostrophe (hers, his, its, ours, yours, theirs).

12o. **To form the possessive case of a singular noun, add an apostrophe and an *s*.**

EXAMPLES   a boy's cap   Marcia's pen
           the baby's toy   book's cover

● EXERCISE 7.   Write a sentence for each of the following words. Use the word in the possessive case.

1. Bob	6. nobody
2. Mary	7. Alan
3. soldier	8. dentist
4. yours	9. dime
5. minute	10. hers

12p. **To form the possessive case of a plural noun not ending in *s*, add an apostrophe and an *s*.**

EXAMPLES   mice's tracks
           men's club
           children's games

12q. **To form the possessive case of a plural noun ending in *s*, add only the apostrophe.**

EXAMPLES   cats' basket   four days' delay
           brushes' bristles   the Carsons' bungalow

● EXERCISE 8.   First write the plural form for each of the following words. Then after each plural form, write a sentence using it as a possessive.

1. horse	6. student
2. carpenter	7. fireman
3. dollar	8. relative
4. mouse	9. week
5. person	10. speaker

● EXERCISE 9. Rewrite each of the following expressions in the possessive case. Insert an apostrophe in the right place.

1. food for the dog
2. the jobs of the men
3. the hats of the ladies
4. the success of the woman
5. the grades of the students
6. the choice of the voters
7. the brooms of the witches
8. the candidate of the party
9. the licenses of the drivers
10. the duties of the examiners

Contractions

A *contraction* is a word made by combining two words and omitting some letters. An apostrophe takes the place of the letters that are left out.

EXAMPLES there is   there's
          we are   we're
          they have   they've

12r. Use an apostrophe to show where letters have been omitted in a contraction.

Perhaps the most common contraction is that made by shortening *not* to *n't* and combining it with a verb. The spelling of the verb is usually unchanged.

is not	isn't	has not	hasn't
does not	doesn't	have not	haven't
do not	don't	had not	hadn't
was not	wasn't	should not	shouldn't
were not	weren't	would not	wouldn't

12
0-r

When *n't* is added to *shall, will,* or *can,* the spelling of the verb changes.

shall not	shan't [the *ll* is dropped]
will not	won't [*o* replaces *ill*]
cannot	can't [one *n* is left out]

Contractions are often formed by joining nouns or pronouns with verbs.

I am	I'm	let us	let's
you have	you've	we shall	we'll
you are	you're	she would	she'd
he had	he'd	Sam is	Sam's
she has	she's	they are	they're
Harry will	Harry'll		

Its and It's

The word *its,* being a personal pronoun in the possessive case, does not have an apostrophe, just as other personal pronouns (*his* and *hers*) do not have apostrophes.

The word *it's,* meaning *it is* or *it has,* is a contraction and requires an apostrophe.

EXAMPLES   Its fur is thick. [*Its* is a pronoun in the possessive case; no apostrophe is needed.]

It's time for school. [*It's* is a contraction meaning "it is." The apostrophe takes the place of the missing letter.]

It's been a great disappointment. [*It's* is a contraction of *it has.* The apostrophe takes the place of the letters *ha* in *has.*]

Write *it's* (with an apostrophe) only when it means "it is" or "it has."

Whose and Who's

The word *whose* is a pronoun in the possessive case. It has no apostrophe.

The word *who's* is a contraction meaning *who is* or *who has*. It requires an apostrophe.

EXAMPLES   Whose book is this? [*Whose* is a possessive pronoun meaning "To whom does it belong?"]

Who's ready for a swim? [*Who's* is a contraction meaning "Who is?"]

Who's been eating the pie? [*Who's* is a contraction meaning "Who has?"]

● EXERCISE 10.   Write the numbers 1–20 on your paper. After each number, write *C* if the sentence is correct. If it is not correct, copy the word requiring an apostrophe, and insert the apostrophe.

1. The weatherman says that its going to snow tonight.
2. Wed better be sure our car has antifreeze.
3. Last year we didnt put antifreeze in our car until December.
4. We werent prepared for snow in October, and neither was our car.
5. Ill never forget my fathers words.
6. He said simply, "Well, the old cars had it this time."
7. And he wasnt far wrong.
8. The old car and its radiator were frozen solid.
9. We couldnt open the doors or raise the hood.
10. We wont forget all those days of walking.
11. I wonder whos ringing the doorbell.
12. Didnt Roger bring his skates?
13. Im certain well be on time.

14. Whose turn is it to bat?
15. Dont you think theyll win the championship?
16. Toms a good swimmer, but he cant dive.
17. Its almost ten o'clock, isnt it?
18. Our camera club didnt hold its annual picnic this year.
19. Theyll come before its too late, Im sure.
20. Look at my bike; there isnt a scratch on its paint.

● Exercise 11. Think of a suitable contraction for the blank in each of the following sentences and write it on your paper after the sentence number.

1. —— my lunch?
2. —— building sand castles on the beach.
3. We —— solve the problem.
4. —— that in your yard?
5. —— a bullfrog.
6. —— go into the water yet.
7. —— the supplies ready?
8. Why —— he here?
9. It —— time to go.
10. They —— ridden in a plane before.

● Review exercise C. For the sentences that are correct, write *C*. In the other sentences, copy the words that need apostrophes, and insert the apostrophes.

1. Arent you interested in lightning?
2. People havent always understood lightning.
3. The Greeks believed that thunder on the right before a battle showed the favor of Zeus.
4. Because the Romans didnt want to imitate the Greeks, they regarded thunder on the left as showing their chief gods favor.
5. The Persians werent so sure about lightning as a favorable omen.

6. They decided that lightning couldnt indicate anything but divine wrath.
7. Its been only two hundred years or so since lightning was properly understood.
8. Benjamin Franklins experiments proved that lightning is a form of electricity.
9. Lightning still has its fascination for man, but its now generally regarded as a natural phenomenon.
10. During a years time the average person will see many flashes of lightning.

Plurals

12s. **Use an apostrophe and *s* to form the plural of letters, numbers, and signs and of words referred to as words.**

EXAMPLES   Your *o*'s look like *a*'s, and your *u*'s look like *n*'s.

There are three *5*'s in the telephone number.

One sign of poor writing is too many *and*'s.

There are two *o*'s, two *k*'s, and three *e*'s in *bookkeeper*.

HYPHENS

The hyphen is used (1) to indicate that a word has been broken at the end of a line and (2) to show that two or more words are being used together as one.

If there is not room for a whole word at the end of the line, you may divide it with a hyphen. Dividing

12s

words at the end of a line, however, should be avoided
as much as possible.

12t. Use a hyphen to divide a word at the end
of a line.

EXAMPLES

In my opinion, what this salad needs is a cucumber.

Will you and Marguerite help me set the table for supper?

That intersection at Elm and High is a bottle-
neck for eastbound traffic.

**(1) Words must be divided so that each syllable
can be pronounced as it is pronounced in the complete word.**

WRONG   Mr. Morgan looked at the board with a pu-
zzled expression.

RIGHT   Mr. Morgan looked at the board with a puz-
zled expression.

(2) Words of one syllable may not be divided.

WRONG   Exercises like push-ups develop the strength of the arm muscles.

RIGHT   Exercises like push-ups develop the
strength of the arm muscles.

**(3) Words may not be divided so that one part is
a single letter.**

WRONG   The seating capacity of the new gym is e-
normous.

RIGHT   The seating capacity of the new gym is enormous.

12u. Use a hyphen with compound numbers from twenty-one to ninety-nine and with fractions used as adjectives.

EXAMPLES   There are twenty-nine days in February in Leap Year.

Congress may overrule a President's veto by a two-thirds majority. [*Two-thirds* is an adjective modifying *majority*.]

The pie was so good that only one sixth of it is left. [*Sixth* is a noun modified by the adjective *one*.]

● EXERCISE 12.   Write the numbers 1–5 on your paper. After each number, write a word or words to fit the blank in the sentence. Be sure to use hyphens where they are needed.

1. January, March, May, July, August, October, and December are the months that have —— days.
2. —— of the moon is visible from the earth, but the other half can be seen only from outer space.
3. In twenty years I will be —— years old.
4. If a quarter of the money has been spent, we must still have about —— percent of the original amount.
5. The last day of school this year will be June ——.

● REVIEW EXERCISE D.   Copy the following sentences and insert whatever punctuation marks are necessary: commas, colons, underlining (for italics), quotation marks, and apostrophes. The punctuation already supplied is correct.

1. Whos read Little Women?
2. There are four sisters in the novel Meg Jo Beth and Amy.

12
t-u

3. Beth is a frail gentle girl who is content to stay home with Marmee the girls mother.

4. Meg the oldest sister marries early.

5. Jo on the other hand vows to be an old maid.

6. Shes interested in being a writer and she spends her spare time making up plays for the entertainment of her sisters.

7. Amy is a pretty curly-haired girl who wants to be an artist.

8. The girls have these characteristics in common kindness unselfishness and loyalty.

9. The book of course takes its title from the four sisters.

10. Its generally known that Louisa May Alcotts models for the four girls were her three sisters and herself.

● REVIEW EXERCISE E.   Copy the following sentences and insert whatever punctuation they need.

1. Youll need the following materials for the art course a brush an easel and some water colors.

2. Whos taken my copy of Life? demanded Dean.

3. Robert Burns a Scottish poet wrote the poem Flow Gently, Sweet Afton.

4. Its hard to decide whose story to read.

5. We thought that we were taking a short cruise but it turned out to be a weeks trip.

6. At 8 15 on March 1 1956 we ate the last of our provisions.

7. The next morning one of the crew shouted Land ho!

8. We werent at all sorry to be back in the harbor of Charleston South Carolina.

9. I didnt expect admitted the convict to be caught.

10. Our car license number is easy to remember because it starts with two 7s and ends with two 4s.

● REVIEW EXERCISE F. Write ten sentences, following the instructions below.

1. a sentence containing an appositive
2. a sentence using a colon before a list of items
3. a sentence which states a complete date
4. a sentence containing *its*
5. a sentence containing a parenthetical expression
6. a sentence containing the title of a book
7. a sentence using the possessive case of *ladies*
8. a sentence using *whose*
9. a sentence containing a broken quotation
10. a sentence containing an indirect quotation

CHAPTER 13

Spelling

Improving Your Spelling

Spelling is easy for some people and hard for others. It is a necessary skill because one's education is sometimes judged by ability to spell. With a little effort you can master some useful spelling rules and a few important exceptions.

GOOD SPELLING HABITS

1. *Keep a list of your own errors.*

Spelling, as you probably have discovered, is a very personal matter. What is a hard word for one person is easy for another. You should keep a list of the words that you misspell, either as a part of your English notebook or in a separate spelling notebook. When you misspell a word, follow these three steps:

a. See the word correctly spelled. Make a mental picture of what the word looks like.

b. Hear the word. Pronounce the word correctly by syllables several times.

c. Write the word correctly. Write the word on your spelling list, dividing it into syllables and putting in the main accent mark. Then write the word several times on a sheet of scratch paper.

2. *Use the dictionary as a spelling aid.*

When in doubt about the spelling of a word, look it up. Guessing is much easier, but if you wish to be sure, open the dictionary. After a while you will have the dictionary habit.

3. *Spell by syllables.*

Break down long words into short syllables. It's not possible to spell all words by syllable, but if you make a habit of using that method, you'll find that your spelling will quickly improve.

4. *Avoid mispronunciations that lead to spelling errors.*

Good spelling often results from good pronunciation. If you say *gov-ern-ment*, it's more than likely that you will spell the word correctly. If you say *arctic*, you probably will remember to include the first *c*. Poor spelling often results from these errors in pronunciation:

a. the omission of a letter: reconize for recognize, suprise for surprise
b. the addition of a letter: athalete for athlete, enterance for entrance
c. the change of one letter to another: seperate for separate, excape for escape
d. the interchanging of the position of letters: calvary for cavalry, prespiration for perspiration

5. *Revise to avoid careless spelling errors.*

Many spelling errors are a result of carelessness rather than ignorance. Reread your papers and correct errors that you may have made in haste.

SPELLING RULES

Many words fall under one or another of the following spelling rules. If you master these rules, you will help yourself to spell correctly. Remember, however, that there are many exceptions, and you must simply memorize words that do not follow the rules. List such words in your notebook, and review them often.

ie and ei

Words containing these pairs of letters have probably appeared on everyone's problem list at some time.

13a. Write *ie* when the sound is long *e*, except after *c*.

EXAMPLES   chief, brief, believe, yield, receive, deceive

EXCEPTIONS   seize, leisure, neither

Write *ei* when the sound is not long *e*, especially when the sound is long *a*.

EXAMPLES   sleigh, veil, freight, weight, height

EXCEPTIONS   friend, mischief

You may find this time-tested verse a help.

> *I* before *e*
> Except after *c*,
> Or when sounded like *a*,
> As in *neighbor* and *weigh*.

If you use this rhyme, remember that *i* before *e* refers only to words in which this combination of letters stands for the sound of long *e*, as in the examples under 13a.

● EXERCISE 1.   Write the following words, supplying the missing letters (*e* and *i*) in the correct order. Be able to explain how the rule applies to each. Do not write in the book.

1. s . . ze
2. n . . ther
3. rec . . ve
4. h . . ght
5. fr . . nd
6. br . . f
7. dec . . ve
8. l . . sure
9. misch . . f
10. w . . ght

11. . . ght
12. rec . . pt
13. sl . . gh
14. fr . . ght
15. th . . r
16. n . . ghbor
17. c . . ling
18. shr . . k
19. r . . gn
20. p . . ce

–cede, –ceed, and –sede

13b. Only one word in English ends in *–sede*—*supersede;* only three words end in *–ceed*—*exceed, proceed,* and *succeed;* all other words of similar sound end in *–cede.*

EXAMPLES   concede, recede, precede

PREFIXES AND SUFFIXES

13c. When a prefix is added to a word, the spelling of the word itself remains the same.

A *prefix* is a letter or a group of letters added to the beginning of a word to change its meaning.

13
a-c

EXAMPLES

in + audible = inaudible

im + mature = immature

dis + appear = disappear

mis + sent = missent

il + legal = illegal

un + natural = unnatural

over + run = overrun

re + read = reread

● EXERCISE 2. Write the numbers 1–20 on your paper. Then write these words in order, spelled correctly.

1. il + legible
2. un + avoidable
3. in + appropriate
4. il + logical
5. mis + spent
6. over + rated
7. un + necessary
8. un + counted
9. im + partial
10. in + offensive
11. im + mortal
12. mis + spell
13. over + ripe
14. over + run
15. dis + satisfy
16. dis + approve
17. im + passable
18. mis + understand
19. over + rule
20. mis + lead

13d. When the suffixes *–ness* and *–ly* are added to a word, the spelling of the word itself is not changed.

A *suffix* is a letter or group of letters added at the end of a word to change its meaning.

EXAMPLES   sudden + ness = suddenness

truthful + ly = truthfully

final + ly = finally

EXCEPTIONS   Most words ending in *y* do not follow this rule. Instead, the *y* is changed to *i*.

kindly + ness = kindliness

day + ly = daily

13e. Drop the final *e* before a suffix beginning with a vowel.[1]

EXAMPLES	drive + ing = driving love + able = lovable
EXCEPTIONS	Words ending in *-ce* and *-ge*, however, usually keep the silent *e* in order to preserve the soft sound of the final consonant. notice + able = noticeable change + able = changeable pronounce + able = pronounceable

13f. Keep the final *e* before a suffix beginning with a consonant.

EXAMPLES	agree + ment = agreement state + ment = statement plate + ful = plateful false + hood = falsehood
EXCEPTIONS	argue + ment = argument true + ly = truly

● EXERCISE 3. Write correctly the words formed as follows.

1. hopeful + ly
2. care + ing
3. sincere + ly
4. write + ing
5. desire + able
6. smile + ing
7. true + ly
8. hope + ing
9. advance + ment
10. shave + ing

[1] Vowels are the letters *a, e, i, o, u,* and sometimes *y.* All other letters of the alphabet are *consonants.*

13
d-f

13g. With words ending in *y* preceded by a consonant, change the *y* to *i* before any suffix not beginning with *i*.

EXAMPLES   pry + ed = pried
happy + ness = happiness
bounty + ful = bountiful

Words ending in *y* preceded by a vowel do not change their spelling before a suffix.

EXAMPLE   key + ed = keyed

13h. With words of one syllable ending in a single consonant preceded by a single vowel, double the consonant before adding *–ing, –ed,* or *–er.*

EXAMPLES   sit + ing = sitting
hop + ed = hopped
dip + er = dipper

With a one-syllable word ending in a single consonant which is *not* preceded by a single vowel, do not double the consonant before adding *–ing, –ed,* or *–er.*

EXAMPLES   reap + ed = reaped; heat + ing = heating
[The final consonant is preceded by two vowels.]

● EXERCISE 4.   Write correctly the words formed as follows.

1. bay + ing
2. silly + ness
3. drop + ed
4. slam + ing
5. embody + ment
6. swim + er
7. cry + ed
8. hurry + ed
9. tap + ing
10. leap + ed

THE PLURAL OF NOUNS

English is a peculiar language in its formation of plurals. You learn a half-dozen rules—then you encounter an exception! You usually add *–s* to form a plural; but you know that the plural of *sheep* is *sheep*. The plural of *goose* is *geese*, but the plural of *mongoose* is *mongooses*. The plural of *radius* is *radii*, but the plural of *circus* isn't *circi*.

Here are a few rules that *will* help you. Learn them and their exceptions, and you will be well on your way to mastering the formation of plurals.

13i. Observe the rules for spelling the plural of nouns.

(1) The regular way to form the plural of a noun is to add an –s.

EXAMPLES boy, boys   task, tasks

(2) The plural of nouns ending in *s, x, z, ch,* or *sh* is formed by adding –es.

The *e* is necessary to make the plural form pronounceable.

EXAMPLES moss, mosses   birch, birches
wax, waxes   dish, dishes
waltz, waltzes

● EXERCISE 5. Write the plural of the following nouns.

1. pencil	3. stitch	5. church	7. buzz
2. crash	4. address	6. fox	8. witch

13
g-i

(3) The plural of nouns ending in *y* preceded by a consonant is formed by changing the *y* to *i* and adding *-es.*

EXAMPLES   lady, ladies   guppy, guppies

(4) The plural of nouns ending in *y* preceded by a vowel is formed by adding *-s.*

EXAMPLES   toy, toys   tourney, tourneys

(5) The plural of most nouns ending in *f* is formed by adding *-s.* The plural of some nouns ending in *f* or *fe* is formed by changing the *f* to *v* and adding *-s* or *-es.*

EXAMPLES   Add *-s:*
        gulf, gulfs   belief, beliefs

    Change *f* to *v* and add *-s:*
        knife, knives   life, lives

    Change *f* to *v* and add *-es:*
        half, halves   thief, thieves
        loaf, loaves   wolf, wolves

(6) The plural of nouns ending in *o* preceded by a vowel is formed by adding *-s;* the plural of nouns ending in *o* preceded by a consonant is formed by adding *-es.*

EXAMPLES   *o* preceded by a vowel—add *-s:*
        patio, patios   ratio, ratios

    o preceded by a *consonant*—add *-es:*
        tornado, tornadoes   Negro, Negroes

EXCEPTIONS   Eskimo, Eskimos   silo, silos

Notice that the plural of most nouns that end in *o* pertaining to music is formed by adding *-s:*

        piano, pianos   alto, altos
        solo, solos   trio, trios

Some of these are exceptions to the rule; others are not.

(7) The plural of a few nouns is formed in irregular ways.

EXAMPLES   child, children mouse, mice
     woman, women foot, feet
     ox, oxen   tooth, teeth

● EXERCISE 6.   Write the plural of the following nouns.

1. turkey	11. valley
2. loaf	12. self
3. studio	13. contralto
4. man	14. chimney
5. chief	15. potato
6. journey	16. baby
7. monkey	17. ditty
8. soprano	18. tomato
9. thief	19. child
10. puppy	20. echo

(8) The plural of compound nouns consisting of a noun plus a modifier is formed by making the modified noun plural.

EXAMPLES   sister-in-law, sisters-in-law
     coat-of-arms, coats-of-arms
     man-hour, man-hours

(9) The plural of a few compound nouns is formed in irregular ways.

EXAMPLES   eight-year-old, eight-year-olds
     tie-up, tie-ups
     drive-in, drive-ins

(10) Some nouns are the same in the singular and the plural.

EXAMPLES   deer, sheep, salmon, Portuguese

(11) The plural of numbers, letters, signs, and words considered as words is formed by adding an apostrophe and –s.

EXAMPLES   1800   1800's
            B   B's
            &   &'s

● EXERCISE 7.   Write the plural of the following expressions.

1. side-wheeler   6. thirteen-year-old
2. moose   7. trout
3. mother-in-law   8. governor-elect
4. 1930   9. Chinese
5. m   10. commander-in-chief

● REVIEW EXERCISE A.   Write the plurals of the following nouns. After each plural, write the number of the rule (1–11) that applies. Use the dictionary if you are in doubt.

1. wish   13. volcano
2. elf   14. hero
3. rally   15. leaf
4. twelve-year-old   16. p and q
5. valley   17. woman
6. roof   18. thief
7. rodeo   19. squash
8. briefcase   20. radio
9. postman   21. loaf
10. goose   22. pulley
11. mix   23. appendix
12. house   24. mouth

25. scenario
26. church
27. camera
28. lady
29. buffalo

30. ax
31. alley
32. box
33. motto

WORDS OFTEN CONFUSED

The words that follow are often confused with each other. Study the explanations and do the exercises that follow. Make sure that you can spell and pronounce each word correctly.

---

accept	*to receive; to agree to* The Lanfords would not *accept* our gift.
except	*with the exclusion of; but* Everyone *except* Larry agreed.

---

advice	*a recommendation for action* What is your father's *advice?*
advise	*to recommend a course of action* He *advises* me to take the camp job.

---

affect	*to act upon; to change* Does bad weather *affect* your personality?
effect	*result; consequence* What *effect* does the weather have on your personality?

---

already	*previously* We have *already* studied that chapter.
all ready	*all prepared* or *in readiness* The launching crew is *all ready* for the signal to blast off.

● EXERCISE 8.   Write the numbers 1–10 on your paper. After each number, write the word from the pair in parentheses that will make the sentence correct.

1. By the time the group arrived, Jody had (already, all ready) cooked supper.
2. One of the purposes of the Cabinet is to (advice, advise) the President.
3. The soft music had a soothing (affect, effect) on the worried man.
4. The children were (already, all ready) for the sleigh ride.
5. The St. Lawrence Seaway has had several important (affects, effects) on North American trade.
6. The snow has melted everywhere (accept, except) in the mountains.
7. The doctor's (advice, advise) was to take a vacation.
8. We were happy to (accept, except) the invitation to the party.
9. Our reading usually (affects, effects) our composition.
10. Your (advice, advise) got me into trouble!

altar	*a table or stand at which religious rites are performed* There was a bowl of flowers on the *altar*.
alter	*to change* Another hurricane may *alter* the shoreline beyond recognition.
altogether	*entirely* It is *altogether* too cold for swimming.

all together   *everyone in the same place*
Will our class be *all together* on the trip?

———

brake   *a device to stop a machine*
Car owners must have their *brakes* checked periodically.

break   *to fracture; to shatter*
Don't *break* that mirror!

———

capital   *a city, the location of a government*
Do you know the *capitals* of the fifty states?

capitol   *the building in which a legislative body meets* [usually capitalized]
Nearly every visitor to Washington goes to the *Capitol*.

———

cloths   *pieces of cloth*
I need some more cleaning *cloths*.

clothes   *wearing apparel*
I have outgrown all of my *clothes*.

———

● EXERCISE 9. Write the numbers 1–10 on your paper. After each number, write the word from the pair in parentheses that will make the sentence correct.

1. The Romans' (cloths, clothes) were loose and light.
2. In England one can still see remains of (altars, alters) built by prehistoric tribes.
3. A bicyclist can wear out his (brakes, breaks) going down a steep mountain.
4. You should use soft (cloths, clothes) to clean silver.

5. The cold weather did not (altar, alter) our plans for a vacation at the beach.
6. Sacramento is the (capital, capitol) of California.
7. Put the pieces of the vase (altogether, all together) and I will try to repair it.
8. A nation may (brake, break) a treaty that no longer serves its interests.
9. On the dome of the (capital, Capitol) stands a large bronze statue of Freedom.
10. The audience was (altogether, all together) charmed by the speaker's wit.

---

coarse   *rough, crude, large*
The *coarse* sand acts as a filter.

course   *path of action; series of studies;* also used in the expression *of course*
What is the best *course* for me to take?
You may change your mind, *of course*.

---

complement   *something that completes*
A predicate nominative is one kind of *complement*.

compliment   *to praise someone; praise from someone*
Miss Bryant *complimented* Jean on her speech.
Thank you for the *compliment*.

---

council   *a group of people who meet together to discuss or advise*
The mayor's *council* has seven members.

councilor   *a member of a council*
The mayor appointed seven *councilors*.

counsel	*advice* or *to give advice* You need legal *counsel* on this matter.
counselor	*one who advises* Miss Higgins is the guidance *counselor* for the seventh grade.

---

desert	*a dry, sandy region* [pronounced des'ert] The cactus is a common flower in the *desert*.
desert	*to abandon, to leave* [pronounced de·sert'] A good sport does not *desert* his teammates.
dessert	*the final course of a meal* [pronounced des·ert'] Let's have ice cream for *dessert*.

● EXERCISE 10.   Write the numbers 1–10 on your paper. After each number, write the correct one of the words in the parentheses.

1. The city (council, counsel) will not meet unless seven of the ten (councilors, counselors) are present.
2. During his wanderings Odysseus received (council, counsel) from Athena, the goddess of wisdom, on the best (coarse, course) to follow.
3. Mustard and piccalilli are the usual (complements, compliments) of hot dogs.
4. We are eager to see the new puppy, of (coarse, course).
5. Anne is preparing the (desert, dessert) tonight.
6. Marilyn made a skirt out of (coarse, course) burlap.

7. The leader would not (desert, dessert) his men.
8. I want your (council, counsel), not your (compliments, compliments).
9. After several days on the hot (desert, dessert), the men began to see mirages.
10. Our camp (councilor, counselor) advised us to eat fruit for our (desert, dessert).

---

formally   *with dignity; following strict rules or procedure*
We must behave *formally* at the reception.

formerly   *previously; at an earlier date*
Formerly, men thought travel to the moon was impossible.

---

hear   *to receive sounds through the ears*
You can *hear* a whisper through these walls.

here   *this place*
How long have you lived *here*?

---

its   a personal pronoun showing possession
That book has lost *its* cover.

it's   contraction of *it is* or *it has*
It's the coldest winter anyone can remember.

---

lead   *to go first, to be a leader* [present tense]
Can you *lead* us out of this tunnel?

led   past tense of *lead*
Eisenhower *led* the Allied troops in the Normandy invasion.

lead   *a heavy metal*
There is no *lead* in a *lead* pencil.

---

loose   *to unfasten, to free; to be free; not tight*
Loose that rope, please.
How did the dog get *loose?*
This belt is too *loose.*

lose   *to suffer loss*
Fred will *lose* the argument if he doesn't check his facts.

---

passed   *went by; past tense of pass*
Three ice cream trucks have *passed* in the last five minutes.

past   *that which has gone by; beyond; by*
A good historian makes the *past* come alive.
That era is *past.*

● Exercise 11.   Write the numbers 1–10 on your paper. After each number, write the word from the group in parentheses that will make the sentence correct.

1. The man who (formally, formerly) (lead, led) the band moved to Alaska.
2. We do not expect to (loose, lose) any of our back-field men this year.
3. We (passed, past) three stalled cars this morning.
4. "Why did you (lead, led) us (hear, here)?" the boys demanded.
5. Odysseus was the only man to (hear, here) the sirens' song and live to tell about it.
6. We have been (lead, led) into a trap.
7. How did the ship get (loose, lose) from its moorings?
8. The men are to dress (formally, formerly) for the banquet.

9. "I think (it's, its) time for a quiz," announced Mrs. Ferrari.
10. Have you seen the school bus go (passed, past) yet?

---

peace *quiet order and security*
Peace is more than merely the absence of war.

piece *a part of something*
Here is a pretty *piece* of silk.

---

plain *unadorned, simple, common; also a flat area of land*
Colonial architecture was *plain* and practical.
A broad, treeless *plain* stretched before them.

plane *a flat surface; a tool; an airplane*
Use an inclined *plane* to move that chest.
I have just learned how to use a carpenter's *plane*.
Have you ever flown in a jet *plane?*

---

principal *the head of a school; also chief, main*
The *principal* spoke of the *principal* duties of students.

principle *a rule of conduct; a fundamental truth*
Action should be guided by *principles*.

---

quiet *still and peaceful; without noise*
The forest was very *quiet*.

quite *wholly or entirely; also to a great extent*
Some students are *quite* sure of their future plans in junior high school.

---

shone   past tense of *shine*
             The moon *shone* softly over the grass.
shown   *revealed;* past participle of *show*
             Mr. Cross has *shown* me how to do the
             experiment.

● EXERCISE 12.   Write the numbers 1–10 on your paper. After each number write the word from the group
in parentheses that will make the sentence correct.

1. Each drop of water (shone, shown) like crystal.
2. Motor vehicles are one of the (principal, principle)
   sources of air pollution in our cities.
3. If you don't hurry, you'll miss your (plain, plane).
4. Gandhi was dedicated to the (principal, principle)
   of (peace, piece).
5. My father has (shone, shown) me how to change
   a tire.
6. It is clear that Barry is acting on (principal, principle), not from personal motive.
7. On Christmas Eve we always have eggnog and a
   (peace, piece) of fruitcake.
8. "What a (quiet, quite) Fourth of July," Mr. Bas-
   com remarked.
9. "For once," the (principal, principle) announced
   with a smile, "you don't have to be (quiet, quite)."
10. Ralph Waldo Emerson recommended "(plane,
    plain) living and high thinking."

---

stationary   *in a fixed position*
               Is that gear *stationary?*
stationery   *writing paper*
               Have you any white *stationery?*

than   a conjunction used in comparisons
Alaska is bigger *than* Texas.

then   *at that time*
If you will see me after class, we can talk about it *then*.

---

their   possessive form of *they*
Can you understand *their* dialects?

there   *a place;* also used in the expression *there are*
Let's meet *there*.
There are three new girls in gym class.

they're   contraction of *they are*
They're all from California.

---

threw   past tense of *throw*
Ted *threw* me the mitt.

through   a preposition
I can't see *through* the lens.

● EXERCISE 13.   Write the numbers 1–10 on your paper. After each number write the word from the group in parentheses that makes the sentence correct.

1. That noise is from a jet plane going (threw, through) the sound barrier.
2. The stars seem to be (stationary, stationery), but we know that (their, there, they're) moving at speeds up to thirty miles per second.
3. Is Lake Erie larger (than, then) Lake Huron?
4. The pitcher (threw, through) a curve.
5. A (stationary, stationery) store usually sells pens, twine, and other items, too.

6. I would rather live now (than, then) in the Middle Ages.
7. The students brought (their, there, they're) displays for the science fair.
8. A moving target is harder to hit (than, then) a (stationary, stationery) one.
9. Betty can't get (threw, through) to Rochester because the circuits are busy.
10. (Their, They're, There) first rehearsal will be after school today.

---

to	a preposition We are going *to* California.
too	*also; to an excessive degree* Audrey is going, *too*. I ate *too* much pie.
two	a number We caught *two* fish.

---

weak	*feeble; not strong* May's illness has left her very *weak*.
week	*seven days* Let's practice again next *week*.

---

weather	*the condition of the air, the atmosphere* The *weather* seems to be changing.
whether	a conjunction expressing *doubt* We don't know *whether* it will work.

---

who's	contraction of *who is* or *who has* *Who's* going to the museum?
whose	possessive form of *who* *Whose* report was the most original?

your   possessive form of *you*
          What is *your* middle name?

you're   contraction of *you are*
          You're expected at the Wallaces in an hour.

● EXERCISE 14.   Write the numbers 1–10 on your paper. After each number, write the word from the parentheses that makes the sentence correct.

1. (Who's, Whose) the present secretary of state of the United States?
2. We built (to, too, two) snowmen on our front lawn.
3. "(Your, You're) late," my friend complained.
4. Would you be able to stand the (weather, whether) in Alaska?
5. That sounds like a (weak, week) excuse to me.
6. (Your, You're) dog is (to, too, two) sleepy to do his tricks.
7. "(Who's, Whose) boots are these?" Mrs. Allen asked.
8. The pilot had to decide (weather, whether) to parachute to safety or try to land the crippled plane.
9. Final exams start next (weak, week).
10. We are driving (to, too, two) New Orleans for Christmas.

● REVIEW EXERCISE B.   Write the numbers 1–20 on your paper. Copy the words from the parentheses that will make the sentences correct.

You may be familiar with the play *Macbeth*, a tragedy by William Shakespeare. The (1. principal, principle) character, Macbeth, was (2. altogether, all together) (3. to, too, two) ambitious for his own good.

When he heard three witches prophesy that he would be the new king, he (4. accepted, excepted) (5. their, there, they're) prediction as true and decided to bring it to pass immediately. His wife did not remain (6. quiet, quite). She was willing for Macbeth to kill the king. Her (7. advice, advise) was to act at once. In fact, her (8. council, counsel) was largely responsible for his (9. coarse, course) of action.

When the king visited Macbeth's castle, Macbeth and his wife greeted him with (10. complements, compliments). They were (11. already, all ready) to proceed with their plan. That night while the king was sleeping, Macbeth slipped (12. past, passed) the guards and (13. threw, through) the door into the king's chamber. As the king slept, Macbeth plunged a dagger into his heart. Nothing now could (14. altar, alter) Macbeth's plan to be king. But this deed had its (15. affect, effect) on Macbeth's conscience. He gained the throne but lost his (16. peace, piece) of mind. From that night on, while others slept, Macbeth lay awake. Macbeth had murdered the king, and he had murdered sleep, (17. to, too, two). His bloody deed (18. lead, led) him on to still other crimes which eventually caused Lady Macbeth to (19. loose, lose) her sanity and Macbeth to (20. loose, lose) his life.

● REVIEW EXERCISE C. Write the numbers 1–20 on your paper. Copy the words from the parentheses that will make the sentences correct.

Last March my family could not decide (1. weather, whether) to visit Boston or Philadelphia. Finally we decided on Boston, the (2. capital, capitol) of Massachusetts. We drove (3. to, too, two) the city in three days. Even my parents could not conceal (4. their, there, they're) excitement. We did not (5. loose, lose) a moment. Boston (6. formally, formerly) was "the hub of the universe," and we discovered that (7. it's, its) still a fascinating city. Everyone in my family (8. accept, except) me had eaten lobster, and I had my first one in Boston. I was not (9. altogether, all together) certain how to eat the lobster, but this doubt did not (10. affect, effect) my appetite. My parents insisted that a banana split was a strange (11. desert, dessert) to follow lobster, but I would not (12. altar, alter) my order. After the banana split, I wanted a small (13. peace, piece) of pie, but my father told me to be (14. quiet, quite).

While in Boston we often walked up and down the streets just to (15. hear, here) the strange accent of the Bostonians. (16. Their, There, They're) especially noted for (17. their, there, they're) pronunciation of *a*'s and *r*'s.

We had not been in Boston long before the (18. weather, whether) bureau predicted a big snowstorm for the area. Since we had not taken the proper (19. cloths, clothes) for snow, we decided to return home. On the way back we were (20. already, all ready) making plans for another visit to Boston.

COMMONLY MISSPELLED WORDS

No matter how many spelling rules you learn, you will find that it is helpful to learn to spell certain common words from memory. The fifty "demons" below are words that you should be able to spell without any hesitation, even though they all contain spelling problems. Study them in groups of five until you are sure of them.

The longer list that follows contains words that you should learn this year if you do not already know them. They are grouped by tens, so that you may conveniently study them ten at a time.

FIFTY SPELLING DEMONS

ache	easy	shoes
again	every	since
always	friend	straight
answer	guess	sugar
blue	half	sure
built	hour	tear
busy	instead	though
buy	knew	through
can't	know	tired
color	laid	tonight
cough	minute	trouble
could	often	wear
country	once	where
doctor	ready	women
does	said	won't
don't	says	write
early	seems	

TWO HUNDRED SPELLING WORDS

absence	aisles	arithmetic
absolutely	among	assistance
acceptance	announce	associate
accommodate	anxiety	attacked
accumulate	apology	attendance
achieve	apparent	attitude
acquire	appreciation	attorney
across	Arctic	basis
advertisement	arguing	beginning
against	argument	believe

benefit
bicycle
bough
bouquet
brief
brilliant
bureau
business
candidate
career

careless
carrying
ceased
ceiling
choice
college
committee
completely
conceive
conscience

conscious
control
courteous
criticize
curiosity
decision
definite
depth
describe
description

desirable
divide

divine
efficiency
eighth
eliminate
embarrass
equipment
especially
exactly

excellent
execute
existence
experience
experiment
explanation
extremely
familiar
favorite
February

field
fierce
finally
foliage
foreign
fortunately
forty
fourth
genius
genuine

government
governor
grammar
guarantee

height
heir
heroes
humorous
hungrily
icicles

imaginary
immediately
independent
inoculate
intelligence
interest
interpret
judgment
knowledge
laboratory

leisure
license
liquor
loneliness
luxury
magazine
marriage
mathematics
meant
medicine

mischief
muscle
museum
necessary
Negroes
nervous

ninety	religion	thorough
occasion	repetition	tongue
occur	rhythm	tragedy
occurrence	safety	
	satisfy	transferred
opinion	scene	treasury
opportunity	schedule	tries
originally	seize	university
particularly	sense	unnecessary
patience		unusually
perceive	separate	useful
performance	shining	using
permanent	similar	vacuum
personal	society	vague
physical	speech	
	strength	various
picnic	studying	veil
possess	stupefy	vicinity
preferred	succeed	villain
privilege	success	violence
probably		warrior
professor	surprise	wholly
pursue	suspicion	whose
realize	sympathy	writing
receive	technique	yield
recommend	temperament	
	temporary	
referred	theory	

CHAPTER 14

Manuscript Form

Standards for Written Work

A manuscript is any typewritten or handwritten composition, as distinguished from a printed document. In your schoolwork this year and the years ahead, you will be writing more and more manuscripts. You should learn the correct form for your written work now, and follow it in all your papers.

14a. Follow accepted standards in preparing manuscripts.

Your teacher will find it easier to read and evaluate your papers if they are properly prepared. There is no single correct way to prepare a paper, but the rules below are widely used and accepted. Follow them unless your teacher requests you to do otherwise.

1. Use white paper $8\frac{1}{2} \times 11$ inches in size for typewritten papers and ruled composition paper for handwritten ones.

2. Write on only one side of the sheet.

3. Write in blue or black ink or typewrite. If you type, double-space the lines.

4. Leave a margin of about two inches at the top of the page and margins of about one inch at the sides and bottom. The left-hand margin must be straight; the right-hand margin should be as straight as you can make it.

5. Indent the first line of each paragraph about one-half inch from the left.

6. Write your name, the class, and the date on the first page. Follow your teacher's instructions in the placement of these items.

7. If your paper has a title, write it in the center of the first line. Do not enclose the title in quotation marks. Skip a line between the title and the first line of your composition.

8. If the paper is more than one page in length, number the pages after the first, placing the number in the center, about one-half inch down from the top.

9. Write legibly and neatly. Form your letters carefully, so that *n*'s do not look like *u*'s, *a*'s like *o*'s, and so on. Dot the *i*'s and cross the *t*'s. If you have to erase, do it neatly.

14b. Learn the rules for using abbreviations.

In your writing, you should spell out most words rather than abbreviate them. A few abbreviations, however, are commonly used.

The following abbreviations are acceptable when they are used with a name: *Mr.*, *Mrs.*, *Dr.*, *Jr.*, and *Sr.* If they do not accompany a name, spell out the words instead of using the abbreviations.

EXAMPLES   **Mr.** Hastings   **Dr.** Eustace

              Mrs. Galzone   Frank B. Nolan, **Jr.**

14
a-b

Have you called the **doctor?**
Paul is a **junior** partner of the firm.

The abbreviations *A.M.* (*ante meridiem*—before noon), *P.M.* (*post meridiem*—after noon), *A.D.* (*anno Domini*—in the year of our Lord), and *B.C.* (*before Christ*) are acceptable when they are used with numbers.

EXAMPLES   The meeting is called for 3:30 **P.M.**

Augustus Caesar lived from 63 **B.C.** to precedes [Notice that the abbreviation *A.D.* **A.D.** 14. the number, while *B.C.* follows it.]

Abbreviations for organizations are acceptable if they are generally known.

EXAMPLE   That man is wanted by the **FBI.** [Abbreviations for government agencies are usually written without periods.]

14c. Learn the rules for writing numbers.

Numbers of more than two words should be written in numerals, not words. If, however, you are writing several numbers, some of them one word and some more than one, write them all the same way. Always spell out a number that begins a sentence.

EXAMPLES   Dick and I set out **twenty-three** strawberry plants this morning.

From Malvern take Route **202.**

Jerry started with **120** baby chicks, but now he has only **90.**

Two hundred and fifty-seven seniors graduated from Franklin High School this morning.

Write out numbers like *seventh*, *fifty-third*, and so on. If they represent the day of the month, however, it is customary to use numerals only.

EXAMPLES   I was the **first** [not 1st] customer at the bank this morning.

Flag Day is June 14 [or the **fourteenth of June**; not June 14th].

14d. Learn the rules for dividing words at the end of a line.

Sometimes you do not have room to write all of a long word at the end of a line. It may look better to start the word on the next line; but if doing that would leave a very uneven right-hand margin, you will have to divide the word, using a hyphen after the first part. Review the rules for dividing words on pages 243–44. Remember that you should try to avoid dividing words when you can; usually a slightly irregular margin looks better than a broken word.

14e. Learn the standard correction symbols.

In marking your papers, your teacher may use some or all of the symbols given below. If you memorize these symbols, you will understand at once what is wrong in your paper. If you are not sure how to correct your error, use the index of your book to find the section that you need to review.

14
c-e

ms	error in manuscript form or neatness
cap	error in use of capital letters
p	error in punctuation
sp	error in spelling
frag	sentence fragment
ss	error in sentence structure
k	awkward sentence
nc	not clear
rs	run-on sentence
gr	error in grammar
w	error in word choice
¶	You should have begun a new paragraph here.
t	error in tense
∧	You have omitted something.

Instead of working exercises for this chapter, apply what you have learned here to every paper that you write. Remember that the appearance of your written work makes an impression on the reader. If your papers show evidence of orderly care, your teachers will give you credit for it and will be better able to evaluate the content of your writing.

PART FOUR

Sentence Structure

CHAPTER 15

Sentence Fragments and Run-on Sentences

Developing Sentence Sense

To punctuate a sentence correctly, you must know where it begins and ends. That sounds obvious enough, but obvious things are not always easy to do. Two very frequent errors in student writing are the *sentence fragment* and the *run-on sentence*. The first of these results from writing a period, question mark, or exclamation point before a thought is completed. The second results from omitting one of these end marks where it is needed to separate two complete sentences. To avoid these errors in your own writing you must develop "sentence sense"—the ability to tell when you have written a complete thought.

Fortunately, you already have a strong sentence sense as far as the spoken language is concerned. Without thinking about it, you make your voice fall or rise to signal the end of a sentence. And by developing the habit of "listening" to the sentences you write, you can make use of your experience as a native speaker. As you study this chapter, let your ear help you decide where the period or other end mark belongs.

THE SENTENCE FRAGMENT

A sentence expresses a complete thought. When only a part of a sentence is written with a capital letter at the beginning and a period or question mark or exclamation point at the end, the result is a sentence fragment.

15a. A fragment is a separated part of a sentence that does not express a complete thought.

In each of the following examples, a part of a sentence has been punctuated as though it were a whole sentence. These sentence fragments are printed in *italics*. If you read only the fragments aloud, you will notice that they sound incomplete.

FRAGMENTS   All of the Texans in the Alamo were killed. *Including W. B. Travis and Davy Crockett.*

With his hands in his pockets and a grin on his face. Joe did not look the least bit worried.

Lefty can strike out anybody in the league. *When he can get the ball near enough to the plate.*

Detecting Fragments

If your ear leads you to suspect that you have written a sentence fragment, there are two tests that you can use to be certain. First look for a subject and a verb. If you do not find both, you have a fragment.

FRAGMENTS   Including W. B. Travis and Davy Crockett.

With his hands in his pockets and a grin on his face.

Neither of these examples has a subject or a verb. (The word *including* can be a part of a verb phrase, but it is never a verb by itself.)

Looking for the subject and verb will help you spot many fragments but not all of them. Some fragments have both.

FRAGMENT   When he can get the ball near enough to the plate. [*He* is the subject; *can get* is the verb.]

If the suspected fragment has both a subject and a verb, a second test can be applied. Ask yourself whether the group of words expresses a complete thought. Separated from the rest of its sentence, the fragment above does not make sense by itself. It leaves the reader wondering what happens "when he can get the ball near enough to the plate."

● EXERCISE 1. Number your paper 1–20. Read the following groups of words, preferably aloud. If the group of words is a sentence, put an *S* after the proper number. If the group of words is a fragment, put an *F* after the number.

15a

1. In the center ring of the circus.
2. When the clown came on.
3. The ringmaster was smartly dressed.
4. On a wire stretched high above our heads.
5. Because no nets were used.
6. Sensing the dangerousness of the act, the crowd fell silent.
7. The dogs were dressed in evening clothes.
8. Since the elephant was well trained.
9. The graceful trapeze artists.
10. When the animal trainer put his head in the lion's mouth, the audience gasped.
11. Riding bareback was a beautiful girl.
12. Munching popcorn and drinking lemonade.
13. The man juggled cups and saucers.
14. During the tightrope walker's act.
15. With a cartwheel the acrobat landed in the ring.
16. After making a human pyramid.
17. For the grand finale the band played a march.
18. As each performer reappeared for the last time.
19. Bowing to the audience.
20. He was rewarded with loud applause.

● EXERCISE 2.   Some of the following items consist of two or more sentences. Others contain a fragment. Number your paper 1–10 and write *S* for items containing only sentences, *F* for items containing a fragment.

1. Betsy can't have the meeting at her house. Because her little brother has the measles.
2. Electricity is everywhere around us. It is in the air and in the ground.
3. We cleaned the three little fish. Hoping that nobody would ask to see our catch.

4. Senator Margaret Chase Smith began her career as a schoolteacher. Working for $8.50 a week.

5. I promised to go to the movies with Elaine. Who would never forgive me if I went swimming instead.

6. About 380,000 boys belong to the Future Farmers of America. Founded in 1928, it is a national organization that helps to develop leadership.

7. Pollyanna never gossips. If she can't think of something nice to say about another girl, she doesn't say anything.

8. The Smithsonian Institution in Washington, D.C., was established in 1846. Through a bequest from James Smithson. He was an English scientist.

9. If I can go, I'll call you before six. Otherwise, go without me.

10. "A stitch in time saves nine" is an old proverb. Which can be applied to many daily situations.

Correcting Fragments

The simplest way to correct a fragment is to rejoin it to the sentence from which it has been separated. Study the following examples and notice how the fragments are put back into the sentences in which they belong.

FRAGMENT The Tigers were expecting to be invited to the Rose Bowl. Until they lost three straight games.

CORRECTED The Tigers were expecting to be invited to the Rose Bowl until they lost three straight games.

FRAGMENT Hansel and Gretel could not find the bread crumbs. Because the birds had eaten them.

CORRECTED   Hansel and Gretel could not find the bread crumbs because the birds had eaten them.

FRAGMENT   Ann spent the whole afternoon at the beach. Gathering shells for her collection.

CORRECTED   Ann spent the whole afternoon at the beach gathering shells for her collection.

● EXERCISE 3.   Some of the following items consist of two sentences. Others contain a fragment. If the items contain complete sentences, write *S* beside the appropriate number on your paper. If an item contains a fragment, rewrite it, joining the fragment to the sentence.

EXAMPLES   1. I will speak to the principal about you. You will be hearing from him before long.

           1. *S*

           2. Lefty practiced his pitching every afternoon. Hoping to become more accurate.

           2. *Lefty practiced his pitching every afternoon, hoping to become more accurate.*

1. Anyone can have a watch like this. If he is willing to eat enough cereal.
2. George's excuse was ingenious. No one had ever been locked in the schoolbus before.
3. Sue is finally going to have her party. The one that she postponed three weeks ago.
4. The playoff game is at six o'clock tomorrow. Unless, of course, it rains.

5. I heard a call for help and swung the boat around. To find Jack floundering in the waves.
6. We are going to the beach tomorrow. If the day is warm.
7. Saturday was cold and rainy. With very good prospects for snow.
8. His car won't start because the battery is low. He says I left the headlights on all night.
9. First, I do my math homework. Which often takes me a long time.
10. We did not play softball this afternoon. Because Fred and Jim had to stay after school.

Two Common Fragments

Two kinds of fragments are especially common in the writing of junior high school students. One of these is the fragment containing a word ending in *–ing: talking with his men, hurrying to work, studying his assignment.* A word that ends in *–ing* and looks like a verb (*talking, hurrying, studying*) cannot stand as the verb in the sentence unless it has a helping verb with it (*is talking, have been hurrying, will be studying*).

When you use a group of words containing an *–ing* word, do not separate this group from the sentence.

FRAGMENT	The officer tried to hide his worries and fears. While talking with his men.
CORRECTED	The officer tried to hide his worries and fears while talking with his men.
CORRECTED	While talking with his men, the officer tried to hide his worries and fears.
FRAGMENT	The boy forgot the time. Studying his assignment.

CORRECTED	The boy forgot the time, studying his assignment.
CORRECTED	Studying his assignment, the boy forgot the time.

Another common fragment is the group of words beginning with a word such as *after, although, because, if, since, unless, when, while.*

FRAGMENT	My brother will finish college this spring. If he passes all his courses.
CORRECTED	My brother will finish college this spring if he passes all his courses.
CORRECTED	If he passes all his courses, my brother will finish college this spring.
FRAGMENT	The mouse ran the maze. Because it wanted the cheese.
CORRECTED	The mouse ran the maze because it wanted the cheese.
CORRECTED	Because it wanted the cheese, the mouse ran the maze.

● EXERCISE 4.   The following groups of words are all fragments. Before or after each one, add enough words to make a sentence. Write each sentence on your paper, using correct punctuation and supplying capital letters where they are needed.

EXAMPLE   1. after the girl finished dancing
      1. *The audience applauded loudly after the girl finished dancing.*

1. when he reached the top of the mountain
2. counting his money
3. although the sea was rough
4. if he had not sneezed when he did
5. moving stealthily through the jungle

6. because she was chosen the most beautiful girl in the pageant
7. unless something is done
8. chattering among themselves
9. lying on its back
10. while the skyscraper was being constructed

● EXERCISE 5.   Decide which of the following expressions are sentences and which are fragments. Write *S* for each sentence after the proper number on your paper. Add enough words to each fragment to make it a sentence.

EXAMPLES
1. As the sun set behind the mountain.
1. *As the sun set behind the mountain, the natives began their ceremonial dance.*

2. Jujitsu is fascinating to watch.
2. *S*

1. Standing near the edge of the water.
2. When the fire was finally extinguished.
3. Before leaving, the guide gave us instructions.
4. While listening to the waves hit the beach.
5. Living alone on the island, the hermit makes everything he needs himself.
6. After the door was bolted.
7. If you think it is so easy!
8. The celebrity needed no introduction, being a native of the town.
9. Before we boarded the ship.
10. Half walking and half crawling down the road.
11. The sailors felt relieved when land was sighted.
12. Our dog lay down quietly, waiting for us to notice him.
13. Because he forgot the date.
14. Unless the train is late.

15. Although he had never played baseball.
16. Whimpering, the child went to bed.
17. Waiting impatiently for the storm to end.
18. If a person does not have a sense of humor.
19. While visiting the museum, we met some students from India.
20. Since the house was built many years before.

THE RUN–ON SENTENCE

Your sentence sense will help you to avoid another common writing fault, the *run-on sentence*. Fragments occur because the writer ends a sentence too soon. Run-on sentences, on the other hand, occur because the writer does not put a period or other end mark at the close of a sentence. Instead, he runs on into the next sentence or uses only a comma between sentences.

15b. A *run-on sentence* consists of two or more sentences separated only by a comma or by no mark of punctuation.

RUN-ON   Finally, the supplies were delivered the settlers rejoiced.

CORRECTED   Finally, the supplies were delivered. The settlers rejoiced.

RUN-ON   The police were called, they sped to the scene of the crime.

CORRECTED   The police were called. They sped to the scene of the crime.

● EXERCISE 6.   The following are examples of run-on sentences. Number your paper 1–10. Decide where each sentence should end. Then write the last word of each complete sentence, the punctuation that it should have, and the first word of the next sentence. Do not forget the capital letter.

EXAMPLE 1. Mercury is the closest planet to the sun, it is also the smallest planet.

1. *sun. It*

1. The stars, as well as the planets, are in motion, some of them move rapidly.
2. We do not see the stars move they are so far away that they seem to be motionless.
3. Pluto is far from the earth, a large telescope is needed to see it.
4. Mars is a desert of reddish rock, sand, and soil it is called the red planet.
5. Mars has some vegetation, an area of vegetation the size of Texas has developed on the planet in a few years' time.
6. The largest planet is Jupiter its diameter is eleven times the diameter of earth.
7. The atmosphere of Jupiter contains many gases, they are probably in a slushlike state because of the extremely cold surface of the planet.
8. Saturn is the second largest planet we are particularly interested in the rings of Saturn.
9. The rings are composed of billions of particles undoubtedly ice is one of the components.
10. Venus is a planet we are studying closely, it is slightly smaller than the earth.

● EXERCISE 7. Some of the following items are correctly punctuated sentences. Others contain run-on sentences. Put an *S* beside the proper number on your paper for each correctly punctuated sentence. For run-ons, write the last word of the first complete

15b

sentence, the punctuation it should have, and the first word of the next sentence. Do not forget the capital letters.

1. Jason was one of the mighty heroes of Greek legend, the story of his struggle to find the golden fleece is well known.
2. Jason's father was driven from his throne by his wicked brother, Pelias.
3. To protect Jason, his father took him to a remote mountain top.
4. There the boy was reared by the Centaur, a creature who was half man and half horse.
5. Later Jason learned of his right to the throne he decided to win back his father's kingdom, he returned to his home and confronted Pelias.
6. Although the wicked king pretended to welcome Jason, he plotted against the young man's life.
7. He sent Jason in search of the golden fleece, hoping that the young man would be killed.
8. When Jason finally arrived in the land of the golden fleece, he was told by the king of the land that he could carry away the fleece only if he performed a certain feat, he had to yoke two fire-breathing bulls and plant a field with dragon's teeth.
9. When he planted the seeds, gigantic warriors sprang up, and Jason had to slay each one.
10. With the help of Medea, the king's daughter, he was able to perform the feat and win the fleece.

● EXERCISE 8.   Number your paper 1–25, to correspond with the line numbers in the paragraph below. The paragraph contains many run-on sentences. Decide where each sentence should end, and write its last word beside the number of its line. Put a period, exclamation mark, or question mark after it; then write the first word of the next sentence, using a capital letter.

1   President Washington chose the site for the
2   White House, but he never lived in the building.
3   The cornerstone was laid in 1792, John Adams
4   moved into the building in 1800. The building was
5   then much smaller than it is now. The East Room,
6   a room used today for formal functions, was un-
7   completed, Mrs. Adams hung her wash in it.

8   In 1814 the White House was burned by the
9   British, the structure had to be rebuilt, again in
10   1950 the White House was rebuilt because it was
11   unsafe. By 1952 the reconstruction was finished,
12   President Truman returned to it from Blair House,
13   where he had lived during the rebuilding process.

14   Today the White House has 132 rooms and
15   20 baths, it has five passenger and service eleva-
16   tors. Many of the rooms are famous, the East
17   Room, the Red Room, and the Blue Room are
18   especially well known, they are used for formal
19   and informal receptions. The White House is open
20   from 10 A.M. to noon Tuesday through Saturday,
21   but, of course, only the public rooms may be
22   visited. Each day crowds line Pennsylvania Ave-
23   nue to see the Executive Mansion, one should be
24   in line early if he plans to go on a tour of the
25   White House.

● REVIEW EXERCISE. This exercise contains complete sentences, fragments, and run-ons. Number your paper 1–20. After each number write *S* for correct sentence, *F* for fragment, and *R* for run-on sentence.

1. Man has long wondered at the noises of animals, can animals communicate with each other?

2. After several years of research.
3. Scientists are convinced that some animals have more effective communication systems than man has.
4. The porpoise can mimic man's voice, but it speaks eight times faster than man.
5. Making a tape recorder essential.
6. In order to slow the porpoise's voice down enough for scientists to study it.
7. Porpoises can imitate human laughter, they can also imitate a "bronx cheer."
8. There is some evidence that porpoises can manage to learn words and phrases.
9. Which they repeat with humanlike rhythm and enunciation.
10. After the porpoise has listened to a person who has a Southern accent.
11. It can mimic the accent.
12. A knowledge of communications among animals may help us communicate with creatures on other planets, should there be any, consequently funds are being provided for such research.
13. Animals do communicate with each other, we know that.
14. Porpoises can learn the meaning of certain words.
15. Because they do tricks after hearing words like *fish* and *jump*.
16. Can you imagine yourself communicating with a porpoise, or does this seem impossible to you?
17. Perhaps one day after getting down close to the surface of the water.
18. You will carry on a conversation with a porpoise.
19. Or maybe some other animal.
20. At one time people laughed at the idea of space travel however today we know that man can travel through space.

CHAPTER 16

Correcting and Improving Sentences

Achieving Sentence Variety

Most of us, when we write, are so busy thinking about what we are going to say that we pay little attention to how we say it. Often the result is writing that consists of choppy, abrupt sentences that are monotonously alike, or rambling sentences that are tiresome to read. Correcting such writing is easy if you will take time to revise your compositions before making a final copy to hand in. This chapter will show you how to spot poorly written passages in your own writing and how to improve them.

CORRECTING A CHOPPY STYLE

Reading a paragraph full of short, choppy sentences is like riding with a driver who keeps jamming on the brakes. Just when you think you are going somewhere, you are pulled up short by a period. When several choppy sentences are related in thought, the passage in which they appear can usually be made smoother and clearer if they are combined into longer sentences.

16a. Combine short, related sentences by using compound subjects.

A compound subject consists of two or more simple subjects joined by a conjunction such as *and* or *or* and having the same verb. In the following examples, the compound subjects are printed in heavy type.

EXAMPLES Your **books** and your **lunch** are on the table.

Roses, carnations, and **violets** were growing in the garden.

You can combine short sentences by putting the ideas they contain into a single sentence with a compound subject. The words that usually connect a compound subject are *and, or, both—and, either—or, neither—nor*. The choice of the conjunction depends upon the meaning of the sentence. In the following examples the compound subjects and the connecting words are printed in heavy type.

EXAMPLES Spain tried to establish a colony in old California. Russia also tried.

Both Spain and Russia tried to establish a colony in old California.

Chemical foam will smother an oil fire. Sand will also smother an oil fire.

Sand and chemical foam will smother an oil fire.

John will not be at the party tomorrow. Alan will not be there either.

Neither John nor Alan will be at the party tomorrow.

● EXERCISE 1.   Combine each pair of sentences by writing one sentence with a compound subject. Be sure the subject and verb agree in number.

1. Blocks of snow are used by Eskimos to make shelters. Walrus hides are also used.
2. Tahiti is an island in the South Seas. Mooréa, another island, is there too.
3. Green cannot be used for the uniforms. Neither can blue.
4. Riding boots are part of a cowboy's wardrobe. A bandanna is also part of his outfit.
5. Tom and Andy were late for the meeting. So was Pete.

16b. Combine short, related sentences by using compound verbs.

A compound verb consists of two or more verbs that have the same subject and are joined by a conjunction. In the following examples, the compound verbs are printed in heavy type.

EXAMPLES   The bugler **arose** at dawn and **woke** the campers.

The heavy rain **flooded** highways and **washed** out bridges.

Short sentences that have the same subject may be combined by putting the ideas they contain into one sentence with a compound verb. The connecting words most frequently used are *and, but, or, either—or, neither—nor, both—and*. In the following examples, the compound verbs and conjunctions are printed in heavy type.

16 a-b

EXAMPLES   He changed his shirt. He put on a different tie.

He **changed** his shirt **and put on** a different tie.

She wrote a composition before supper. She did not finish her history assignment.

She **wrote** a composition before supper **but did** not **finish** her history assignment.

The lost pilot had not reported his position. He had not radioed a call for help.

The lost pilot **had neither reported** his position **nor radioed** a call for help.

● EXERCISE 2.   Combine each pair of short sentences into a single sentence with a compound verb.

1. We applied for the job yesterday. We were hired immediately.
2. The sergeant awakened his men. He led them to the waiting truck.
3. Tom was late this morning. He missed the assembly.
4. Margaret cleared the table. She did not have time to wash the dishes.
5. Chris pulled to the curb. He let the driver pass.

● REVIEW EXERCISE A.   Combine each of the following groups of short sentences into one sentence by using a compound subject or a compound verb.

1. The seventh grade will be dismissed at two o'clock. The eighth grade will be dismissed at the same time.
2. He swung hard at the first pitch. He missed it.
3. Jack and Betty left for town at eight o'clock. Jimmy went with them.

4. Jerry set a pail of paint on the bottom step. He forgot to mention it.
5. Harry will meet me after school. He will drive me downtown.
6. Mother was waiting at the station. Dad was there, too.
7. The girls went riding from different stables. They met at the halfway point on the bridle path.
8. Doris prepared our breakfast. She also packed a lunch for each of us.
9. The guest speaker had not yet arrived. The president of the club was also late.
10. Al may pitch for the Tigers. On the other hand, it may be George.

16c. Combine short, related sentences by making them into a compound sentence.

A compound sentence is made up of two or more simple sentences usually joined by *and*, *but*, or *or*. A compound sentence, therefore, will have two or more subjects and two or more verbs.

s   v   s   v

EXAMPLE   The sun rose, and the air became warm.

When you use a compound sentence, you tell your reader to think of the two ideas together. Do not combine short simple sentences into a compound sentence unless the ideas are closely related and equal in importance.

RELATED IDEAS   We had won the football game, and we all felt like celebrating.

UNRELATED IDEAS   We had won the football game, and my dad picked us up in his car.

16c

EQUAL IDEAS   Mary brought her mandolin to the
                   party, and Sandra brought her gui-
                   tar.

UNEQUAL IDEAS   Mary brought her mandolin to the
                   party, and it was Leonard's birth-
                   day.

● EXERCISE 3. Most of the following items consist
of two or more closely related ideas. Combine these
ideas into a single compound sentence, using *and, but,*
or *or* as the connecting words. A few items contain
unrelated or unequal ideas. In such cases, write *C*
after the appropriate number to show that the ideas
are better expressed in separate sentences.

1. The British troops marched toward Lexington.
   The minutemen quickly gathered there to oppose
   them.
2. Martha got useful clothes for Christmas. Tom got
   a box of toys.
3. Mother invited the new neighbors to dinner. They
   used to live in Detroit.
4. You think fishing is fun. I think it's a very boring
   sport.
5. Mr. Jones planted apple and plum trees around
   his house. Now he has fruit as well as shade.
6. Jimmy left school early. Tom and Eddie stayed
   late.
7. A century ago, farmers depended on horses for
   power. Today they use tractors.
8. Catching sight of the watchman, Tony dived into
   the pool. Andy climbed out and ran.
9. Nora brought Mary a birthday present. Brenda
   also brought one. Lucy forgot hers.
10. Horseback riding is my favorite sport. Horses are
    as different from one another as people.

16d. Combine short, choppy sentences into one sentence by using such words as *after, although, as, because, before, if, since, so that, when, whether,* and *while* to show the relationship between the ideas.

Sometimes the ideas expressed between two simple sentences have a special relationship with each other. For example, one sentence may explain *why, where, how,* or *when* the action in the other sentence took place. Therefore, some simple sentences can best be combined by beginning one of them with a word that expresses exactly how the two ideas are related. Study the following examples. Notice how the relationship between the ideas has been expressed by the joining words.

EXAMPLES Tom had lost his library card. He couldn't complete the assignment.

Tom couldn't complete the assignment **because** he had lost his library card.

The judge listened to the lawyers' arguments. He called a recess to consider his ruling.

After the judge had listened to the lawyers' arguments, he called a recess to consider his ruling.

The judge called a recess to consider his ruling **after** he had listened to the lawyers' arguments.

The children were playing in the yard. Their mother hid the Christmas presents in a closet.

16d

While the children were playing in the yard, their mother hid the Christmas presents in a closet.

The mother hid the Christmas presents in a closet **while** the children were playing in the yard.

Jerry practiced hard for the track meet. He was defeated in the broad jump.

Although Jerry practiced hard for the track meet, he was defeated in the broad jump.

Jerry was defeated in the broad jump **even though** he had practiced hard for the track meet.

Notice that your choice of a connecting word depends on the meaning you wish to give. Become familiar with the following list of words and learn to use them effectively in your writing.

after	before	until
although	if	when
as	since	whether
because	so that	while

● EXERCISE 4.   Combine each of the following groups of sentences into a single sentence by using one of the words listed above. Choose the connecting word that will best show how the two ideas are related.

1. The Indians did not needlessly kill the buffalo. They knew that their food and shelter depended upon herds of buffalo to hunt.
2. White hunters reached the prairies. A change occurred.
3. White men began slaughtering buffalo in great numbers. The herds began to dwindle in size.

4. Some white men spoke out against such wholesale killing. The slaughter continued.
5. The Indians watched the white hunters reduce the herds. Their anger grew bitter.

16e. When combining short sentences into a single sentence, be careful to choose a connecting word that expresses the exact relationship between the main ideas.

Notice that the connecting word may be placed at the beginning of the new sentence or in the middle of it. Remember also that, in combining short sentences into one sentence, your purpose is not only to make your writing smoother but also to make your meaning clearer. The word you choose to join two ideas must express the exact relationship you wish to show between the ideas.

For example, we can use a number of connecting words for these two sentences: *President Lincoln watched a play in Ford's Theater. John Wilkes Booth shot him.* But not all the connecting words would express a meaning that makes sense.

INCORRECT   Because President Lincoln watched a play at Ford's Theater, John Wilkes Booth shot him.

INCORRECT   Whenever President Lincoln watched a play at Ford's Theater, John Wilkes Booth shot him.

These combined sentences may read smoothly, but *because* and *whenever* do not convey the correct relationship between the two ideas. Booth did not shoot Lincoln *because* he watched the play; nor did he shoot him *whenever* he watched the play.

16e

CORRECT **As** President Lincoln watched a play at Ford's Theater, John Wilkes Booth shot him.

or

While President Lincoln watched a play at Ford's Theater, John Wilkes Booth shot him.

● EXERCISE 5.   Combine each of the following pairs of sentences by using the appropriate connecting word in parentheses. The connecting word need not come at the beginning of the new sentence.

1. The gale increased in force. The bridge swayed dangerously. (*as, although*)
2. The rainbow glistened brilliantly. The rain had fallen in torrents. (*until, after*)
3. Kit Carson's wife urged him to remain at home on the ranch. He guided Frémont's party to California. (*although, because*)
4. They burned the useless brush. New forage grass would grow up. (*as, so that*)
5. Mr. Bogard took Ellen's picture. She did not look her best. (*when, because*)
6. The doctor gave her polio vaccine. She will not catch polio. (*although, so that*)
7. The plow turned the rich, black soil. Birds darted into the furrow to snap up grubs and worms. (*as, until*)
8. Mother gave Nora a present. Today was her birthday. (*because, while*)
9. Fire burned the protective covering of grass and brush. Heavy rains caused severe soil erosion. (*although, after*)
10. Andy wants to go with us. He will have to get up early. (*so that, if*)

● EXERCISE 6.   Combine each of the following groups of two sentences into a single sentence, using such connecting words as *after*, *although*, *as*, *because*, *before*, *if*, *since*, *so that*, *when*, *whether*, *while*. Choose the connecting word that expresses exactly the relationship you see between the ideas.

1. He overhauled the motor car. It ran much better.
2. Lincoln's parents were poor people. He became President of his country.
3. The shadow of the earth crept over the moon. Astronomers took photographs of the eclipse.
4. He had sanded the table top. He varnished it.
5. John should be the guide. He is the only one among us who knows the way to camp.
6. Alan worked very hard. He did not finish the job that day.
7. A storm had grounded all planes. Mr. Adams came home by train.
8. The huge redwood quivered, swayed, and fell with a great crash. The children watched breathlessly.
9. His friends were playing ball in the street. Jack was mowing the lawn and feeling very sorry for himself.
10. Harold bought some new safety equipment for his boat. He wanted to be ready for any emergency.

CORRECTING A RAMBLING STYLE

Sometimes, instead of writing short, choppy sentences, a person will go to the opposite extreme and run many sentences together, punctuating them as a single sentence. Using *and*, *so*, *but*, and *and then* as connectives, he will loosely tie a long succession of thoughts into a sentence that rambles on and on.

16f. Correct a rambling style by combining ideas and avoiding the overuse of *and*, *but*, and *so*.

The first step in correcting a rambling passage is to break it into separate complete sentences. The second step is to combine some of the short sentences that result into better sentences.

Read the following example of a rambling sentence. Then read Step 1 in which the sentence has been broken up into six sentences. Next read Step 2, which shows how these sentences are combined and improved through the ways suggested in rules 16a–d.

> The afternoon was hot and sultry and so we asked my big brother Bill to drive us to the lake and he was willing and so he backed his old junk heap out of the garage and we got into our bathing suits and piled into the "heap" and we started out on our great adventure.

Step 1. Break up the passage into shorter sentences.

> The afternoon was hot and sultry. We asked my big brother Bill to drive us to the lake. He was willing. He backed his old junk heap out of the garage. We got into our bathing suits and piled into the "heap." We started out on our great adventure.

Step 2. Combine some of the short sentences into longer ones by using compound subjects and verbs, and by using the words listed on page 302.

> Because the afternoon was hot and sultry, we asked my big brother Bill to drive us to the lake. He was willing and backed his old junk

heap out of the garage. After we got into our bathing suits, we piled into the "heap" and started out on our great adventure.

In revising your writing, of course, you will not need to copy it twice. You will do Step 1 in your mind and write your revised version, Step 2, only once.

● EXERCISE **7.** Correct the rambling style of the following passages. First, in your mind, break the passage into shorter sentences. Then combine these sentences into varied, better-written ones by using compound subjects and compound verbs, compound sentences, or the words listed on page 302. Be careful not to change the meaning of the original passage.

1. The boys had seen Jim's father start the outboard motor by yanking on the starting cord, and they decided to try it themselves, so they got into the boat and Andy pulled the cord, but the engine unfortunately was in gear and the throttle was wide open, so the motor caught with a roar and the boat leaped ahead and it shot up onto the beach.

2. Janey and Nora said that their first skiing lesson was a very upsetting experience, for the first time that Janey stood up, her skis slid out from under her, and she made a deep *sitzmark* in the snow, and the first time that Nora stood up on her skis they slid right out from under her, too, and she also made a deep *sitzmark* in the snow. Janey played safe, then, by sitting on her skis as she started down a slope, but she started going too fast, and she got scared, and she screamed. She was headed straight for a tree, and she tried to veer to one side, and she got her skis tangled, and she pitched headfirst into the snow.

16f

CORRECTING A MONOTONOUS STYLE

If all the sentences in a passage begin the same way, the writing will be dull. Such monotony can be avoided by occasionally varying the beginnings of sentences.

16g. Correct a monotonous style by varying the beginnings of sentences.

(1) To vary sentences, begin with an adverb.

EXAMPLE The door suddenly flew open.
    Suddenly, the door flew open.

● EXERCISE 8. Change the following sentences to begin with an adverb.

1. He handed over the letter reluctantly.
2. George grudgingly admitted that we were right.
3. He banged his fist repeatedly on the table.
4. We shall first take up old business.
5. The baby set up a howl instantly.
6. The mountains appeared in the distance gradually.
7. The old man slowly climbed the steps.
8. We went swimming yesterday.
9. The clerk eagerly took the money.
10. The natives eyed the stranger suspiciously.

(2) To vary sentences, begin with a prepositional phrase.

EXAMPLES The coach had a few words to say after the game.
    After the game, the coach had a few words to say.

    A quart jar of pennies stood on the table.
    On the table stood a quart jar of pennies.

● EXERCISE 9.   Change the following sentences to begin with a prepositional phrase.

1. We had traveled three hundred miles before lunch.
2. The game was tied in the last inning.
3. I was afraid to try that strategy after my last experience.
4. She wore a heart-shaped locket around her neck.
5. He had just one dime in his pocket.
6. Mr. Olivani has taught the same grade for twenty years.
7. He waited for fifteen minutes despite the rain.
8. I suddenly remembered the answer after the test.
9. Everyone is expected to remain quiet throughout the program.
10. I thought ours the most original of all the skits.

● REVIEW EXERCISE B.   Revise the following passages. Remember that your goal is to produce clear, well-written, varied sentences. You may not need to change every sentence. Read each passage carefully before you begin your revision.

1. Andy planted a vegetable garden. So did Pete. Andy fertilized his garden. Andy irrigated it often. Pete also fertilized and irrigated his garden. Andy sprayed his growing vegetables with insect killer. He wanted his garden free of crawling eaters. Andy warned Pete against pests. Pete couldn't be bothered. Andy raised some fine vegetables. Pete raised a bumper crop of bugs and cutworms.

2. Joan and Elsie had colds when they visited their aunt in Hollywood but they remember the stay as a very exciting time, for they took a bus tour past the big homes of the movie stars, they shopped on Hollywood Boulevard—they couldn't come home without

16g

312 Correcting and Improving Sentences

gifts for the family—and then Joan went alone to see a live television show, and Elsie spent a day in bed to shake off her cold, but the next day Joan stayed in bed for the same reason, and Elsie went to a crowded movie premiere at Grauman's Chinese Theater, and on the last day of their visit they promised to go to bed early and their aunt took them to Disneyland.

Summary

Use the following methods to give clearer meaning to what you write and to make your style more interesting and varied.

1. Combine short, related sentences by using compound subjects.

2. Combine short, related sentences by using compound verbs.

3. Combine short, related sentences by making them into a compound sentence.

4. Combine short, choppy sentences into one sentence by using such connecting words as after, although, as, because, before, if, since, so, so that, when, whether, while.

5. Correct a rambling style by avoiding the overuse of and, but, and so.

6. Correct a rambling style by using connecting words such as when, because, before, etc., to show the proper relationship between ideas.

7. Correct a monotonous style by using adverbs, adjectives and prepositional phrases to vary the beginnings of sentences.

PART FIVE

Composition

CHAPTER 17

Narration
and Description

Telling what happened and telling what something is like are two of the most common uses of language. Hardly a day passes in which you do not do one or the other in your conversation. Telling what happened is *narration;* creating a word picture of something is *description.*

If you have tried writing narration or description, you have probably found that it is more difficult to tell about events and people and things on paper than it is by the spoken word. When you are speaking, you use gestures, facial expressions, and tone of voice to carry part of your meaning and hold the listener's attention. When you write, your words have to do the whole job.

Learning to do the job with words alone requires careful thought and a good deal of practice. However, you do not have to learn to write narratives and descriptions by trial and error. People have been telling stories and describing things for thousands of years and in that time they have naturally given some thought to the best way of going about these kinds of writing. The principles you will study in this chapter will help you solve some of the general problems that arise in writing narrative or description.

WRITING NARRATIVES

"And then what happened?" is not just a child's question. Adults often ask it, too. Everyone likes a story. The story may be about far-off places and strange events or about very familiar things. In either case, people are curious about things that happen to others.

Your readers will be interested in what has happened to you. Making mistakes, having fun, finding new friends, being frightened, making difficult decisions—these and many other things that you have experienced are your best sources for stories. And you are the only one who can write them.

Planning a Narrative

17a. Plan a narrative before you write it.

Planning your narrative is important. Unless you plan, you may omit essential parts of your story or get the details so mixed up that your reader is confused and the story spoiled.

A story plan should tell:

1. *Time:* when the incident occurred
2. *Place:* where the incident occurred
3. *People:* who were involved
4. *What happened:* a summary (in a sentence or two) of what happened
5. *How you felt:* a summary (in a sentence or two) of how you felt at the time

Suppose that you have been asked to write a story about a personal experience. You think a while and decide, for example, to tell a story about an accident you had on a fishing trip. When you have jotted down notes for each heading, your finished story plan might read:

1. *Time:* last summer, while I was fishing
2. *Place:* on the dock at Lake Wyandot
3. *People:* me, crowd of scouts, my father, a doctor
4. *What happened:* I grabbed at my fishing line and hooked my own thumb
5. *How I felt:* angry with myself for having a silly accident in front of all those people

This plan serves as a general outline and as a guide to what you should put into your story. The items of this plan should be clear and definite. As you write, *stick to your outline.*

A common error in story writing is to begin in the wrong place. If, for example, in developing this outline into a story, you begin by telling how you left home in a rainstorm, where you stopped for breakfast, the names of friends who waved to you as you passed, you would be confusing your reader with unnecessary details. Your story is about an accident you had while fishing, so begin the story on the dock at the lake, with the fishing.

● EXERCISE 1.   Draw up a story plan for the following story. Remember the five items of the plan: *Time; Place; People; What happened; How the writer felt.*

Johnny Burt and I had a good lesson in obeying signs last summer. When we were camping with our folks in Mount Cato State Park, Johnny and I went

17a

on a hike. We started climbing the trail up Mount Cato at daybreak, and reached the top by mid-day. We were tired and hungry.

"Let's shortcut, going down," I said to Johnny after we had eaten our sandwiches.

He pointed to a sign.

"It says hikers should stay on the trail."

"We'll be careful. Come on!" I said.

We were very careful. The trail zigzagged down the mountain in gentle switchbacks, but we cut straight down between zigs and zags. When we came to a slope of loose rock that our weight might have moved into a bad rock slide, we went around it on the trail. Farther down, we returned to the trail again to avoid a slope so steep that we might have broken our necks trying to climb down it. But all the rest of the way we took shortcuts, clinging to shrubs and trees as we made our way down. We arrived at camp with no more hurts than briar scratches.

We had been careful, but not careful enough. We had caught poison oak. We had such a bad case that our eyes swelled shut, and we spent a week in bed—so miserable we could hardly stand it!

● EXERCISE 2.   Prepare a story plan about something that happened to you. The following suggestions may help you find the right incident. Save your plan. You will use it later as an outline for a narrative.

1. An automobile breakdown in a deserted place
2. An attempt to imitate someone older than you
3. An embarrassing moment
4. A quarrel with a friend
5. Overcoming a fear
6. A scheme for making some money
7. Your first baby-sitting assignment

8. An unexpected visitor
9. Training a pet
10. A difficult decision

17b. **Make sure that your story has a beginning, a middle, and an end.**

Generally, your story should be at least three paragraphs long. Usually it will be longer. The first paragraph is the beginning or introduction to your story. The last paragraph, of course, is the ending. The longest part of your story is the middle, which may consist of several paragraphs.

The beginning. The beginning of a narrative should arouse the reader's interest and get him quickly into the story. It usually gives the *time* and the *place* and introduces the *people*. Unless the reader is supposed to be surprised, the beginning should give him a hint of what is going to happen.

The middle. This part of the narrative is mainly devoted to *what happened*. It deals with the important events in the order they occurred. But only the *important* events belong. It is very easy to stray from the point of your story in the middle. Only those details that the reader has to know should be included.

The end. The end of a narrative should satisfy the reader's curiosity about *what happened* and tell him *how you felt* about it. Sometimes the way in which you tell about the final event will show your reader your attitude toward it. At other times, a brief comment will help him to see the point.

17b

● EXERCISE 3.   Turn back to the narrative in Exercise 1. Be able to identify the beginning, middle, and end. Would the point be clearer if the writer had added a concluding sentence such as "Johnny and I certainly learned the hard way"? Be able to give the reasons for your answer.

● EXERCISE 4.   Write a narrative of about two hundred words on the plan you worked out for Exercise 2. Introduce *time*, *place*, and *people* in the beginning.

Narrative Details

17c. Make your details specific.

A vague and general story is likely to bore the reader. A good narrative gives the reader the feeling that he is actually witnessing the events. To achieve this, the details must make a strong and definite impression.

Look once more at the story in Exercise 1 (page 317). The long paragraph, telling how the boys climbed down the mountain, begins with the sentence, "We were very careful." But the writer does not stop with this general statement. He gives vivid details to show how careful the boys were.

Vivid details do more than tell what happened. They *show* what happened. Suppose you were writing a narrative based on the story plan on page 317. The last two items of the plan are

4. I grabbed at my fishing line and hooked my own thumb.
5. I was angry with myself for having a silly accident in front of all those people.

These two bare statements give an idea of *what happened* and *how you felt*, but they do not hold the reader's interest or make the story vivid. Specific, vivid details will show what happened:

> When I started to swing the fish onto the dock, it flopped off the hook and fell back into the water. The boys groaned, but I was too busy just then to care. I grabbed for my swinging line, realizing that I might hit somebody with my sinker or snag someone with my hook. I was right. I caught my line—by the hook. It stuck into my thumb.
>
> I exclaimed, "Ouch!" That hook felt like a sudden jab of fire into my hand. Then I forgot the hurt in a worse kind of pain. My face got red as I realized everybody was staring at me. What a dumb thing to do! Snag yourself with your own fishing hook like a six-year-old!

● EXERCISE 5. The following situations are ones that might be important parts of a longer narrative. Choose two of these situations and write for each three or more sentences containing specific details that will make the reader feel he is *there*.

EXAMPLE 1. Putting out a brush fire
 1. *The sudden breeze swept the fire out of the small ravine in which we had been camping and onto the broad, dry meadow. We desperately beat at the flames with the one shovel we had and our raincoats. The intense heat of the flames made our faces burn as though we were feverish.*

1. Riding in a roller coaster
2. Taking an important test

17c

3. Being caught in a thunderstorm
4. Riding on a crowded bus (or train or subway)
5. Waiting in line to buy tickets
6. Trying out for a part in a play (or a position on a team)
7. Looking for landmarks in a strange part of town
8. Meeting someone unexpectedly with whom you have quarreled
9. Trying something new for the first time
10. Entering a new school for the first time

17d. Omit unnecessary details.

A common error in writing narratives is to stray from the main idea of your story. If you are telling about how you hooked your thumb while fishing, avoid giving details about the weather or how large a fish someone else caught. These things have nothing to do with your story. One way of deciding whether a detail is necessary is to consult your story plan. If a detail will help to build an item in the plan (*time, place, people, action, feelings*), that detail is likely to be useful and appropriate. If the detail does not apply to any item in the plan, omit it.

● EXERCISE 6. The following narrative contains a number of unnecessary details. Decide which details should be omitted and copy them in a list on your paper.

I woke up in a fright and lay tense in my sleeping bag, listening. Outside the tent I could hear the wind in the pine trees. I heard an owl hoot and a burning stick crackle in the dying campfire. Then I gasped as again I heard the sound that had scared me out of sleep. Just on the opposite side of the tent wall something shuffled and snuffled.

A bear! Sniffing at our camp icebox!

I screamed, "Dad! A bear!" I screamed loud enough to shake pine cones off the trees. My father and brother woke up. People in tents around us woke up and looked out.

Dad rushed out of the tent in his pajamas. My mother, still half asleep, said, "Millie, you should've brought your new green dress."

My brother said angrily, "Quit shouting! Girls should be seen but not heard!"

Outside, Dad was moving his flashlight beam around camp. Flashlights from tents around us shone on our camp. Far in the distance, a train whistled for a crossing.

Suddenly I felt as silly as a dog with its head caught in a bucket. Dad's flashlight showed our icebox resting where it belonged, safe and sound. No bear was in sight. But slowly waddling away, making a shuffling sound in the pine needles, was a fat, harmless little raccoon. I felt so ashamed I wanted to crawl down into the bottom of my sleeping bag. Right then I was one girl who didn't even want to be seen, let alone heard!

Using Dialogue

In a written story, the conversations that people have are called *dialogue*. Using dialogue is one way to make your narratives more lively and to make your characters come to life.

Even though the narratives that you are writing right now are very short, you will still find some opportunities to use dialogue. Before you do, review quickly the rules for using quotation marks on pages

17d

228–34. Remember to start a new paragraph with each change of speaker.

EXAMPLE   "What was that noise?" I asked.

        Jerry rubbed his eyes. "I didn't hear a thing."

        "Then you were asleep."

        Jerry looked at me indignantly. "Asleep? Are you accusing *me*—"

        "Let's not argue," Ray interrupted. "We have to stick together."

● EXERCISE 7.   Choose one of the following situations and write a short dialogue to fit it.

1. A boy attempts to convince his father that his allowance should be raised.
2. Two girls try to persuade a third to come to the beach with them.
3. A student explains to his teacher why an assignment has not been completed.
4. Two boys or two girls disagree about the way to do something.
5. A baby-sitter tries to reason with a small child.

● EXERCISE 8.   Write a narrative of about three hundred words on one of the following topics or on one of your own choice. Plan your story carefully and make sure that it has a beginning, a middle, and an end. Use dialogue if it is appropriate.

1. What I learned from a great disappointment
2. The first trip I took alone
3. A holiday I can never forget
4. The greatest favor anyone has ever done for me
5. Lost!
6. How we won a special award
7. The last day of school

8. A false alarm
9. How I helped win (or lose) a game
10. A practical joke that backfired

WRITING DESCRIPTIONS

The purpose of a description is to make the reader see, hear, or otherwise experience something. The writer must use words to create his impression, and he must choose them carefully.

Descriptive Detail

17e. Use details that appeal to the senses.

Good details are as important in a description as in a narrative. Effective description appeals to the senses. You know what something is like by *seeing* or *hearing* it, or by *smelling*, *tasting*, or *touching* it. The best way to make a reader feel that what you are describing is real is to appeal to his senses. If you are describing a walk on a sweltering summer day, you want your reader to feel the waves of heat, see the people trying in different ways to find relief, smell the hot asphalt in the streets, and perhaps hear the refreshing sound of water splashing in a fountain or pool. A vague or general description is dull stuff. Only vivid details and sharp sense impressions will hold a reader's interest.

Like a good narrative, a good description omits unnecessary details. The main purpose of the description of the summer walk is to give an impression of the effect of the heat. A description of jewelry that you

17e

saw in a store window is not related to this main idea and should be omitted.

● EXERCISE 9.   The following passage describes the summers the author, Thomas Sancton, spent at Boy Scout camp. On your paper, copy the words or phrases that appeal to the senses, give the line in which the word or phrase appears, and indicate which of the senses the word or phrase appeals to. It may appeal to more than one sense.

EXAMPLES   *Wet, line 1, touch*
　　　　　　Steaming, line 13, sight

1　Standing in the wet grass, still yawning and sleepy,
2　we did the morning exercises. Night chill was in
3　the air, but behind our backs the sun was rising,
4　and its warmth crept onto our shoulders. After
5　the exercises we raced along a wagon road to the
6　swimming pool, and as we ran up, shouting and
7　excited, two or three startled frogs made tremen-
8　dous leaps and plumped beneath the glassy sur-
9　face of the water. After the swim we dried our
10　skinny sunburned bodies and ran to the mess
11　hall. . . .
12　　At mealtime we ate ravenously. . . . There were
13　steaming platters of pork and beans and cabbage
14　and stew. As we walked to the long clapboard
15　building with our hair freshly combed and water
16　glistening on our faces, which we washed at the
17　flowing pipe of a big artesian well, we existed in a
18　transport of hunger. In the steamy fragrance of
19　the mess hall we set up a clatter of knives and
20　forks and china, and afterward we went to our
21　cabins and flopped on the bunks in a state of
22　drowsy satisfaction. . . .
23　　During those summers in camp a love grew up

24 in me for the rhythms of nature, for tropical rains
25 that came sweeping through the pines and oaks,
26 for the fiery midday sun, for long evenings, and
27 the deep black nights. Great campfires were lit
28 beside the bayou and a rushing column of lumin-
29 ous smoke and sparks ascended to the cypress
30 trees. Fire gleamed in the water where bass were
31 sleeping in stumps. Campers wandered toward the
32 meeting place, their flashlights swinging in the
33 woods. We sat about the fire, singing, beating
34 deep rumbling tom-toms made of hollowed oak
35 logs. . . .[1]

● EXERCISE 10.   Choose five of the following objects
or situations and write one sentence describing each.
Include words and details that appeal to the senses.

1. Eating cold strawberry ice cream
2. A large old tree
3. A fish swimming near a dock
4. A baseball hitting a catcher's mitt
5. A car stuck in a snowbank
6. Night sounds at a lake or at the seashore
7. A drum majorette in a parade
8. Holding a piece of ice for a long time
9. Faces on a bus or train
10. An excited crowd at a football game

17f. Use adjectives and adverbs effectively.

An adjective, you will remember, describes a noun
or pronoun and tells *what kind*, *which one*, *how
many*. An adverb describes a verb, an adjective, or
another adverb and tells *when*, *where*, or *how*.

17f

[1] From "The Silver Horn" by Thomas Sancton. Copyright, 1944,
by Harper & Bros.

Many of us have times when we are lazy and fall into bad habits of thinking. Often we tend to use the same few adjectives to describe anything we happen to be talking or writing about. Such overused descriptive words become tired and weak and dull. They not only fail to do the job they are intended to do, but they bore the reader.

Among such overused adjectives and adverbs are

nice	neat	awful
swell	funny	good
terrible	terrific	bad
cute	wonderful	really

A good example of how an adjective is overused until it becomes so trite that it carries little meaning is the word *awful*. Look it up in the dictionary. It means *terrible, appalling; worthy of profound respect and fear; sublimely impressive; majestic; inspiring awe,* etc. We use the word to mean *exceedingly great, bad.* For example:

> She had an awful headache.
> They live in an awful neighborhood.
> Della wore an awful dress.
> Mike had an awful time at the party.

The word *awful* has been so weakened, abused, and blunted by overuse that it no longer adds much to a description.

An adjective should be fresh and exact. Replacing a dull, trite adjective with a more exact and fresher word will not only help the reader understand what you mean but will give more force and interest to your writing.

If you replace the word *awful* in the sentences on page 328 with adjectives that tell precisely what is intended, much more meaning results.

> She had an awful headache. [piercing? throbbing? agonizing?]
>
> They live in an awful neighborhood [ugly? crowded? unfriendly? dangerous?]
>
> Della wore an awful dress. [hideous? inappropriate? unfashionable?]
>
> Mike had an awful time at the party. [unhappy? painful? boring?]

● EXERCISE 11. Replace the trite adjective (in italics) in each of the following sentences with an adjective that you think is fresher and more exact. Use your dictionary if you need to. List your new adjectives on a sheet of paper, numbering each one for the sentence in which it belongs.

EXAMPLE 1. We had a *grand* time sailing in the high wind.
  1. *thrilling*

1. He was in an *awful* rage.
2. Dan is a *terrific* dancer.
3. They bought a *swell* new car.
4. My aunt lives in a *cute* house.
5. The policeman found Timmy huddled in a corner, crying in a *funny* way.
6. Nora stayed home because she had a *terrible* cold.
7. Dorothy had a really *awful* case of hives.
8. When Max stepped on the hoe blade, the handle flew up and gave him a *wonderful* shiner.
9. After he finally found his broken bike, he was *good and mad*.
10. Pete was suffering from a *bad* case of stage fright.

Like adjectives, adverbs should be fresh and exact. We tend to overuse some adverbs to such an extent that they lack precise meaning and are trite. For example:

> He was terribly good to me. [frighteningly? surprisingly? extremely?]
>
> She's so terribly shy. [severely? painfully? violently?]
>
> Diamonds are terribly expensive. [excitingly? excessively? savagely?]
>
> Tom is terribly careful about details. [savagely? frighteningly? overly?]

● Exercise 12.   Replace the trite adverb in italics in each of the following sentences with an adverb that you think is fresher and more exact. Use your dictionary. List your new adverbs on a sheet of paper, numbering each one for the proper sentence.

1. They danced together *nicely*.
2. Her father was *terribly* good to her.
3. I kept still when he stole my lunch, but when he called me "Fatty" I got *really* angry.
4. At Christmas they were *awfully* happy.
5. She thanked him so *cutely* that he forgot to be angry.
6. He whirled around and around until he got *wonderfully* dizzy.
7. The renegade *neatly* double-crossed his Sioux partners.
8. He is *really* tall.
9. Nora's new dress was *nice*, but Ellen's was *terribly cute*. (Substitute better adjectives and adverb.)
10. Andy has a *really neat* hot rod, but Tom's new car is a *terrific* job. (Substitute better adjectives and adverb.)

17g. Use adjectives and adverbs sparingly.

Using adjectives and adverbs is such an obvious way of writing a description that we may fall into the trap of using too many, thus cluttering the impression we want to create. You should choose adjectives and adverbs as carefully as you do the details of a description. A few strong adjectives and adverbs create a more vivid and interesting word picture than many weak ones. Be especially careful not to overuse *very*.

● EXERCISE 13. Number your paper 1–10. For each phrase in italics, write one adjective or adverb that will do the work of two words.

1. The *very large* policeman helped the lady across the street.
2. A *very smart* girl won the Science Fair award.
3. That was a *very good* dinner we just ate.
4. In a *very loud* voice he demanded to be seated.
5. He told us a *very funny* joke.
6. The football team played *very well.*
7. He described her costume *very clearly.*
8. He has a *very sad* way of speaking.
9. *Very slowly* he took out his wallet and paid the bill.
10. She has a *very musical* voice.

● EXERCISE 14. Write a short description of about seventy-five words. Be sure to include details that appeal to the senses and to make effective use of adjectives and adverbs. Some suggestions are

1. A street at night
2. A department store on a bargain day
3. My favorite dessert
4. The last inning of a baseball game
5. A Saturday matinee at the movies

17g

17h. Use verbs that help with the work of describing.

The careful selection of verbs also helps to make a description vivid and interesting. Verbs are especially useful in describing action. For example, the following paragraph owes its vivid quality to the use of good verbs. Adjectives like *torrid* help, but the strength of the paragraph depends mainly upon the italicized verbs.

> As the runner *flung* himself across the finish line, he *paled* and *crumpled* in a heap. The torrid sun *had beaten* down his strong body, and the final seconds of the race *had exhausted* the last of his reserves. The crowd *roared* and *swarmed* about him.

● EXERCISE 15.   Use verbs from the following list to improve the sentences given below. If you aren't sure of a meaning, use the dictionary.

staggered	throbbed
dawdled	careened
grimaced	squinted
sprawled	screeched
flailed	chuckled

1. The old man looked into the blinding light.
2. After a hard day, Dad lay in the hammock for a rest.
3. He made a face after taking the medicine.
4. He took his time while eating breakfast.
5. The wounded man walked into Gunsmoke Saloon.
6. He laughed quietly when we asked for a day off.
7. Sam waved his arms in excitement.

8. He swayed to one side to avoid colliding with the man suddenly turning the corner.
9. The painful wound hurt.
10. Above us the owl gave a shrill cry.

Using Description in Narratives

17i. Use description in narratives to make your characters and setting vivid.

Because a good description makes what it describes seem real, it will also help to make a story seem real. Study the following description from Mark Twain's story, "The Celebrated Jumping Frog of Calaveras County":

> And he had a little small bull pup, that to look at him you'd think he warn't worth a cent, but to set around and look ornery and lay for a chance to steal something. But as soon as money was up on him, he was a different dog; his underjaw'd begin to stick out like the fo'castle of a steamboat, and his teeth would uncover, and shine savage like the furnaces.[1]

This dog plays an important part in the story. Because this character has been described effectively, what he does later becomes more vivid and more interesting.

A description of a setting may also play an important part in a story. Here, for example, is the opening paragraph of Stephen Crane's story, "The Open Boat." This story is about four men in a lifeboat struggling

17
h-i

[1] From "The Celebrated Jumping Frog of Calaveras County" by Mark Twain. Reprinted by permission of Harper & Row, Publishers.

against the sea for survival. Notice how the description makes the sea not merely a background but an active part of the story.

> None of them knew the color of the sky. Their eyes glanced level, and were fastened upon the waves that swept toward them. These waves were of the hue of slate, save for the tops, which were of foaming white. . . . The horizon narrowed and widened, and dipped and rose, and at all times its edge was jagged with waves that seemed thrust up in points like rocks.[1]

● Exercise 16.   Write a description of a setting (no longer than one hundred words) which might be used in a narrative.

● Review exercise A.   Write a description of from one to two hundred words. Here are some suggestions:

1. A crowded beach or pool
2. An amusement park
3. A parade
4. Your block
5. A state or county fair
6. An ice-skating rink
7. An impressive natural setting such as the Grand Canyon
8. A crowd at a sporting event

● Review exercise B.   Write a narrative of about three hundred words. If you like, you may use the same setting you wrote about in Exercise 16.

[1] Reprinted from *Stephen Crane: An Omnibus*, edited by Robert Stallman. Reprinted by permission of Alfred A. Knopf Incorporated.

CHAPTER 18

The Paragraph

Structure and Development

Unless a piece of writing is extremely short, it is usually divided into parts called paragraphs. A paragraph, first of all, is something you can see. It usually consists of several sentences, and it is set off from the preceding paragraph by its first line, which starts a short distance in from the left margin. In addition to being a physical division on the page, a paragraph is a unit of the writer's thought. Just as he uses punctuation marks within a sentence to show which words belong together, the writer uses paragraphs to show which sentences are closely related.

THE STRUCTURE OF A PARAGRAPH

18a. **A paragraph is a series of sentences developing one topic.**

A good paragraph develops only one topic or idea. When the writer moves on to another topic or to a different part of the topic he has been discussing, he begins a new paragraph to help his reader follow his train of thought.

18a

The main idea in the following paragraph is stated in the first sentence. The rest of the paragraph consists of a series of sentences that explain or clarify the main idea.

> The average cowhand is so conscious of brands that in season and out of season, appropriately and inappropriately, he brands whatever he comes across. He whittles brands on sticks, he burns them into the planks of branding chutes, on pasture gates, on the anchor posts of windmill towers. He smears them with axle grease across the doors of barns and garages. He paints them with charcoal on the rock walls of canyons in which he has made a campfire. He carves them into his spur traps, leggings, and saddle—above all, into his boot tops. More pistols were etched with cattle brands than were ever notched for dead victims. Many a cook has stenciled the ranch coat of arms into the top crust of that gala-day treat—a wild plum cobbler . . . [1]

The Topic Sentence

18b. The topic of a paragraph is stated in one sentence. This sentence is called the *topic sentence.*

In the following paragraphs, the topic sentence is printed in heavy type. Note that the other sentences in the paragraph support the topic sentence by giving additional information.

[1] From "The Heraldry of the Range" by J. Frank Dobie. Reprinted by permission of the author.

The electric motor has greatly eased housekeeping. A willing, tireless helper, the electric motor operates the dishwasher, cleaning glassware and china far better than tired hands can do the job. A motor runs the garbage disposal that cuts waste into particles that can be washed down the drain. An electric motor operates the vacuum cleaner and the wax polisher. A motor even drives the clothes washer and the dryer.

The origin of furniture as we know it goes back to ancient Egypt. The Egyptians had stools, chairs, chests, tables, and beds, examples of which can be seen in museums today. They put such everyday objects in their tombs. They also painted scenes of daily life on the walls of the tombs. Some of these were indoor scenes which showed furniture in great use. Many centuries later, when the sealed tombs were opened, examples of both the real and the painted furniture were found.

In the paragraphs you have just read, the topic sentence is the first sentence. This is its usual position, and often its most effective one. A topic sentence at the beginning tells the reader what the paragraph is going to be about. Knowing this, the reader is able to follow the writer's idea easily. However, the topic sentence may be in any position and is sometimes the last sentence in the paragraph.

● EXERCISE 1. Read the following paragraphs carefully. Decide which sentence in each paragraph is the topic sentence. Write the topic sentence on your paper after the number of the paragraph.

18b

1

We associate masks with Halloween and fancy-dress balls, but in the past the mask has been an important prop in drama and in religious rites. Witch doctors among African tribes and shamans of American Indian tribes wore masks in their medicine dances and religious rituals. Oriental actors wear masks when performing classic plays that are centuries old. The plays of ancient Greece were performed by actors wearing masks that represented gods and forces of nature or the emotions the characters were supposed to feel. Even in England, during the Elizabethan period, masks were worn by actors in a type of brief court play called "the masque."

2

The sport of archery has long been associated with tales of romance and valor. We all know the story of Robin Hood and his band of merry archers who roamed Sherwood Forest. We know too of William Tell, whose skill with a bow saved his life. Many a tale set in early England tells of picturesque and colorful archery contests. In fact, these contests were often the main events at country fairs.

3

Carrying a load of freight or a man, a camel can go for ten to sixteen days without water and can travel long distances over hot, shadeless sands. It can store as much as fifteen gallons of water in its peculiar stomach. Until the automobile and the airplane were invented, the camel was the only means men had for crossing the deserts of Asia and Africa. It is small wonder that the camel is called the "ship of the desert."

4

The sense of touch, which is far more complicated than most of us realize, consists of nine different kinds of senses. There is the sense of touch, as we usually think of it, of pressure, of heat, cold, and pain. Each of these senses reports to the brain by different receptor cells. In addition, we have a vibratory sense, lodged in our bones, that reports vibrations. We have a two-point discrimination sense (awareness of being touched at different places). We have a position sense that enables us even with closed eyes to tell the position of an arm or leg in relation to the rest of the body. Lastly, we have an equilibrium sense, with receptors in the canals of the inner ear, that enables us to keep balance.

The Concluding or Clincher Sentence

At the end of a paragraph, a writer will sometimes restate in different words the topic sentence he used at the beginning. A concluding sentence of this kind is sometimes called a *clincher sentence* because it clinches the point made in the paragraph.

While such a sentence may provide a helpful summary of a long and complicated paragraph, it is likely to seem tacked on in a shorter paragraph. Do not use the concluding sentence unless you think it is necessary to summarize the paragraph.

Steamboat travel made New Orleans one of the nation's great ports. — topic sentence

Through that city, the products of the central plains of North America were shipped out and the goods needed by the people of the plains were shipped in. The Mississippi

River developed into a great trade route. Every year, more boats puffed up and down the mighty river, carrying more freight. In 1820, there were sixty steamboats traveling the western rivers. By 1840, their number had increased to more than three hundred and was rising rapidly. In 1860, over a thousand were in service. With the coming of the steamboat the amount of freight handled by the port of New Orleans increased in only a few decades from five million to 185 million dollars worth.[1]

— concluding sentence

● EXERCISE 2.   Each of the following topics can be treated in a paragraph. Choose three topics from the list that interest you, consider what you would say in a paragraph on each of these subjects, and then write a topic sentence for each of your choices.

1. The advantages of traveling by train (or automobile or bicycle)
2. How to survive in the wilderness
3. A mistake that turned out to be lucky
4. The best (or worst) thing about television commercials
5. A dish that anyone can make
6. An argument that no one can win

[1] From *Story of the American Nation* by Mabel B. Casner, Ralph H. Gabriel, Edward L. Biller, and William H. Hartley. Reprinted by permission of Harcourt, Brace & World, Inc.

7. Why you think there should (or should not) be billboards along our new roads
8. How an accidental event changed your way of thinking
9. Your favorite after-school activity
10. The best day of the week

● EXERCISE 3. Using one of the topic sentences you wrote for Exercise 2, write a paragraph of about one hundred words.

DEVELOPING A TOPIC SENTENCE

The topic sentence tells what the paragraph is going to be about. Although it may be about a specific person or thing, the topic sentence usually makes a fairly general statement. It tells the reader that something is true. The rest of the sentences in the paragraph show more fully what the writer means in his topic sentence.

The other sentences in a paragraph should develop the topic sentence, making its generalized meaning clear and definite. For example, the following topic sentence states an idea that we can understand:

> The student who joins a school club can expect many benefits.

But we will understand this sentence better when we know what the specific benefits are. The sentences that follow this topic sentence should develop the idea by telling just which benefits the writer has in mind.

There are a number of different ways to develop a topic sentence. In this book, you will study three of the most important of them.

18c. **A topic sentence may be developed by giving details.**

If the topic sentence of a paragraph says, "Many strange things happened in the San Francisco earthquake of April 18, 1906," the reader expects some of these things to be mentioned. The other sentences in the paragraph would probably tell what particular strange things happened, thus supporting the topic sentence.

Read the following paragraph. Notice how the sentences support the one topic sentence by adding to the idea already stated.

Practically all the clothes worn by the pioneers were homemade. At first the pelts of deer and other fur-bearing animals were used in making clothing. When sheep became common, wool came increasingly into use. The wool was sheared and washed, combed, spun into yarn, and dyed with coloring made from bark, berries, and leaves. Then it was woven into cloth. The process was, of course, long and laborious. Nevertheless, every pioneer girl learned to spin and to weave in order to be able to make the clothes her family would need.

topic sentence

details supporting the topic sentence

concluding sentence

18d. A topic sentence may be developed by giving examples.

Examples, which are simply a kind of detail, are often useful in illustrating the point of a topic sentence. The examples given should be as specific as possible and should have a clear relation to the main idea.

As the season advances, other mysterious comings and goings take place. — topic sentence

Fish called capelin gather north of Russia in the deep, cold water of the Barents Sea. Flocks of birds such as auks, fulmars, and kittiwakes follow and prey upon their shoals. Cod gather off the shores of Norway and Iceland. Birds which in winter fed over the whole Atlantic, or the whole Pacific, make for some small island. The entire breeding population arrives there within the space of a few days. Whales suddenly appear off the coastal banks where the shrimplike krill are spawning. But where the whales came from or by what route no one knows.[1]

paragraph developed by examples

[1] Reprinted by permission from *The Sea Around Us* by Rachel L. Carson, Young Reader's edition adapted by Ann Terry White, by arrangement with Oxford University Press. © 1958 by Golden Press, Inc. Text copyright 1950, 1951, 1958 by Rachel L. Carson.

18
c-d

18e. A topic sentence may be developed by telling an incident.

Sometimes, a brief story, that is, an incident or an anecdote, is used to illustrate the point of the topic sentence.

Bold, reckless Sir Francis Drake was the kind of man who inspires legends. — topic sentence

Englishmen of his time were ready to believe almost any story about Drake. And why not? Many Spaniards feared him more than any other English sea captain. He had seized Spanish treasure ships in the Caribbean and raided Spanish seaports under the very muzzles of Spanish cannon. . . . According to one of the legends, Drake was bowling on a lawn in Plymouth when news arrived that the Spanish Armada had been sighted approaching the English coast. The Royal navy, with Drake second in command, was anchored in Plymouth Harbor. It was ready to fight the battle that might decide the fate of England. Drake paused in his game, holding the bowling ball in his hand as he listened to the breathless messenger. "We have time

incident developing topic sentence

enough to finish the game and beat
the Spaniards, too," he said. Then
he turned his back and sent the ball
rolling down the green.

● EXERCISE 4. Read each of the following paragraphs carefully. Find the topic sentence and write it on your paper after the proper number. After each of the topic sentences, indicate whether the paragraph develops it by details, by examples, or by an incident.

1

A community of ants is a highly organized place. One ant in each community is the queen. Some members are hunters who go out and search for food which they bring back to the group. Other ants are herders who take care of "ant cows" (aphids) which produce milk on which the ants feed. Many of the ants are farmers: they harvest grass seed and store it in the nest; some grow "mushroom gardens" by preparing special beds of chewed leaves on which grows a fungus that is a chief item of diet for the group. There are ant warriors who own slaves: they sally out in raids on other ant groups, steal the young, and raise them to be workers. In every ant community, some ants take responsibility for the young, feeding them, cleaning them, keeping their quarters sanitary and healthful.

2

In 1675, the normal way to get from New York City to Philadelphia was on foot, and the trip took from three to five days. By 1775, horse-drawn coaches had lessened the time to two days. About sixty years later, a railroad connected the two cities; and by the twentieth century, fast planes and automobiles had been developed. Now we can cover the distance in a few minutes by jet airliner. In less than three hundred

18e

years, the ever-increasing speed of travel has completely changed our ideas of distance.

3

When we upset Nature's balance in the relationship of wildlife to its surroundings, the results can be very unfortunate. Some years ago, in order to increase the number of deer in the Kaibab Forest, all the wolves and coyotes and mountain lions were killed by state hunters. As a result, the deer increased rapidly, multiplying in a fifteen-year period from four thousand to over a hundred thousand. The sick and weak deer, which the wolves and lions would have killed, survived. However, the enlarged herd was more than the range could feed. In two severe winters, sixty thousand deer starved to death. The herd kept dwindling, down to ten thousand animals. Damage did not stop there; the range had been so severely overgrazed that disastrous soil erosion occurred.

4

One of the many secrets of success can be expressed as "Try just a little harder." This lesson was driven home unforgettably to an oil driller in Texas named Conley. After a long effort to reach oil, he quit drilling on one site and moved away. Soon after, the driller of another well, close to Conley's, sank his well just one foot deeper than Conley's had gone. He struck oil and brought in a rich well. Conley never forgot the lesson. If he had drilled *just one foot deeper*, he, too, would have struck oil. Ever after, when drilling a well, he always sank the hole to the depth his experts recommended and then went one foot deeper.

● EXERCISE 5. Some of the topic sentences below can be developed into paragraphs by giving details. Others can be developed by examples or incidents.

Choose three suitable topics and develop one by using details, one by examples, and one by incident. You may substitute one or more topic sentences of your own if you like.

1. Professional football is very different from college football.
2. Earning his own spending money is good experience for a boy.
3. Raising a puppy requires much skill and patience.
4. Learning to be a fisherman takes practice.
5. Habits can be hard to break.
6. Training rules for athletes are very strict.
7. You cannot count on first impressions.
8. Anyone who goes to the beach on a hot summer day should take precautions against sunburn.
9. Giving a good party takes careful planning.
10. The old-time movies we see on television certainly give us a good idea of how movies have changed.

UNITY IN THE PARAGRAPH

18f. Every sentence in a paragraph should support the main idea expressed in the topic sentence.

The topic sentence of a paragraph states the topic or part of a topic that the paragraph will deal with. Every sentence in the paragraph should serve to make the meaning of the topic sentence clearer and more definite. Any sentence that strays from the idea expressed in the topic sentence, however interesting it may be in itself, breaks the train of thought and confuses the reader.

18f

A paragraph in which all of the other sentences stick to the idea expressed in the topic sentence is said to have *unity*.

The following paragraph contains one sentence, printed in heavy type, that does not support the topic sentence. Notice how this sentence distracts the reader from the idea of the variation in density of the stars, the topic that the paragraph is really about.

Stars vary in weight or density. The range of density is, in fact, surprising. At one extreme are gigantic bubbles of gas, very hot but composed of particles so far apart that such stars (like Antares) have a density of one-thousandth the density of the air we breathe. **The new two-hundred-inch telescope at Mount Palomar is opening up vast new frontiers of astronomical research.** At the opposite extreme are stars like the companion of Sirius, so dense that if a cubic foot of their material were brought to earth, it would weigh as much as ten large locomotives! Even the scant amount of this material that would cover the bottom of a teacup, astronomers say, would weigh a ton.

● EXERCISE 6.   Three of the following paragraphs include a sentence that does not bear on the main idea and thus destroys the unity of the paragraph. Find the unnecessary sentence and copy it beside the proper number on your paper. If there is no unrelated sentence in a paragraph, write *C* beside the number.

1

Everyone uses tin cans, but few people know much about them. A tin can, first of all, has very little tin in it. The can is made of tin plate which is over 98 percent steel with only a coating of tin. A firecracker exploded under an inverted tin can makes a satisfying roar. Coating a metal with tin is a process which has been known a long time. As long ago as 55 B.C., the early Romans coated copper vessels with tin in order to make them suitable as food containers. In recent years, however, great improvements in the manufacture of tin cans have been made. Some mills roll strips for tin plate at a speed of 70 miles per hour. Today, over twenty-one billion tin cans are used to contain packed food.

2

Coal is a vital ingredient in the manufacture of steel. Over 60 percent of the 100 million tons of coal used in making steel is converted into coke. The loss of iron and steel through rusting is a great waste each year. For every ton of iron ore dumped into a blast furnace, a ton of coke must be added. The coke, burning with intense heat, melts the iron. In addition, the coke supplies the carbon which, next to the iron, is the most important element in steel.

3

The family pleasure boat of today will be vastly improved in the future. It will be built of plastic that is stronger than steel and will not corrode. Motive power will be provided by gas turbine or turbojet engines capable of operating at 100 miles per hour, or even by sun-powered engines that will convert sunlight into electricity to run a motor. People managing boats should have automobile drivers' licenses. Once under way, the boat will lift out of the water and travel on metal vanes, or hydrofoils, that will increase the speed of the craft up to 50 percent.

4

For a number of years, scientists and engineers have been making a strange kind of music in their laboratories. The sounds they work with are no dulcet tones. Some are a thousand times more intense than a clap of thunder, yet they are inaudible to the human ear. These sound waves are capable of performing an amazing amount of useful work, from washing dishes to drilling square holes in steel. They can locate submarines and schools of fish under water. They can improve the combustion of oil in a burner, and they can also help to find it deep in the earth.[1]

COHERENCE IN PARAGRAPHS

In addition to sticking to the point, the sentences in a paragraph should flow smoothly and naturally from one to the next. When they do, the paragraph is said to have *coherence.* The ideas in a coherent paragraph have a clear and logical relation to each other.

In many paragraphs, coherence can be achieved by simply putting the details or examples or incidents in the paragraph in a logical order. A paragraph about baking a cake will tell how to mix the batter before it says anything about putting the cake pan in the oven. Sometimes, however, you will need to give the reader a clue to the way in which one sentence is related to another or to the topic sentence.

Within paragraphs in this part of the chapter, you will study first the ordering of details and then some of the ways of helping the reader follow your train of thought.

[1] From "Sound Waves at Work" in *The Lamp,* Standard Oil Company (New Jersey).

Organizing Details

The natural way of telling a story is to give the events in the order they happened. This way of organizing information is called *chronological*—the order of time. Chronological order is useful in other kinds of writing as well as narratives. For example, a paragraph explaining how to make a box kite or how to thread a sewing machine can best be managed by simply taking each step in order. The example below uses chronological order to explain a process.

A simple electromagnet can be made by wrapping insulated wire around a spool, then sticking a long spike or bolt up through the hole. When the ends of the wire are attached to the poles of a battery and a current is sent through the coils around the spool, the spike inside the spool is made magnetic. It loses its magnetism, however, as soon as the current is stopped.

Just as it is natural to take up events in the order they happen, it is natural to describe objects by their position in relation to each other. In the following example, the various details are organized *spatially*, or by position.

A typical theater of ancient Greece resembled a huge bowl partly imbedded in a hillside. Seats were cut into the hillside in tiers and looked much like the seats in a modern football stadium. In the center of the bowl there was a circular playing space for the chorus and the actors. Behind this space was a building that the actors used as a dressing room. The wall of this building that was closest to the playing area served as a backdrop for the playing area. In the later days of the Greek theater, side wings were added to this backdrop and were equipped with doors through which the actors could make entrances and exits.

A paragraph that deals with ideas that do not involve time or position requires a different kind of order. In such a paragraph, the details or examples may be organized in order of their importance. The order may be from least to most important or the other way around. Either method, if followed consistently, should result in understandable arrangement.

> Student self-government has many benefits for young people. Students are less likely to resent rules they have made themselves than rules handed down to them by adults. Penalties devised by students are likely to fit the crime, and students generally accept such punishments as fair and deserved. Student opinion will favor obeying regulations that the students themselves have made. But most important of all, the experience that students gain in making and enforcing their own rules will help them to understand the need for laws among civilized peoples.

● **EXERCISE 7.** Each of the following topics can be treated in a single paragraph. Number your paper 1–8 and indicate which kind of order—chronological order, spatial order, or order of importance—you would use in developing each topic.

1. The life cycle of an insect
2. The advantages of learning to dance
3. The arrangement of a room in your house

4. How a basketball court is laid out
5. The best method of artificial respiration
6. Your reasons for belonging to the Boy Scouts, the Girl Scouts, or some other organization
7. The duties of a cheerleader
8. The preparation of a favorite dish

● EXERCISE 8.   Choose one of the topics from Exercise 7 that you think should be developed chronologically and write a paragraph using this kind of order.

● EXERCISE 9.   Choose one of the topics in Exercise 7 that you think should be developed by order of importance and write the paragraph.

Connecting Sentences Within Paragraphs

In a good paragraph the thought flows easily from one sentence to the next. Putting your ideas in an understandable order will help the reader to follow your thinking, but you can help him still more by giving some thought to the relation between your sentences. If you are developing your paragraph in chronological order, you can make the order of events readily understandable to the reader by using such expressions as *first, meanwhile, later, afterward, finally,* etc. Paragraphs organized spatially are likely to need expressions like *next to, in front of, beside, between,* and *behind.* Words like these, which help to make the organization of the paragraph clear to the reader are called *transitional devices.*

Still other transitional devices express the relationship between ideas. Some of these, like *and, but,* and *or,* are used mainly within sentences; others are used to link the idea of one sentence with the one that precedes or follows. Some examples are *however, furthermore, as a result, in fact, yet,* and *therefore.*

The transitional devices in the following paragraph are printed with underscores. Notice how they help the reader grasp the relation of the supporting sentences to each other and to the topic sentence.

More people are visiting our national parks now than ever before. In fact, there are more visitors than the parks are prepared to handle. Our park system is equipped to receive 25 million visitors a year. However, more than 50 million visitors now pass through annually. And even this vast number falls far short of the enormous total of 80 million people expected to visit our parks annually in the late sixties. Despite insufficient funds for establishing new campsites and shelters, the National Park Service is making every possible effort to provide for the comfort and safety of its guests. However, the Park Service needs more support from both the public and the government if it is to succeed in making our great natural playgrounds available to all who wish to enjoy them.

— topic sentence

transitional devices

— concluding sentence

● EXERCISE 10. Transitional elements have been omitted in the following paragraph. For each blank, choose an appropriate transitional expression from the list below and write it beside the proper number on your paper. You may use some of the transitional expressions more than once if you need to. You will not need all of them.

actually	then
after a short while	nevertheless
after that	therefore
first	meanwhile

The old-time beekeeper had a clever way of locating a cluster of wild bees. Equipped with a small wooden box that had a sliding cover, he would go to a meadow. __1__, he would find a bee in a flower and capture it in his box. __2__, he would pull back the cover and release the bee. __3__, since he knew that the pollen-laden insect would make a "beeline" to the tree where the wild bees were clustered, he would carefully note the direction of the flight. He would __4__ move to the other side of the meadow, capture another bee, release it, and note the direction in which it flew. He knew that both bees had headed home by the most direct route. __5__, he knew that the cluster of bees must be located at the point where his imaginary lines crossed. __6__, it was easy to capture the swarm in a large net and move it to his own orchard. __7__, the beekeeper was performing a simple application of mathematics.

● REVIEW EXERCISE. Choose one of the topics below, decide what you would like to write about it, make up a topic sentence, and then develop it in an interesting paragraph. Underline the topic sentence and any transitional expressions you use.

1. A favorite program (radio, TV, disc jockey, singer, band, etc.)
2. Someone I admire
3. A great performance (athletic, stage, movie, etc.)
4. How seventh grade is different from sixth
5. A needed reform
6. An experience with bad weather
7. My vacation home
8. An unusual relative
9. How to stay healthy
10. Baby-sitting techniques
11. Today's fads in dress
12. Why girls (boys) annoy me
13. A shop project (crafts, art, etc.)
14. A disaster
15. Rules in my home
16. Imaginary companions
17. Why my marks aren't better
18. Foods I can't eat (don't like)
19. Another school I attended
20. Why I believe (or do not believe) in luck

CHAPTER 19

The Whole Composition

Planning and Organizing a Longer Piece of Writing

Much of what you learned about paragraphs in Chapter 18 applies to the composition as a whole. The paragraph consists of sentences closely related in meaning; the composition is made up of related paragraphs. Like the paragraph, the composition focuses on a single idea, which is often stated near the beginning.

Because compositions consist of a number of paragraphs, it stands to reason that the topic must be bigger or more fully treated than that of a paragraph. Usually the composition deals with an idea that has several parts, each of which can be discussed in a separate paragraph. For example, a composition comparing winter sports with summer sports may have two paragraphs, one dealing with each kind. Similarly, a composition on carelessness as a cause of accidents may have one paragraph on accidents in the home, another on accidents on the highway, another on boating accidents, and so on. Often the composition has a short introductory paragraph stating the topic. It may also have a short concluding paragraph that sums up what has been said in the same way as the concluding sentence does for the content of a paragraph.

CHOOSING A TOPIC

Although the topic of a composition will usually be broader than that of a paragraph, it should not be too broad. A composition of the kind you will be writing this year is still a short piece of writing. Avoid choosing a topic so large that you would have to write a book to do it justice.

19a. Choose a subject that you know something about.

Knowing your subject is the first principle of good writing. It is easy to make general statements like, "Life as we know it cannot exist on the planet Mars." You have to know something about the subject to provide the supporting details. General statements are useful to introduce or sum up a number of specific statements, but the specific statements, the details, have to be there. It is the details that really inform your reader, and knowing details means knowing your subject.

(1) You may choose a topic from your own experience.

The subjects you know best are to be found in your everyday life—in your interests and hobbies, your experience with friends and family, your memories of places you have seen and things you have done. Perhaps you can build and fly model airplanes or design a dress or make hand puppets. Perhaps you know how to throw a boomerang, ride a surfboard, or apply theatrical makeup. Whatever your interests happen to be, they are bound to provide you with material you can handle successfully in compositions.

(2) You may choose a topic from other sources.

Naturally there are many things that you come to know about at second hand. Possibly you have become interested in space travel, the War Between the States, or a famous person from history through a chance reading of a magazine article. If so, you may have followed up your original interest by reading other articles and books or watching television programs on your subject. Information that you collect in this way becomes part of your experience, too.

● EXERCISE 1.   The following topics are intended to suggest things that you might write about. Some of them you may know about from personal experience; others you may have read about. Choose one topic of each kind and write only the title that you would use for a composition on this subject. Indicate after each title whether you know about the topic mainly from personal experience or from other sources. You may substitute similar topics of your own if none of these suggestions fits your interests. Consider your choice carefully, for you will later be asked to write a composition on one of them.

1. How a cat teaches her kittens to keep clean
2. Breaking a bad habit

19a

3. Careers in aviation (or science or teaching or the theater)
4. The work of the Peace Corps
5. Your reasons for admiring a famous person
6. How to make a model plane
7. The importance of first impressions
8. Making friends in a new school (or a new neighborhood)
9. Shopping at a general store (or a supermarket)
10. An invention that changed history

19b. Limit the topic.

Once you have found a subject to write about, you must decide whether it is too big to handle in the time and space you have to work with. Big subjects are *not* easier to write about than smaller ones. The bigger the subject, the more detailed knowledge you will have to include in your composition. A composition on "The War Between the States" would have to be book length to cover the subject; on the other hand, one on the importance of the Battle of Gettysburg could be managed in a reasonable amount of space.

● EXERCISE 2.   Each of the following topics is too broad to be covered in a short composition. Choose five and find for each a more limited topic. Write the narrower topic beside the proper number on your paper.

EXAMPLE   1. Careers in aviation
           1. *The duties of a stewardess*

1. Pets
2. Earning money during vacation
3. Clothes

4. Sports
5. Automobiles
6. Fashions
7. Courtesy
8. Conservation
9. Science
10. Television programs

19c. Determine the purpose of your composition.

In limiting your topic, you must consider the purpose of your composition. Taking a particular attitude toward your subject will help you define that purpose. The topic "Television" is too big. However, the narrower topic "My favorite television program" does indicate a purpose—to explain why a particular program is your favorite. If your purpose were to show how much can be learned from certain programs, your topic might be "The educational benefits of television." Another topic, "The dangers of watching too much television," indicates a third purpose and still another way of limiting your topic.

● EXERCISE 3.   Choose three of the topics you wrote for Exercise 2. State what your purpose would be if you were to write a composition on each of these topics. You may revise your topics if you wish.

EXAMPLE	*Original topic*	*Sports*
	Narrowed topic	*How to be a good outfielder*
	Purpose	*To explain what skills an outfielder needs and show how to develop these skills.*

19
b-c

● EXERCISE 4. Write a composition of about two hundred words on one of the two topics you chose for Exercise 1. At the top of your paper, state the purpose of your composition. Be sure that all the details support this purpose.

PLANNING THE COMPOSITION

19d. Plan your composition before writing.

A clear, well-organized composition always has a plan behind it. The best kind of plan is an outline, like the one on page 367, which gives the main and supporting ideas in the order you will write about them. Before you reach the stage of making an outline, however, you must think of ideas and details to put in your composition.

(1) List your ideas.

After you have chosen a topic, make a list of the ideas that seem to fit within the topic. Do not worry at this point about organizing your ideas. Jot them down as they come to you.

Title of Composition: Training a Dog
Purpose: To show how a dog may be trained to respond to simple commands

what obedience training is	repetition of command
need for firmness	some obedience commands—sit, lie down, heel
need of praise	
a dog's desire to please	a dog's intelligence
using the words of command	give one command at a time

(2) Group your ideas under headings.

Now you are ready to decide what the larger divisions of your composition will be. Find the ideas that belong together and group them under a common heading. Sometimes this heading will be one of the ideas you have already jotted down. At other times you will have to supply the heading. For example, in the list for "Training a Dog," two ideas, *a dog's desire to please* and *a dog's intelligence*, seem to belong together. What larger idea do they share in common? Since both intelligence and the desire to please are qualities that make a dog easy to train, these ideas can be grouped under *qualities needed for training*. Similarly *what obedience training is* and *some obedience commands—sit, lie down, heel—*can be grouped under a larger idea, *obedience training*.

The complete list of notes can be grouped as follows:

Qualities needed for training	heading
desire to please	related
intelligence	ideas
Obedience training	heading
what obedience training is	
obedience commands—sit, lie	related
down, heel	ideas
Some rules for training	heading
praise as an incentive	
firmness	
repetition of command	related
one command at a time	ideas
using words of command	

19d

● EXERCISE 5.   The ideas for each of the following topics should be grouped under two major headings. First write the topic as a title. Then write the two headings and the ideas that belong under each of them. In topics 1, 2, and 3 the major headings are included in the list of ideas. You supply the headings for topics 4 and 5.

EXAMPLE   1. How to build a signal fire: choose location; pick dry wood for start; look for high ground; find clear space; choose green wood to make smoke; build fire to make visible sign.

1. *How to Build a Signal Fire*
   I. *Choose location*
      look for high ground
      find clear space
   II. *Build fire to make visible signal*
      pick dry wood for start
      choose green wood to make smoke

1. Autumn activities: Halloween party; sports; school dance; football; social activities; hiking
2. How to fry an egg: procedure; pan; pancake turner; grease; equipment and materials; egg; heat grease in pan; add egg and cook
3. How to find a book: card catalogue; sources of information; asking librarian; biography shelved by subject's name; system of placing books on shelves; fiction by author's name
4. Our drama club: getting members; casting a play; electing officers; rehearsing; performing the play; writing the club constitution; choosing a play
5. Description of my cat: lying by fire; pouncing; playing; sleeping; running smoothly

(3) Arrange your ideas.

The final step in planning a composition is to arrange your ideas in the order they will appear in your composition.

Outlining

19e. Make an outline for a composition.

An outline is a guide to your subject which not only shows your ideas in their correct order but also indicates their relative importance. Here is the form of a typical outline:

I. First main idea
  A. Supporting idea
  B. Supporting idea
II. Second main idea
  A. Supporting idea
  B. Supporting idea
  C. Supporting idea
    1. Supporting detail
    2. Detail
    3. Detail
III. Third main idea
  A. Supporting idea
  B. Supporting idea

Notice that Roman numerals precede the main headings, followed by capital letters and Arabic numerals for subtopics. Notice that each level of the outline is indented.

Notice too that there are at least two subtopics for each major heading. Subtopics are divisions of a more important topic. It is impossible to divide a piece of

19e

land, a cake, or a topic into less than two parts. A correct outline will not show

    I. Main idea
       A. Supporting idea [There should be at least
          two supporting ideas here.]
    II. Main idea

The order in which you arrange the ideas in your outline will depend on your subject. Sometimes you will arrange them in chronological order or in order of importance. Often the ideas themselves will suggest the proper order. For example, these ideas obviously should follow the order of time: *the beginning of our trip, incidents during our trip, the end of our trip.*

How can the main ideas for the composition "Training a Dog" be arranged? One idea, *Obedience training*, is clearly more specific than the others, since it involves specific commands. Furthermore, *Qualities needed for training* is the most general idea and should probably be discussed first. Thus the main ideas would be arranged in the order of general to specific:

    I. Qualities needed for training
    II. Some rules for training
    III. Obedience training

Now the supporting ideas should be arranged with some indication of their relative importance. Notice, for example, that the specific commands, *heel, sit, lie down,* are really developments of the idea, *Obedience commands* and should be treated as details under this idea.

Notice in the sample outline on page 367 that a fourth main idea has been added to provide a conclusion to the composition. The role of a conclusion will be discussed later in this chapter.

TRAINING A DOG

I. Qualities needed for training
   A. Intelligence
   B. Desire to please
II. Some rules for training
   A. Importance of firmness
   B. Teaching one command at a time
      1. Repetition of command
      2. Using words of command
   C. Praise as an incentive
III. Obedience training
   A. Definition
   B. Obedience commands
      1. Heel
      2. Sit
      3. Lie down
IV. The qualities of a good master

● EXERCISE 6.   Copy the incomplete outline at the left. Fill the blanks with the items at the right.

POLISHING SHOES

I. Materials
   A.
   B.
   C.
   D. Brushes
      1.
      2.
II.
   A. Removing loose dirt
   B.
   C.
   D. Using polishing brush

Small brush
Wax polish
Procedure
Polishing cloth
Applying polish evenly
Rag
Polishing with cloth
Polishing brush

● EXERCISE 7.   Arrange the following ideas and details into an outline. Your outline, like the one on page 367, should have three levels.

GIVING A PARTY

Main Ideas:

> Cleaning up after the party
> Preparing for the party
> Entertaining at the party

Supporting ideas and details:

> Making a guest list
> Washing dishes
> Suggesting party games
> Cleaning the room
> Inviting guests
> Preparing refreshments
> Serving refreshments
> Making decorations
> Sandwiches
> Greeting guests
> Ice cream
> Cake
> Making everyone feel at home
> Soft drinks

● EXERCISE 8.   Prepare an outline on a subject of your own choice. If you wish, use one of the topics suggested in Exercise 1, page 359. Later you will use this outline to write a composition. Be sure your outline has the following:

a. a title
b. a statement of purpose
c. at least two main headings
d. supporting ideas for each main heading

The Parts of a Composition

19f. Be sure that your composition has an introduction, a body, and a conclusion.

In Chapter 17 you learned the importance of a beginning, a middle, and an ending in narratives. Similarly, other kinds of compositions need an introduction (beginning), a main discussion, or body (middle), and a conclusion (ending).

The *introduction* should state the purpose of the composition. A good way to indicate purpose is with a statement of fact. Notice that the sample composition on pages 370–71 begins, "A dog has two qualities that make him one of the easiest animals to train." This statement of fact not only leads to a discussion of these qualities but also indicates the purpose of the composition—to tell how to train a dog.

The *body* is the longest part of a composition. It contains most of the information and must fulfill the purpose you have set out to accomplish. In the sample composition below, the body consists of the second, third, and fourth paragraphs, corresponding to parts II and III of the sample outline.

The *conclusion* should sum up the main points of the composition. It need not be long or complicated. Notice that the conclusion of the sample composition, while discussing the qualities of a good master, also restates two of the basic rules for training a dog.

The composition that follows was developed from the outline on page 367. The outline topics appear in the right margin in shortened form to show the relationship of outline and finished composition.

19f

Training a Dog

A dog has two qualities that make him one of the easiest animals to train. His intelligence helps him to learn quickly and to understand what you want. His desire to please makes him eager to learn and obey.

introduction

qualities for training—I, A–B

Before learning about specific commands, you should know some general rules about training a dog. First, always be firm. Being firm does not mean being harsh or cruel to your dog. It means making sure your dog understands very clearly that he must obey you even if he is playful or not paying attention. Next, teach only one command at a time. Always use the same words of command, and repeat the lesson every day until your dog has learned it. Finally, praise your dog when he has done well. Praise is one of the greatest rewards you can give a dog, and it will help him to learn.

body

importance of firmness—II, A

one command at a time—II, B

praise as incentive—II, C

The basic kind of training to give a dog is obedience training, which teaches certain simple commands. A dog that has learned obedience com-

obedience training defined—III, A

mands, like "heel," "sit," or "lie down" has formed the habit of obedience and other commands will come easily to him. One of the basic commands is "heel," because it controls a dog when he is moving. To teach your dog this command, jerk his leash and give the word of command whenever he moves ahead or steps behind you. Praise him when he moves to the correct position. In time he will obey even when he is not on a leash. Another command, "sit," is taught by jerking the leash and pushing the dog's haunches as you give the word of command.

To teach a third important command, "lie down," put your dog in a sitting position, and pull the leash almost tight. Then bring your free hand down on the leash, gently forcing the dog into the desired position as you say the command.

In training a dog, the master's qualities are as important as the dog's. A dog learns best from a patient, kind master, who is firm in giving commands and ready to reward his dog with praise.

obedience commands—III, B

1. "heel"

2. "sit"

3. "lie down"

conclusion

qualities of a good master—IV

19g. Revise your composition.

There are at least five things you should do before you hand your composition in. Try to follow the same procedure for each composition. Good habits of revising will be useful whenever you have writing to do.

1. Strike out words or phrases—even whole sentences—that may confuse a reader who does not know your subject as well as you do. Don't be afraid to cut.

2. Look hard at each adjective and adverb. If it isn't really needed, take it out.

3. Cut unnecessary words from the beginning of your sentences. Some students fall into the bad habit of beginning many sentences with words like *well* and *oh*. Such a beginning may be acceptable in conversation, but it is awkward in written work.

4. Check all the punctuation by reading the composition aloud. Remember that full pauses are likely to require periods.

5. Check the spelling of all words.

At first, planning and writing a good composition may take more time than you have previously spent on writing. But as following the steps given in this chapter grows into a habit, you will find that you have become a much better writer and writing a composition has become easier.

● EXERCISE 9. Write a composition based on the outline you made for Exercise 8. Perhaps you have had second thoughts about the ideas for the composition. If so, revise your outline. Your teacher may want you to hand it in with your composition. Be sure to revise your composition carefully before you hand it in.

Summary

1. Choose a subject you know, either from personal experience or reading.
2. Limit your topic, and decide the purpose of your composition.
3. Jot down ideas.
4. Organize these ideas in an outline.
5. Revise carefully.

19g

CHAPTER 20

Writing Explanations and Reports

Steps in Organizing Information

Writing explanations, reports, and book reports involves some of the same problems as writing other compositions. You must carefully choose words that will exactly convey your meaning. You must select and organize details. You must be sure that every sentence and paragraph is perfectly clear. In addition, there are some special problems. In writing an explanation, you must often divide a process into a series of steps. To write a report, you must gather information and then put the information in your own words. In a book report, you must give an accurate idea of the book's content and present solid reasons for your opinion of the book.

EXPLANATIONS

Usually, to answer the question *Who? What? When?* or *Where?* you need little time and only a few words. But to answer the question *How?* you need to explain a relationship or process. This kind of explanation requires time and thought.

20a. Write explanations which are complete, clear, and accurate.

Before you can explain something, you must be sure that you understand it yourself.

If you are going to explain how to make or do something, think of the important steps and present them in the order they must be performed. Make the order clear by using transitional words like *first*, *next*, *then*, and *finally*. Give each step simply, clearly, and briefly without leaving any gaps or omitting essential information. If you use technical terms or unfamiliar words, make their meaning clear to the reader. Be sure to mention all necessary equipment and materials.

EXAMPLE   HOW TO BUILD A CAMPFIRE

First, collect three kinds of fuel: tinder to start the fire, kindling (small pieces of wood), and larger wood. Various items will serve as tinder—shredded bark, wood shavings, clumps of dry grass, newspapers, or anything else that catches fire easily. In addition to fuel, get three wet or green logs.

Next, put two of the logs at an angle to each other with the open side facing the wind. Between the angle of the logs place the tinder, the kindling, and finally the larger wood. Set fire to the tinder. When the larger wood has caught fire, place the cooking pan on the logs where they meet. After the fire has burned a while, cover the open side of the fire with the third log.

20a

● **EXERCISE 1.** Write an explanation of something you can do well. Present the steps in the order in which they must be performed. Be sure that your explanation is clear, complete, and accurate.

Here are some suggestions:

1. How to polish a car
2. How to bake your favorite cake
3. How to make decorations for a party
4. How to ride a surfboard
5. How to make a box kite
6. How to make a bed
7. How to hem a dress
8. How to prepare an exhibit for a science fair
9. How to fix a frayed electric cord
10. How to take flash pictures with a camera

20b. Give examples and comparisons to help convey what you mean.

When you are explaining something that is unfamiliar, complicated, or technical, help your reader to understand the explanation by giving a simple example or a comparison with something familiar. Notice in the following paragraph how a comparison makes a basic principle of health easy to understand.

> Your body is like a bank in which you deposit good food, good exercise, recreation, rest and sleep, good thinking, and good work. If these deposits are regular, you will be able to withdraw more than enough energy for work and play. You will be able to get more than enough material for good growth.[1]

[1] From *You and Your Resources* by Paul F. Brandwein, et al. Reprinted by permission of Harcourt, Brace & World, Inc.

In the following paragraphs, a simple example is used to explain a complicated term.

> Labor ... could not contribute much to our production without tools. These tools ... are parts of what economists call *capital.* ...
>
> If you have ever read the novel *Robinson Crusoe*, you will remember that when Crusoe was shipwrecked he had a whole island of land to supply his raw materials. He had his own labor to apply to the raw materials of the land. But he would not have been able to create a comfortable life for himself if he had not also had a chest of tools that he was able to salvage from the wreck of his ship. Those tools were his capital.[1]

● EXERCISE 2.   Match the subjects in the first column with the examples or comparisons in the second column which you think would help to explain the subjects.

1. Man's nervous system
2. Your city council
3. The force of gravity
4. Fractions
5. The development of a living organism

a. A magnet
b. Telephone lines and a central switchboard
c. A tadpole becoming a frog
d. Your club passing or defeating a motion
e. Slices of a pie

A picture, the Chinese say, is worth a thousand words. Using an illustration, a map, a chart, or a diagram will often help your reader to understand your explanation.

[1] From *Our American Economy* by Richard W. Lindholm and Paul Driscoll, New York: Harcourt, Brace & World, Inc., 1959.

20h

20c. Use illustrations, maps, charts, or diagrams that might help the reader better understand what is being explained.

Review the sample explanation on page 375. Although a person following these directions can easily build a campfire, the explanation can be made still clearer by including the following illustration:

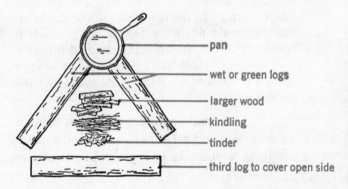

- EXERCISE 3. From the following list of subjects for explanations, choose five for which you could use illustrative material—illustrations, maps, charts, diagrams, and graphs. List these five subjects on your paper, along with a sentence or two indicating what illustrative material might be used.

EXAMPLE 1. *How to set a table. To help explain how to set a table, I would use a diagram showing the position of the plate, cup, glass, and silverware for one place setting.*

1. How to paddle a canoe
2. How to develop a roll of film
3. How to find Yellowstone Park

4. How a particular football play is executed
5. How to set up a tent
6. How to thread a sewing machine
7. How to apply makeup
8. How to make a model plane
9. How the earth rotates on its axis
10. How to find your way by the stars

REPORTS

As you go on in school, you will be asked to write more and more reports in English, social studies, and science. The purpose of such reports is to develop your ability to gather facts, organize them, and write about them in your own words. Writing a report is not difficult if you go about it in a logical way and follow a few simple rules.

20d. Be sure you understand the assignment.

Obviously you cannot write a good report unless you fully understand the assignment. Listen carefully to your teacher and ask questions if you need to. Be sure you know how long your report is supposed to be and what kind of material it is to cover.

For example, if you have been told to write a report on "The Wild Flowers of Death Valley," you might describe the tall white gravel ghost, the low, egg-shaped turtle bush, the purple and yellow lupines, the sage and juniper, and the waving fields of yellow mustard. It would be a mistake to describe the burros and horned toads. You would also be wandering from your topic if you told about the huge twenty-mule

20
c-d

teams and the old stagecoaches. You would not be following instructions if you described the rugged salt flats and towering snowy peaks, fascinating as these are.

20e. Gather all the necessary information for the report.

Usually the best place to begin gathering information is the reference section of the library. An encyclopedia or other general reference work will give a good introduction to the subject and furnish many facts. Often you will find further information in a specialized reference work. (See pages 455–62 for instructions on using reference works.)

Suppose you want to write a report on Ernest Thompson Seton, who did so much to start the Boy Scouts of America. You will find a biographical sketch of him in the *World Book Encyclopedia*, in the volume marked *S*. Or, you are asked to write something about the material cork. In the same encyclopedia, in volume *C*, you will find an article on cork. If you want to write on a scientific topic such as helicopters or refrigeration, you will probably find articles on these topics by looking in a large encyclopedia or in the table of contents or index of a one-volume encyclopedia, such as the *Lincoln Library of Essential Information*.

More specialized reference works are also available. Suppose you want to get information—for a report, or for your own use—on how to play chess or anagrams or charades. You would find it in such a book as *The Complete Book of Games* by Clement Wood and Gloria Goddard.

Your teacher or school librarian will help you find the special reference book you need.

◆ NOTE   You may also wish to use other books than reference books. Such books may be found by consulting the card catalogue in the library. See pages 451–54 for instructions in using the card catalogue.

● EXERCISE 4.   Choose a topic for a report which you will later write. Review the material in the previous chapter on limiting your topic. (See pages 360–61.) Be sure your topic is not too large to cover in one report.

Find information on your topic in at least three different reference works or other books. On a sheet of paper write the name of your topic. Number 1–3. After each number give the title and author (if given) of your reference work or book, the volume number (if necessary), and the number of the page on which you found your information.

If you have difficulty in thinking of a topic, here are ten suggestions. Some of these topics are too broad to cover in a short report and have to be limited to a more specific topic.

1. The Navaho Indian
2. History of some state flowers, state birds, or state songs
3. Stamp collecting
4. An outstanding athlete
5. The history of the Boy (Girl) Scouts
6. Contributions of minority groups
7. A colorful event in the history of your state
8. Nuclear submarines
9. The history of Braille
10. The Olympic games

20e

Taking Notes

After locating sources of information about your topic, your next step is to select facts for your report, that is, to take notes. Carefully write down each item of information that you think should be in your paper. Be careful to get your facts straight and to note the source.

When taking notes, do not copy the exact words of an encyclopedia or any other book without using quotation marks. In general, do not use quotations unless they are particularly apt or striking. A good report is written in the writer's own words, not in the words of his sources. Taking notes in your own words will help you avoid the bad habit of copying. A teacher can easily tell the difference between your writing and a passage from a book. Be ready to hand in a list of your sources with your report, if your teacher requests it.

Suppose you have chosen to write a report on the importance of salt. On page 272 of the *Modern Wonder Book of Knowledge* you would find information about the necessity of salt to human and animal life and the importance of salt to industry. You would want to take separate notes about each of these facts. Your first note might be:

1. Salt is necessary to human life. There is not enough salt in the food we get; we therefore have to add salt in cooking. We also add salt to make food taste better.

Then you would take notes about some of the other facts you might use in your report. In volume *S* of the *World Book Encyclopedia* you would find other useful facts about the importance of salt which you would record in your notes. Your final notes for the report might look like this:

From the *Modern Wonder Book of Knowledge*, p. 272:

1. Salt is necessary to human life. There is not enough salt in food we get; we therefore have to add salt in cooking. We also add salt to make food taste better.
2. Many animals also need salt. Wild animals get it at salt licks. Farmers provide rock salt for domestic animals.
3. Salt preserves food.
4. Salt is used in many industrial processes.
5. "In fact, next to water, salt is the most used substance on earth."
6. This country uses about 110 pounds of salt every year for each person in it.

From *World Book Encyclopedia*, volume *S*, p. 6340:

1. Salt is used to season food.
2. Salt is used to preserve meat and fish—salt pork, herring, fish fillets, etc.
3. Salt is used to make chemicals for industry—hydrochloric acid, soda ash, sodium carbonate, caustic soda.
4. Salt is used to harden soap.
5. Salt is used in making pottery glaze.
6. Salt is used to improve clearness of glass.
7. Salt is used as a medicine—as a throat gargle and as an emetic for someone who has swallowed something poisonous.
8. Salt is soothing and restful in bath water.
9. Salt is so highly valued that in some places it has been used as money. (In Central Africa salt is packed in reed hampers worth about sixty cents

each. A man could formerly buy a wife with ten hampers, but now he needs about thirty!)

10. A large part of the caravan trade across the Sahara is in salt.

11. The importance of salt to man is shown in history. Roman soldiers were paid in salt. Our word *salary* comes from the Latin word for salt. To say that a man is "worth his salt" or that he is the "salt of the earth" is to praise him.

● EXERCISE 5.   Refer back to the three sources which you used in Exercise 4. From each source, write at least three notes about your topic. Make sure that each of your notes is accurate, that it is in your own words, and that it is directly related to your topic. These notes are the second stage of the report that you will later write.

Organizing Your Notes

20f. Organize your information.

Now that you have gathered the information for your report in the form of notes, you must prepare them for use.

Read your notes. You will discover that some information is duplicated. You may also find that some statements do not fit into the topic as you have limited it. Your job now is to organize the information that you will use.

Ask yourself: What are the most important ideas in these notes that I have gathered? Write a list of these main ideas.

Here is a list of ideas based on the notes on salt.

1. Salt is used in manufacturing.
2. Salt is used as medicine.
3. Salt is needed by both man and animals in order to live.
4. Salt is used by man more than any other substance except water.
5. The value of salt is recognized in history by its use as money and as a mark of honor.

Are these ideas listed in the order that you will use them? Which idea should come first in your report? Which last? Where do the other ideas belong?

When you have arranged these ideas in a sensible, logical order, you will have a rough outline for your report. (Review pages 365–67.) Here is a rough outline for the report on salt.

SALT
   I. Used by man more than any other substance except water
  II. Needed by both man and animals
 III. Used as medicine
  IV. Used in manufacturing
   V. Recognized as valuable through the ages

● EXERCISE 6.   Choose the main ideas from the notes which you have taken for Exercise 5. Organize them into a rough outline like the one above. This rough outline is the third stage of your report.

After you have made your rough outline of main ideas, your next step is to organize the other details under your main ideas. Here is a complete outline for the report on salt.

SALT

I. Widely used by man
   A. About 110 pounds used in our country every year for each person
   B. An important item in caravan trade across the Sahara
   C. Next to water, the most widely used substance on earth

II. Needed by both man and animals
   A. Needed in man's diet
   B. Used to season food
   C. Needed by wild animals
   D. Rock salt provided for farm animals

III. Used as medicine
   A. Mixed with water and used as a throat gargle
   B. Given to persons who have swallowed poison
   C. Soothing and restful in bath water

IV. Used in manufacturing
   A. Used in making chemicals for industry
   B. Used to harden soap
   C. Used to make a glaze on pottery
   D. Used to improve the clearness of glass

V. Recognized as valuable through the ages
   A. Used as pay for Roman soldiers
   B. Used in such proverbs as "salt of the earth," and "worth his salt"
   C. Thirty hampers of salt the price of a wife in Central Africa

● EXERCISE 7. Using the main ideas which you have written for Exercise 6 and the notes which you have written for Exercise 5, prepare a complete outline for your own report. (To review outlining, see pages 365–67.)

Writing the Report

By now you have chosen or been assigned a topic for your report, gathered information and made notes on your topic, and organized your notes in the form of an outline. What remains is to write the report and then to revise it.

20g. Use your own words in writing the report.

A report copied word for word from books shows you can find information but nothing more. A report in your words shows you can use the information.

It is tempting to copy a passage from a book. You may feel that the passage does a better job of organizing and conveying the information than you do. But copying is not writing. Putting the information in your own words means that you have learned it and organized it, and perhaps even added to it, yourself. You can increase your skill in writing reports only by seeking to understand the information and striving to find the best words possible to communicate it.

● EXERCISE 8.   Using your outline and your notes, write a first draft of your report. Be sure the report is in your own words.

20h. Check and revise your report.

All writing assignments may contain errors, some minor and some serious. Since a report may contain errors of fact as well as writing errors, you should be especially careful in checking and revising it. A useful way of writing your report is to write a first

20
g-h

draft, and then to check it for accuracy and improve the writing. Your last step is to write the final copy of the report.

After you have written the first draft, you are ready to improve it.

First, read it over for *content:*

(a) Does the report cover the subject adequately?

(b) Are all the facts accurate?

(c) Have you included a list of sources in your report?

Next, read it over for *construction* and *style:*

(a) Do the title and opening paragraph arouse the reader's interest?

(b) Is there a concluding paragraph?

(c) Is each paragraph well constructed, with a topic sentence and supporting details or examples?

(d) Are the facts in your report well organized?

(e) Are the sentences varied, and have you avoided fragments and run-on sentences?

Finally, check for matters of form:

(a) Does the paper have a heading—name, class, and date?

(b) Is there a title, and is it capitalized properly?

(c) Is there a one-inch margin at the left, a slightly narrower one at the right?

(d) Are the pages numbered? Is your name on each page?

Here is the final copy for the report on salt.

THE WORTH OF SALT

Although we would miss salt if it disappeared from the dinner table, few of us are aware of salt's true importance. Each person in the United States uses about 110 pounds of salt yearly. In the Sahara, a large part of the caravan trade is devoted to carrying and selling salt. According to one authority, next to water, salt is the most widely used substance on earth.

Like water, salt is not a luxury but a necessity. Man needs it in his diet in order to live. Since he does not get enough of it from food, he must add it to his meals. As a seasoning, salt improves the flavor of our food. Animals need salt as much as man does. Wild animals search for salt licks to get their salt, while farmers provide rock salt for domestic animals to lick.

Salt can also be used as a medicine. When it is mixed with water, it becomes a throat gargle. It can be given as an emetic to persons who have swallowed poison. When it is put in hot water, it makes a soothing, restful bath.

Much salt is used in manufacturing processes. For instance, it is used to harden soap, to make a glaze on pottery, and to improve the clearness of glass. Large quantities of salt are used in making chemicals for industry.

Through the ages man has recognized the value of salt. In the days of the Roman Empire, soldiers were paid their wages in salt. Common sayings like "salt of the earth" and "worth his salt" emphasize the importance of this mineral. In recent times, a man in Central Africa could buy a woman with salt. At first, a reed hamper of salt was worth about sixty cents, and a man needed only ten hampers to make his purchase. When inflation came, he needed thirty hampers!

Sources: *Modern Wonder Book of Knowledge,*
page 272.
World Book Encyclopedia, volume *S,*
page 6340.

● EXERCISE 9.   Prepare the final copy of your report. If your teacher wishes, hand in your outline and first draft with it.

WRITING BOOK REPORTS

Another special writing assignment that you will be called upon to do is the book report. A book report always gives two kinds of information: what the book is about and what you thought of the book.

20i. In giving an idea of the book's content, avoid getting bogged down in details.

Many students who write a summary of a book's content begin with the first incident of the book, go on to the next incident and then the next. They soon find that they have a long, tedious account which includes every single incident in the book. A report on a book should tell only the book's highlights. It should be carefully planned.

The kind of information you give in your summary will depend on the type of book. A report on a novel should indicate the background of the story—the time, the place, and the main characters. It should also give a general idea of what happens and mention some of the chief incidents. A report on a nonfiction book should indicate the importance of the subject, according to the author, and briefly describe several parts of the book. A report on a biography should indicate why the person written about is important enough to be the subject of a biography and mention several of the chief incidents in that person's life.

20j. Give specific reasons for liking or disliking a book.

Here are two statements of opinion about a book.

POOR   I liked this book because I am interested in the War Between the States.

BETTER   This book deals with the progress of the War Between the States—from the moment Fort Sumter was fired on to Lee's surrender at Appomattox. Besides making the reader feel that he is present at all the events, the author explains the causes of the War Between the States, and shows why particular battles were won and lost and why the South eventually lost the war. This book is both exciting and informative.

The student who wrote the first statement of opinion would certainly receive a poor grade. Saying that he likes books about the War Between the States does not indicate why *this* book about that war is a good book. The second student gives details to support his conclusion, that the book is both exciting and informative. Furthermore, he indicates not only why he personally liked the book, but why it may generally be considered a good book (inclusiveness, clear and vivid writing, explanation of causes).

In your book reports, give the specific reasons behind your opinion of the book. Try also to show why others might share your opinion—why, in other words, the book may be called good or poor. These are reasons which should go beyond, "I am interested in the subject of this book"; or, "This book bored me."

**20
i·j**

Some guides for book reports are these:

1. Be sure to give the title of the book and the name of the author.

2. When you refer to the title of the book, be sure to underline it.

3. Be careful in your use of tense. In writing the summary of the book, decide on present tense or past tense and stick to it. Do not shift from present to past or past to present.

4. Refer directly to the characters by name. Do not say "this boy" or "this girl."

● EXERCISE 10. Write a book report. Tell briefly what the book is about. Give solid reasons for your opinion of the book.

CHAPTER 21

Letter Writing

Everyone likes to get letters. One of the first things that people do when they return home after a short absence is to look for mail. Telegrams and telephones are handy in emergencies and on special occasions, but for really keeping in touch with far off friends and relatives there is nothing like a newsy letter.

How often you find a letter in your mailbox depends to a great extent on you. If you write frequent, interesting letters, you are likely to be satisfied with the mail you get in return. If, on the other hand, you are in the habit of waiting until you have more time or until something really exciting comes along to write about, the letters that come for you are likely to be few and far between. Exchanging letters is like carrying on a conversation: one person can't do it all by himself.

THE FRIENDLY LETTER

Have you ever felt, when you sat down to write a letter, that you didn't have much to say? Most of us feel this way at times; but it is rarely, if ever, true.

393

21a. In a friendly letter, write about things that interest you and the person to whom you are writing.

There are several helpful ways of deciding what to put in a letter. Think of the person to whom you are writing. *What would he (or she) like to hear about?* Suppose you're writing to your grandparents. Everyday happenings in the family will interest them. Has someone had a birthday? Taken a trip? Had the measles? Have you taken up a new hobby?

Another kind of material is supplied by the letter you are answering. If you were talking with a friend and he told you about an interesting experience or a piece of luck he had had, you would have something to say about it. If he writes you news about himself, you will want to comment on it in your reply. People often ask questions in their letters about what you are doing and plan to do. The answers to such questions are still another thing to go in your letters.

● EXERCISE 1. Read the letter on the following page and note the items of news that you would want to comment on if you were replying to this letter.

21b. Write friendly letters neatly on appropriate stationery.

You may use tinted paper, if you wish, but white paper of good quality is always suitable. Use a pen and write in blue or black ink. If you can use a typewriter well, it is all right to type a friendly letter.

59 Hobart Avenue
Summit, New Jersey 07901
January 25, 1965

Dear Tony,

    Thanks for the letter and the pictures of San Antonio. I envy you for having the Alamo practically in your backyard. That's a place I would really like to see.

    The big news from the old neighborhood is that we finally got Dad, Mr. Blake, and some of the other fathers to play football with us yesterday morning. There were eleven of us altogether – practically six-man football. Charlie Adams was the extra player. Every time one team got behind they put him on it. You should have seen him grab those passes! You know how small he is. He would sneak right past the safety man and be in the clear before they even noticed him.

    Toward the end of the game, the little kids came around and we let them play. Jimmy Nelson was one of them. I guess he's about eight. When we were all in the huddle he asked me which side I wanted to have win. "Why, our side," I told him. "Which side is that?" he asked me. With a team like that, how can you lose?

    We finally won 36 to 30. The other side gave up when Charlie had to go home for dinner.

    Write soon and let me know what you're doing.

Your friend,
Jack

Write neatly. A letter that is blotched with inky fingerprints, crossed-out words, spatterings, or erasures will make a bad impression on the reader.

Center a short note on the page. Keep equal margins on the sides and on the top and bottom of a long letter. If you are using folding stationery and the letter

21
a-b

is so long that more than two pages are required, use the page order of a book; write the second page on the back of the first, and so on. If you foresee that your letter will be only two pages long, leave the back of your first page blank and start a fresh sheet, or, if your stationery is folded, continue on page three.

21c. Follow generally accepted rules for the form of a friendly letter.

You have seen many letters, and you probably have a fairly clear idea of letter form. Actually, the form is not hard to master. Study the following instructions and example.

1. *Heading*

Write your address in two lines in the upper right-hand corner. Put a comma between the city and the state. Skip a few spaces after the state and write your ZIP code number. Do not use a comma between state and ZIP code number. Write the date on the third line, with a comma between the day of the month and the year. Do not use any punctuation at the ends of the lines in the heading.

2. *Salutation*

Write the salutation a short space below the heading, flush with the left-hand margin. In a friendly letter, the salutation usually begins with *Dear* ——. Put a comma after the salutation.

3. *Body*

Indent the first line of the body of the letter, and use the same indention for the first line of each paragraph that follows. Other lines should begin at the left-hand margin.

4. *Closing*

Begin the closing a little to the right of center. Capitalize the first word of the closing, and put a comma at the end. The closing of a friendly letter is usually *Sincerely, Your friend, With love,* or something similar.

5. *Signature*

Sign your first name beneath the closing, either centered (if your name is shorter than the closing) or lined up at the left with the closing. Do not put any punctuation after your name.

The letter shown on page 395 is in *block style*. That is, the second and third lines of the heading begin directly below the beginning of the first line. Another style that is often used for handwritten friendly letters is *indented style*, in which the heading looks like this:

> 1183 West Street
> Green Bay, Wisconsin 54301
> June 11, 1965

A heading in either block or indented style is appropriate for a friendly letter.

● **EXERCISE 2.** Think of a friend or relative who would like to get a letter from you. With that person's interests in mind, choose several incidents from your recent experience and write a short letter about them.

21c

1183 West Street
Green Bay, Wisconsin 54301
June 11, 1965

Dear Andy,

_____

_____

_____

_____

_____

_____

_____

_____

_____

Sincerely yours,
Walt

Model Form of a Friendly Letter

THE ENVELOPE

You should address the envelope for your letter with care. Quite often letters cannot be delivered because of faulty addressing. Lack of a return address may result in your letter's being lost if your correspondent has moved. Study the following instructions and example.

Place the address of the person to whom the letter is going just below the middle and to the left of the center of the envelope. Place your own name and address in the upper left-hand corner. No title is used before your name in the return address.

Notice that the ZIP code number is included in the address, and is written after the state. The state may be written on a separate line, as in the example, or on the same line as the city. Every word begins with a capital. In the return address, a comma is used between city and state.

```
John Davis
1649 Muir Drive
Port Huron, Michigan 48060


          Mr. Stephen Kinnery
          325 South Ames Street
          Marian
          Indiana   46952
```

A Model Envelope

● EXERCISE 3. Address an envelope for the letter you wrote in Exercise 2.

● EXERCISE 4. For practice in following the correct form for friendly letters, choose one of the following situations and write the letter it suggests. If you prefer to make up a different situation to write about, you may do so.

For girls:

1. Write to someone you know who is living in Europe, asking for information about living conditions in whatever country she is living. Explain that you need the information for a composition. Ask specific questions.

2. As a surprise to your father, you got your mother's permission to plan and prepare a meal. Describe to a friend what you cooked and everything that happened.

3. You have just attended a movie that you know your friend will want to see. Describe it enthusiastically so that she will be sure not to miss it.

4. You have just completed your first baby-sitting assignment. The friend you are writing to has done some baby-sitting, too, but she does not know these particular children. Describe how it went.

5. You have just moved to a different neighborhood and are writing about it to a friend who still lives in your old neighborhood. Tell her what you like or don't like about your new surroundings.

For boys:

1. You have just been to see an important baseball (or football or hockey) game. Both you and the friend you are writing to are fans of the same team. Describe what happened.

2. You have just got a paper route. Write to a friend urging him to get a route or not to, depending upon your experiences in the first week of your new job.

3. You have just moved to a new neighborhood and are writing about it to a friend who still lives in your

old neighborhood. Tell him what you like or don't like about your new surroundings.

4. You are giving your dog a course in obedience training. Write to a friend or relative reporting on your progress. (Use information from the explanation on pages 370–71, if you wish.)

5. You want to set up a darkroom to develop your own photographs. The friend to whom you are writing already has one. Ask him what you will have to buy, how much you will have to spend, and generally how to go about it.

THE SOCIAL NOTE

21d. Social notes are short letters, such as invitations and thank-you notes, written to meet certain social demands.

Everyone has occasion to write social notes now and then, and you should learn to do it properly. The social note has the same form as a friendly letter.

The Thank-You Note

The form of a letter of thanks is the same as that of a friendly letter. Such a letter should be written on personal stationery. The purpose of a letter of thanks is, of course, to show the person who will receive it that you really appreciate the kindness he has done you. However, it will seem less like a duty letter if you say a word about something else as well. Write a thank-you letter as soon as possible after you have received a gift or a favor.

21d

5455 South Blackstone Street
Chicago, Illinois 60615
March 20, 1965

Dear Aunt Jane,

Thank you ever so much for the beautiful blouse you sent on my birthday. It is exactly the right size and the color goes perfectly with the blue skirt Mother made for me.

Maybe I'm getting too old for birthday parties, but when Mother asked me if I'd like to have some of my friends over, I was all for it. I had four for a pajama party Saturday night. I slept all Sunday afternoon!

For my birthday, Daddy gave me plane fare for a trip to Cleveland to visit Ginnie Taylor during spring vacation. I can hardly wait!

Love,
Linda

A Thank-You Note

● EXERCISE 5. Write a letter of thanks for an actual gift or favor you have received. Or, if you prefer, select one of the following situations as the occasion for a letter, and write the letter.

1. You have been out of school for about two weeks because of illness. Your class has sent you a get-well card and a gift. You want to thank them.
2. A friend who lives in another city has sent you a special stamp for your collection.
3. A relative visiting Arizona has sent you samples of petrified wood.
4. A relative whom you have not seen for some time remembers your birthday and sends you a present.

The Bread-and-Butter Note

If you have spent a weekend at the home of a friend, or if you have paid a longer visit to friends or relatives, you should write a letter of thanks to your hostess as soon as you return. If you were visiting someone of your own age, the letter should be addressed to your friend's mother. Such a letter is called a "bread-and-butter" note. It is important for you to show the family that you enjoyed your stay with them and that you appreciate their kindness and generosity.

The form of the "bread-and-butter" note is the same as that for any friendly letter.

● EXERCISE 6. If you have visited someone recently, write a bread-and-butter note expressing your thanks for the hospitality you received. Or, if you prefer, imagine that you were in one of the following situations, and write a bread-and-butter note.

1. You have spent a month of your summer vacation on your uncle's ranch.
2. You have stayed for the weekend with your best friend, who lives on the other side of the city. There was a party Saturday night.
3. Your grandmother has taken you on a three-day

trip to a nearby city, where you went sight-seeing with her.

4. You and your family have visited your aunt and uncle and their family at their summer camp. Their family includes two cousins, Bob and Joan, about your age.

---

532 Fifth Street Southeast
Minneapolis, Minnesota 55414
July 15, 1965

Dear Mrs. Berman,

Everyone is getting tired of hearing me talk about my big weekend at your farm. Jack and I had so much fun. I can't stop talking about it – the swimming and riding, how I didn't learn to milk a cow, the trip to town on Saturday, and your wonderful meals. Mom says I have been spoiled rotten.

I appreciate all the things you and Mr. Berman did to give me a good time. Tell Jack I will write to him soon.

Sincerely,
Al

A "Bread-and-Butter" Note

THE BUSINESS LETTER

Many of the letters which you and members of your family write are not letters to friends or relatives but are business letters: letters ordering goods, asking for information, applying for jobs or entrance into schools, and so on. Such letters are important in our daily life, and they should be correctly written.

21e. Follow generally accepted rules for the form of a business letter.

Use suitable stationery. White paper is appropriate. Write your business letter on a typewriter if you type well. If not, write it in pen and ink. Make your letter look attractive by centering it properly on the page. You will have to figure out in advance how much room you need, and you cannot always make the lines come out exactly right; nevertheless, try to get even margins all around. Keep the letter neat by avoiding erasures, messy blotting, or splotching. Keep your letter brief. If your letter is too long for one page, do not write on the back but continue on a second page. Try to carry over at least three lines onto the second page. Begin them two inches down from the top.

Business letters should be polite and very clear. When writing an order for merchandise, for example, it is important to give full and exact information. Otherwise, exasperating mistakes and delays may result.

The form of a business letter is slightly different from that of a friendly letter. Study the model and explanation on the pages that follow.

21e

1   1811 Kindy Avenue
Covington, Kentucky 41012
May 11, 1965

2   H. C. Laurel Hardware Company
160 North Main Street
Memphis, Tennessee 38103

3   Gentlemen:

4   In the <u>Memphis Scimitar</u> for Sunday,
May 5, you advertise a woodcarving set
for $4.98, postpaid. Please send me this
item.

      I am enclosing a money order for
$4.98.

5   Very truly yours,

6   *John J. Mack*
John J. Mack

A Model Business Letter

1. *Heading*

Write a complete heading: street address on the first line; city, state, and ZIP code on the second line, with a comma between the city and state; date on the third line, with a comma between the day and the year.

2. *Inside Address*

Unlike a friendly letter, a business letter has an inside address placed a short space below the heading, beginning at the left margin. Give the name of the person or firm, or both, to whom you are writing. Give the address, with a comma between city and state and about one-quarter inch space between state and ZIP code number.

The reason for the inside address on a business letter is that in a business office where carbon copies of all letters are filed, it must be clearly indicated on each letter to whom it was addressed. A letter which had only the salutation "Dear Mr. Smith" would not make this clear. You may not keep a file of the few business letters you write; nevertheless, you should follow the regular form used everywhere.

3. *Salutation*

Place the salutation two typewriter spaces (one-quarter inch) below the inside address, flush with the left-hand margin. Follow it with a colon. If you are writing to a firm rather than to an individual, the correct salutation is *Gentlemen.* If you are writing to an individual whose name you do not know, the proper salutation is *Dear Sir* or *Dear Madam.* If you are writing to an individual whose name you do know, the salutation should be *Dear Mr.* ——, *Dear Miss* ——, or *Dear Mrs.* ——.

4. *Body*

The first line of the body of a business letter begins two spaces below the salutation. It may be indented five typewriter spaces (one inch in handwriting) from the left-hand margin. The first line of all succeeding paragraphs should be indented the same distance.

5. *Closing*

The standard form for the closing of a business letter is *Yours truly* or *Very truly yours*. The first word is capitalized. The closing should begin just to the right of the middle of the page and should be followed by a comma.

6. *Signature*

The signature should be placed below the closing and flush with it. Sign your first and last names. If you have typed the letter, type your name several spaces below the closing, and then write your name in ink between the closing and your typed signature. Do not put a title (Mr., Miss, etc.) before your handwritten signature.

The way you fold a business letter depends on the size of the paper and the envelope. If the sheet is the same width as the envelope, fold it up from the bottom and down from the top, as shown in the first three steps of the illustration. If the sheet is wider than the

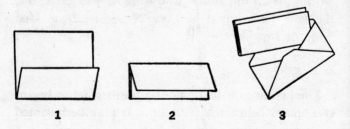

envelope, follow the steps pictured on this page. Fold the paper up from the bottom almost to the top of the sheet. Then fold the right side over a third of the way; fold the left side over that. Always put the folded edge of the letter into the envelope first.

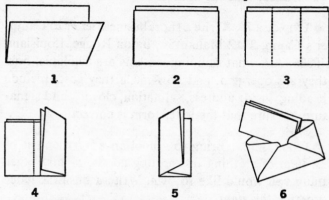

You may have occasion to write business letters requesting information or correcting a mistake, as well as letters ordering merchandise. No matter what the purpose of your business letter, make sure you meet these requirements:

1. *Be clear.* State exactly what you want or whatever information you intend to convey. Tell the reader as much as he will need to know to understand the situation.

2. *Be brief.* Do not put any unnecessary information in your letter, and do not write it in a rambling, wordy style. Be as concise as possible. However, do not leave out any important details; if you do, the reader of your letter will not be able to fulfill your request promptly.

3. *Be courteous.* Your letter will make a better impression if its tone is polite and reasonable. If you must make a complaint in a letter, do so courteously.

The block style is preferred for a business letter; the indented style is not usually used. The envelope for a business letter is addressed the same as that for a friendly letter. The inside address in the letter should be identical with the address on the envelope.

● EXERCISE 7.   Write a short business letter to Camper's Camp, 3412 Mahan St., Baton Rouge, Louisiana 70806. Ask what camping lanterns are available, how they are operated, and how much they cost. Include heading, inside address, salutation, closing, and signature. Be sure that the letter form is correct.

● EXERCISE 8.   Bring to school an advertisement of an item of clothing or sporting goods, or any other thing you would like to own. Write a business letter ordering this item.

Checklist

Friendly letters and social notes
1. Include your address and the date in the heading.
2. Place a comma after the salutation.
3. Include news the other person would like to know or find interesting. Answer any questions your friend may have asked in his last letter.
4. Write as if you were talking face to face, but be careful to organize your thoughts.
5. In a note of thanks, be specific about whatever it is you are grateful for.

Business letters
1. Use block style for the heading, not indented style.
2. After the salutation use a colon, not a comma.
3. Be careful to include all information necessary to understand or act upon your letter.

PART SIX

Speaking
and
Listening

CHAPTER 22

Speaking

Introductions, Giving Directions, Preparing and Delivering a Talk

As you grow older, you encounter new and different types of social situations. More and more you are expected to take part in social conversations and to make and acknowledge introductions. In school, you may have to give a talk in class, or make a report to a club.

Acquiring these skills and learning how to speak effectively in front of a group are not difficult. You need only a few rules—and some practice.

INTRODUCTIONS

You will find that knowing how to introduce people helps to put yourself and others at ease.

22a. Follow the customary methods of making and responding to introductions.

When making an introduction, use any of these expressions:

22a

May I present ——
May I introduce ——
This is ——
I would like you to meet ——
Or simply use the names of the two people.

EXAMPLES   "Al Durgin, may I present Jack Burke?"

"Al Durgin, may I introduce Jack Burke?"

"Al Durgin, this is Jack Burke."

"Al Durgin, I would like you to meet Jack Burke."

"Al Durgin, Jack Burke."

The expressions *may I introduce* and *may I present* are formal. You probably will not have many occasions to use them. You should use whatever words come naturally to you. The important thing is for each person to learn the other's name.

(1) In introducing a boy to a girl and a man to a woman, mention the girl's name or the woman's name first.

EXAMPLES   "Mrs. Blair, may I present Mr. Jordan? Mr. Jordan, this is Mrs. Blair."

"Shirley, I'd like you to meet Bob Gregory. This is Shirley Borden, Bob."

(2) In introducing a younger person to an older person, if there is a distinct difference in ages, speak the older person's name first.

EXAMPLES   "Mom, this is Mary Malone. Mary, this is my mother."

"Mr. Kent, these are my brothers Tom and Matt. This is my chemistry teacher Mr. Kent."

This rule will sometimes take precedence over the first rule, which advises you to introduce a man to a woman. If the man is much older or deserves unusual honor or respect, it is courteous to present the woman to him, speaking his name first.

EXAMPLES   "Dr. Mayberry, may I present Mrs. Dorn, my teacher? Mrs. Dorn, this is Dr. Hugh Mayberry."

"Colonel Johns, this is my sister, Lucy. Colonel Johns."

"Grandfather, this is Julie Gomez. My grandfather, Mr. Hopkins."

(3) When introducing people of the same sex and about the same age, it does not matter which name you speak first.

When someone is introduced to you, be sure to listen for his name. Respond with a smile and a friendly greeting. To people of your own age, you probably say "Hi" or "Hello." "How do you do?" is a customary response among adults. Repeating the name of the person who has been introduced will help to fix it in your mind.

EXAMPLES   "Hello, Judy."

"Hi, Mike and Bud."

"How do you do, Mrs. Fullerton?"

● EXERCISE 1.   Act out the following situations.

1. A mother introduces her seventh-grade son to the new minister of their church.
2. A father brings home the chief partner of his firm and introduces his daughter, who has been lying on the living-room rug, watching television.

3. Two cousins, of the same age, are introduced to each other by their grandmother. (a) Both are boys. (b) Both are girls. (c) They are a boy and a girl.
4. A young man brings home the girl to whom he is engaged. His younger sister is practicing at the piano. He introduces them.
5. A mother and daughter, walking together, meet a boy the mother knows. The mother introduces him.
6. A boy sits reading in the living room when his older sister comes in with her college roommate and introduces them.
7. A boy sits in a restaurant with his parents. A couple the parents know comes to their table. The boy is introduced.
8. A girl is sewing when her brother enters with the boy who has just moved in next door. The boy is introduced.
9. A girl is sitting at a table, studying, when her mother enters with an older woman whom the girl does not know.
10. A boy introduces a new student in his science class to two boys who are walking home with him. (a) The new student is a boy. (b) The new student is a girl.

(4) On some occasions, it is convenient and proper to introduce yourself.

Sometimes you will have occasion to introduce yourself. Simply say: "Hello. I'm Betty Perkins," or "Hi. I'm Jim Blake from Central High," or "How do you do? I'm Charles Blunt from Clifton."

(5) If many people are in a room and you are introducing a newcomer, do not present him to every-

body at once (he wouldn't remember all the names),
but introduce him to small groups.

EXAMPLES   "John Cagle, Al Newlin, this is Ed Ben-
ton."

"Girls, I would like you to meet Edith
Saunders. Edith, this is Irene Newsom,
Louise Ames, and Doris Allen."

(6) Respond to an introduction properly.

Men and boys shake hands when they are introduced. When a girl is presented to another girl, they
usually do not shake hands. When a girl and a boy
are introduced, they may or may not shake hands, as
they wish. If either extends a hand, it is the natural
and gracious thing for the other to shake it.

A boy always stands up when being introduced to
someone. A girl rises when, as a hostess, she greets
a guest. She is not expected to rise when a boy is
introduced to her, but she does rise when she is being
introduced to a woman.

(7) Help to start a conversation when you make an introduction.

When you introduce people, add a friendly remark.
Say something that will help to put the two strangers
at ease and give them something to talk about.

EXAMPLES   "Mom, this is Ellen Knorr. Ellen just entered our school today."

"Rick, this is my friend Jack Simon from
Eastern Prep. Jack is planning to go out
for track, too."

● EXERCISE 2. Act out the following situations.

1. Each person in class will write on a piece of paper his name, a motion picture he has seen lately, a magazine he reads, a favorite radio or television program, a book he has just read, and a hobby or special interest. Select two of these slips of paper. Introduce the two writers to each other, using some of the information on the papers to start a conversation.

2. Newcomers with a daughter about your age move in next door. You see her for the first time and introduce yourself.

3. You are waiting to catch a bus. Standing near you are two young people of your own age, also waiting. You've seen them before but have never talked to them. Introduce yourself.

4. You take your cousin to a party. The young people are all sitting at tables, playing a game. You introduce your cousin. (a) Your cousin is a boy. (b) Your cousin is a girl, a little older than the young people present.

5. In the following introductions, a clue is provided to start a conversation between the people introduced. How would you begin a conversation?

a. "Nora Bates, Sally Morris. Nora, Sally just moved here from Honolulu." (What might Nora say?)

b. "Ed, I'd like you to meet Jeff Roberts. This is Ed Kindy. Ed, Jeff's dad works for a circus." (If you were Ed, what could you say?)

c. "Johnny, this is Pete Sims. Johnny Ryan. Johnny, Pete was asking about the 4–H Club here. He used to be a member in Colorado." (What might Johnny say?)

d. "Larry, this is Dick Perrin. Larry Gold. Larry, Dick is working on a project for the Science Fair, too." (What might Larry ask Dick?)

e. "Alice, I want you to meet Pam Barker. Alice Jones. Alice, Pam wants to join our Spanish Club." (What might Alice say?)

CONVERSATIONS

For all of us, there are times when we can't think of a thing to say, particularly with people we don't know well. A good rule to follow is to talk about the other person. Sometimes the person who has introduced you will give you a clue to the stranger's interests. If you don't know anything about your companion, ask a question.

22b. Learn to converse easily and naturally.

(1) Do your part to get a conversation started.

EXAMPLES   "Dorothy, this is Celia Stern. Dorothy Hannen. Celia, Dorothy's new here. Her folks just moved near you. She doesn't know anybody yet."

"Hi, Dorothy. Welcome to Franklin Park! Did you move into that blue house on the corner?"

"Loren, this is Ed Bender. Ed, this is my brother."

"Hi, Ed. Do you live in this part of town, or are you visiting?"

Look at the person with whom you are talking and follow the conversation. Do not glance around the

22b

room or think about something else. Give your companion the courtesy of your full attention.

(2) Do your part to keep a conversation going.

Once a conversation has been started, be alert to keep it moving. Ask an occasional question to draw out further information, and contribute some ideas of your own on the subject being talked about.

EXAMPLE   "Ben Laurence, Phil Daigle. Ben, Phil just got back from a trip over the Alaska Highway."

"Say, that sounds great. I bet you saw lots of big game."

"Yes, we did. We saw wolves and mink, lots of foxes and wolverines, and bighorn sheep, too."

"See any grizzly bears?"

"One. But he didn't see us. Dad says they've got poor eyesight. I'd sure hate to have one come after me."

"I guess their good sense of smell makes up for their poor eyesight."

Good manners in conversation are based on kindness and thoughtfulness. Bad manners usually arise out of carelessness. You can do much to build a habit of being tactful, considerate, and pleasant in talking to people.

Here are a few tips for conversing:

1. *Select topics of interest to the other person.* Ask questions or mention subjects that you think will be interesting to him.

2. *Use a conversational tone.* Do not mumble and do not shout.

3. *Listen to the other person.* Whatever he has to say, you owe him the courtesy of paying attention. Besides, you may learn something.

4. *Be good-natured.* Try to be pleasant, even though you may differ. Do not mistake argument for conversation.

● EXERCISE 3.   Act out the following situations, including a short conversation. The rest of the class may evaluate the conversational manners of the speakers.

1. You are meeting a friend at his or her home to go to a movie. Your friend's mother answers the door and invites you to wait for a minute in the living room.

2. On a short bus trip, you meet a teacher whom you have not seen since last year.

3. At a ball game, you realize that the person sitting next to you is a classmate you do not know well.

4. On a field trip or tour of a museum, you sit down in a lunchroom next to someone who is in your group but whom you do not know at all.

5. Your parents have just met a family they know and have started talking with the other parents. You and your sister are left with the daughter of the other family, who is a little younger than you.

6. You are going to baby-sit for a family you don't know well. When you arrive, the mother is not ready, and the father takes you into the living room with him and the baby.

7. You are eating lunch in the school cafeteria with three friends. A new student whom you have seen in some of your classes approaches your table hesitantly.

8. You and your brother and parents are visiting your grandmother, whom you have not seen for

several years. You and your brother are left alone with your grandmother, who asks you to tell her about yourselves.

9. You are an usher at the school play. A half hour before the play begins, you notice a girl standing in the hall outside the auditorium, apparently waiting for someone. You know that she is the sister of one of the actors.

10. At a party, the hostess has just introduced you to a girl from the town where she used to live. Then she is called away to greet another guest. You are left with the girl you just met.

TELEPHONING

The telephone is such a frequently used instrument in our lives that it is important to know how to use it efficiently and considerately.

22c. Learn to use the telephone correctly.

When you are talking on the telephone with someone who does not know you, your listener forms a mental image of you. You can influence this image by what you say and how you say it. Here is a list of rules for good telephone manners.

When making calls

1. Be sure you know the correct number and the correct dialing methods. If you get a wrong number, apologize briefly for disturbing the person who answers.

2. Try not to telephone at mealtime or bedtime unless it is an emergency.

3. Identify yourself promptly when someone answers the telephone. If you know the person who answers, be sure to greet him. If the person you are calling is not there, leave your name and number and, if you wish, a brief message.

4. Speak clearly. If you mumble or shout, or have the telephone too far away from you, conversation is difficult.

5. Have a pencil and a piece of paper at hand in case you wish to write down some information.

6. Do not talk too long. It is the responsibility of the person who makes the call to end it.

When receiving calls

1. Answer promptly and identify yourself.

2. Listen carefully and take notes of anything you will have to remember.

3. If the call interrupts you when you do not have time to talk, ask if you may return the call later.

4. Take a message if the call is for someone who is out. Write it down, and then repeat it to be sure you have the message straight. Check the spelling of names and addresses. Be sure to leave the message where the person called will find it.

● EXERCISE 4. Study your telephone directory to learn what kinds of information it contains. Be prepared to answer the following questions: What information is given in the introductory pages? How are government agencies listed? What abbreviations are used through the book? How would such names as De Long, McCrae, Von Heln, De los Rios, and St. Patrick's Church be listed? What is the quickest way to get the police or fire department? What information do the yellow pages contain?

22c

● EXERCISE 5. Write answers to the following questions. To whom would you telephone:

1. If you found a lost child, crying in the street, too young to know his name or where he lives?
2. If your little brother pulled a pot of soup off the stove and the boiling liquid scalded his arms?
3. If you smelled gas in your kitchen or basement?
4. If you saw a rabid dog on your street?
5. If you were helping to plan a picnic for your class and needed weather information?
6. If you found a telegram for someone you did not know that had been mistakenly pushed under your front door?
7. If you saw a fire flaring up in rubbish on the lot across the street?
8. If you saw a car hit a child and race away, leaving the hurt child lying in the street?
9. If you and a friend were in your house alone at night and heard a prowler in the backyard?
10. If you found a special delivery letter left mistakenly in your mailbox?

● EXERCISE 6. With a partner, prepare correct telephone dialogue for one of the following situations: (1) A boy calling to congratulate a friend for having been elected class president. (2) A girl is baby-sitting at the home of Dr. and Mrs. A. R. King. Before leaving, the doctor gives instructions for locating him in case of an emergency call. The girl receives such a call five minutes after he departs. (3) You have been asked to spend a few days with a friend in another town. Telephone him or her to discuss the details of your arrival by train or bus. Using dummy or imaginary telephones, make the call. The rest of the class will comment on your performance.

GIVING DIRECTIONS

All of us occasionally have to ask for help in finding a person or a place in a strange locality. We may be called on by others for such help, too. Or we may be asked to explain how to make fudge, repair a bicycle tire, sew on a button, or start a campfire. Giving clear, concise directions is a useful skill for everyone to have.

22d. Give directions that are orderly, complete, clear, and accurate.

(1) Arrange information in a clear order.

Before giving directions to anyone, go over them in your own mind to simplify the steps and leave out unnecessary ones, and to arrange them in a sensible order that will be easy to remember.

FAULTY   "Just drive to the center of town, take one of the main streets east—if you go right on Boynton you'll have a detour—cross the river, go down the embankment to the motel district. You'll find the Riverside Motel in the middle somewhere."

BETTER   "Drive straight ahead on Center to Main Street. Go right on Main, about one mile, to Riverside Road. Your motel is just beyond the yellow blinker, on the right."

FAULTY   To "break in" a book, you should open the book gently and bend the pages down, to left and right. Each cover, however, should be pressed flat first. Then bend the pages down and press them flat. Do only a dozen or twenty pages at a time. Alternate from side to side as you work.

22d

BETTER   To "break in" a book, hold the book closed and place the spine (back) on a table. Press one cover flat to the table. Gently press the opposite cover flat. Press a dozen or so pages flat on one side. Do the same on the opposite side. Continue pressing small clumps of pages flat, alternating left and right, until the book lies flat, open at the middle.

(2) Give complete information.

When giving directions, make sure that you have included every necessary step. Obviously, by leaving out one necessary turn, you can send the person you are trying to help in the wrong direction.

(3) Review the steps.

After you have given the directions, go over them once more, slowly, to give the other person a chance to fix them in his mind. You might, then, ask him to repeat them to you. In this way you can check on how well he has grasped your instructions. If necessary, you can correct a mistake he has made, or add any necessary detail.

● EXERCISE 7.   Select a well-known building or place of interest in your community and write a set of directions for reaching it from school. In class, the teacher will call upon individuals to read the directions aloud. The class will judge each set on how well it would enable a stranger to reach the place concerned.

● EXERCISE 8.   Prepare a set of directions for one of the following incidents.

1. The phone rings and you answer it. A friend of your father's has just driven into town. He is tele-

phoning from a drugstore on the outskirts of the city. Give him directions to your father's place of employment.

2. You are mowing your front lawn. A car stops at the curb and the driver asks how to get to the bus station. You tell him.

3. A new family has moved in next door. A boy (or girl) of the family, who is your age, asks you how to go to the post office, the junior high school, and the nearest movie theater. Give him directions.

4. A friend calls up to ask where a picnic could be held. Tell him how to get to your favorite picnic site. (If you do not have one, invent one.)

5. A friend telephones you for help. Her mother is not at home and her father is dressing for an important dinner. She has to sew a button on his shirt but doesn't know how. Give her instructions.

6. A father and son are on a fishing trip. Pretend that you are the father, and tell your son how to clean a fish.

7. A librarian from out of town comes to your school. You meet her in the corridor, and she asks where the library is. Give her directions.

8. You and a friend are hiking in the country. He notices some mushrooms that you recognize as poisonous. Give him directions for identifying some poisonous mushrooms.

9. A friend has just been told by her mother that she must take care of her own clothes. She wants to know how to wash and dry a wool sweater. Tell her what she should do.

10. You and your sister have agreed to meet at a local department store to choose a gift for your mother. She is not familiar with the store. Tell her where inside the store to meet you and how to get there.

PREPARING AND DELIVERING A TALK

Occasionally in seventh grade, and more frequently later, you will be called upon to deliver a short talk or book report in one of your classes or at a club meeting. Your task will be easier and more enjoyable if you learn some basic methods of preparing and delivering a talk.

22e. Select a suitable topic.

Select a topic about which you are interested or curious. The enthusiasm you feel for your subject will be reflected in your talk and will help to make your presentation more interesting.

Consider how you can get your listeners interested in the subject. You may spend hours at a particular hobby, for example, but this does not mean that your audience will have the same enthusiasm unless you manage to convey to them some of the pleasure and excitement you derive from this pastime.

Let us assume that you have a topic that interests you and that you think will interest your audience. Your next step is to make sure that your topic is sufficiently narrow in scope to enable you to present the necessary information in the given period of time.

Suppose, for example, you are interested in water sports and want to talk about them. Obviously, you cannot cover all water sports in a short talk. You decide to limit your topic to swimming.

List some ideas that occur to you about swimming: the pleasures derived from the sport, the advantages of knowing how to swim, the various kinds of strokes, how to improve your swimming, outstanding swimmers and their records. As you write these, it becomes clear that the subject is still a large one. You narrow it still further and decide to give a talk on the various types of swimming strokes.

When you are sure of your topic and have thought about what you will say, you are ready to organize your talk.

22f. Organize your material in such a way that your listeners can easily follow you.

At this stage, you may jot down some notes to refer to as you are talking. Write them on 3 × 5 inch cards, so that you can hold them easily in your hand. Remember, however, that you are giving a talk, not reading a speech. Don't write down everything that you will say. A few words or a sentence will remind you of each part of your talk.

A talk may be divided into three sections: (1) the introduction, (2) the body, and (3) the conclusion. These are the beginning, the middle, and the end.

The Introduction

Remember that the first thing you want to do is to attract your listeners' interest and attention. Do not waste your opening statement by saying something like, "This topic is one I have always been interested in." Such a sentence is not likely to make your listeners want to hear more.

Instead, you might have an opening sentence that gives a general statement about swimming or asks a

question about it. In a book report, your opening remark might refer to the main character or setting of
the book.

EXAMPLES   Why is the dog-paddle the first stroke most
swimmers learn?

In two books about life in the West, Ralph
Moody tells how he grew from "Little
Britches" to the "man of the family."

The Body

When you are telling a story or giving an oral book
report, relate the events in the order in which they
happened. This arrangement of incidents is called a
time or chronological arrangement. When you are
trying to persuade or to influence your listeners, you
may indicate your arrangement of arguments in your
opening sentence or paragraph.

EXAMPLE   In this jet age, in which travel is a matter
of hours instead of days, everyone should
know a foreign language. There are at least
three advantages in being able to speak and
understand a foreign language.

This introduction makes it clear that the body of
your talk will present the three advantages.

● EXERCISE 9.   Some of the following topics are suitable for a short talk and others are not, either because
they are too broad in range or too narrow in interest.
Choose a topic and adapt it, if necessary, to make it
more suitable. Then think of an introduction for a
short talk about it. Be prepared to give the introduction and to tell what points you would cover in
the body of the talk.

1. Food from the sea
2. Teacher for a day
3. Sports
4. *Huckleberry Finn*
   by Mark Twain
5. Planting a garden
6. Some safety features of
   automobiles
7. *The Diary of Anne Frank*
8. Training animals
9. Art
10. Piano lessons

The Conclusion

Try to make the conclusion a positive one. One way
to do this is to restate the main idea briefly. Another
way is to ask your listeners to take some kind of
action—read the book on which you've just reported,
vote for a particular candidate for the Student Council, or support some action or cause.

EXAMPLES   Each of these swimming strokes is valuable
for certain situations, as I have explained.
Try one of them the next time you're tired
of the dog-paddle.

If you aren't studying a foreign language
now, shouldn't you consider enrolling in
such a course and joining the jet age?

● EXERCISE 10.   Analyze the following concluding
remarks. Which are suitable? Why? Which are weak?

1. In conclusion, I want to say thank you for your
   patience and good manners during my talk, and I'm
   sorry that I took longer than I intended.
2. I think everyone with an interest in jet planes should
   read this book, even though it is hard to understand
   in some places.
3. So you see, I've learned the hard way, and I'll be
   more cautious next time. Fools rush in where angels
   fear to tread.

4. I've learned that major league baseball is more interesting if you choose one team to follow.
5. Bicycling is fun, and it's a good way to get around. Unfortunately, not everyone has a bicycle.

22g. Learn to deliver a speech effectively.

Stand firmly—but not stiffly—on both feet and speak directly to your audience, looking around the room as you speak so that you can note your listeners' reactions. Your facial expressions, movements, and gestures will influence your audience as much as what you are saying. If you refer to note cards, do so as unobtrusively as possible. You should be looking at your audience most of the time, not at your notes.

Vary the rate, pitch, and inflection of your voice as you do in natural talk. Since your listeners will be aware of your pronunciation and enunciation, you should be especially careful to speak well.

Several kinds of errors mark sloppy speaking. Study the following lists of errors and, if you make any of them, or others like them, practice the correct forms until you are sure of them.

Omitting sounds

probly for *probably*   *kep* for *kept*
reglar for *regular*   *ask* for *asked*
leven for *eleven*   *libery* for *library*

Adding sounds

drownded for *drowned*   *filum* for *film*
athaletics for *athletics* *chimeny* for *chimney*

Running words together

didja for *did you*   *lemme* for *let me*
wanna for *want to*   *commere* for *come here*

● **EXERCISE 11.** For each of the following general topics, suggest one that is sufficiently narrow for a short talk.

1. Pets
2. Jazz
3. Travel
4. Dancing
5. Farming
6. Cooking
7. Television
8. Public speaking
9. Cars
10. School publications
11. Hawaii
12. Alaska
13. How jet propulsion works
14. Geronimo, Indian warrior
15. Snorkeling
16. Surf riding
17. Juvenile delinquency
18. How to select a college
19. Types of humor
20. The advantages of knowing how to type

● **EXERCISE 12.** Using the topic that you developed in Exercise 9 or one from Exercise 11, prepare and deliver a two-minute talk before the class.

22g

CHAPTER 23

Listening

Listening Manners and Skills

How well we learn, how well we get along with others, even how successful we are in life, can depend in many ways on how well we listen. Good listening habits can be acquired and can be improved by practice.

23a. Show good listening manners in an audience and in conversation.

Good listeners learn much from what they hear. They do not hamper the speaker by disturbance. By listening quietly and attentively, they make him feel that what he has to say is worthwhile; and this encourages him to do his best. Furthermore, by listening alertly, they gain the most value from what he says.

It is also important to practice good listening manners when talking to your friends. When you are talking, you expect people to listen to you. When someone else is talking, it's up to you to listen attentively.

To show good listening manners:

1. Look at the speaker. Your expression and posture reveal your interest and appreciation.

2. Do not doodle, read, whisper, or fidget.

3. Ask questions when they are invited, after the talk. Address the speaker politely, and show by your questions that you have listened carefully.

● EXERCISE 1. During the next week, observe the listening manners of audiences you are in: at a movie, in church, at talks in school, and so on. When you get home, write down what you noticed so that you can report to your class at an appropriate time.

23b. Learn some useful techniques of listening.

Whether you are listening to some extemporaneous remarks or a prepared speech, you can apply certain techniques of listening to get the speaker's message.

(1) Listen for the speaker's purpose.

A speaker may be giving you information, entertaining you, expressing his ideas or opinions, or trying to persuade you to a certain point of view. Usually he makes clear at once what his purpose is. If you keep this in mind as you listen, you will be better able to follow his main points and to evaluate what you hear.

(2) Learn to follow a speaker's main points.

After a speaker has made clear what he intends to talk about, your task is to follow his ideas and apply them to your own interests. In an informal discussion,

23
a-b

where there are several speakers, the ideas may not be well organized. The main points will be scattered, and there will be opposing opinions. An important point may be made quietly and unexpectedly. You must think as you listen, separating the main ideas from the details and illustrations.

Listening to a prepared talk is easier, because the main points are likely to be presented in a more organized form. Some speakers give their talks so that the outline shows through. Their opening remarks may be like these: "There are three outstanding qualities that make this book memorable," or "What benefits will result from the passage of this bill?" Sometimes, a speaker even numbers his points *first, second, third.* Some speakers pause as they introduce each important idea.

Another guidepost to listen for in a speech is the use of transitional words or phrases, such as:

so	however
next	furthermore
therefore	finally

Before he closes, a speaker may review the main points he has made. Such a summary provides you with a double check. You should not count on this kind of repetition, but you should be ready to take advantage of it when it appears.

(3) Take notes when necessary.

There are times when it is necessary to support your memory by taking notes. Certainly, you need to take notes on assignments, since you cannot always remember the details of what you are to do. Whenever you want to be sure to retain the information you are hearing, you should jot down notes.

When you have occasion to take notes, keep these questions in mind:

1. What is the speaker's purpose?
2. What do I want to get out of his talk?
3. What main points does he bring out?
4. How well does he support his main points?

Do not try to write down everything a speaker says. Train yourself to listen for the main points and make notes of these. Use whatever words come quickly and naturally to you. Probably they will be a combination of the speaker's and your own. Do not worry about complete sentences or about punctuation—use abbreviations and whatever shortcuts you think of. Your purpose is to get down quickly the essence of what the speaker is saying while still listening to him.

● EXERCISE 2. As a class, discuss one of the following questions. Keep the discussion short; agree in advance how long it should be. After the discussion is over, each student should write down what he understood to be the main points. Then compare the papers.

1. Should all schools provide summer sessions for students who want to make up work or supplement their regular courses?
2. Should colleges give scholarships for athletic skill as well as academic excellence?
3. Does studying grammar help one to speak or write better?

● EXERCISE 3. Ask one student to read aloud to the class the first three or four paragraphs of any chapter in your science or social studies book. The other students will imagine that they are to be responsible for this material two days from now and will take notes as they think necessary. Compare the notes. Do they identify the main ideas?

23c. Listen carefully.

It is important to listen carefully when you are receiving class assignments, work instructions, or directions for doing something. Careless listening can result in grave mistakes. While taking a wrong bus, for example, may result only in losing time and temper, taking a wrong medicine could have serious consequences.

(1) Take down class assignments accurately.

1. Jot down each step of the instructions.
2. Do not interrupt with questions while the assignment is being given. If there is something you do not understand, ask a question as soon as the teacher has finished speaking.
3. Be sure that you have all the instructions and understand them.

(2) Get instructions straight and follow them correctly.

Everyone listens to instructions everyday. Parents and teachers give many kinds of instructions. We may get instructions from a friend in response to a question about how to do something or from a stranger in response to a request for directions. It is important to listen carefully to instructions.

A good check on how well a person grasps and understands instructions is for him to repeat them aloud to the person who gave them. Obviously, this is not practical when a teacher has given instructions to a whole class. However, when instructions are given to an individual, it is wise for the listener to repeat them. By doing so, he fixes them firmly in his own mind; and if he makes mistakes or omissions, he can be corrected.

● EXERCISE 4.   As an exercise in attentive listening, your teacher will read the following instructions to the class. He will read quickly and pause only briefly between instructions. Close your book and carry out the instructions as he reads. You will need pencil and paper.

1. Write *9*, no matter what the sum of 5 and 6 is.
2. If the Northern Lights are not turned on by a switch, write your name without capitals.
3. If you were born in the first six months of the year, multiply your age by 3; if you were born in the last six months of the year, subtract 3 from your age.
4. If you think whales are fish, write the weight of a pound of whalebone; if you think whales are mammals, how many ounces in half a pound?
5. Write *yes*, if the following statement is in error: You are listening to these instructions in German.
6. If two men and two women make two couples, what do four bakers make?
7. If six from twelve leaves an even number, write the opposite of *nearby*.
8. Without touching pencil to paper, write the opposite of *something*.
9. Write the name of the newest state in the Union.
10. If *music* is a five-letter word, write *piano*.

23c

● EXERCISE 5.   The teacher or a student will read the following instructions to the class. No one is to take any notes during the reading. After the reader finishes, the group will write down the directions from memory. When everyone has finished, the reader will reread the instructions, and each student will make whatever corrections and additions are necessary on his paper, and will add up the number of changes he had to make.

Teacher: I am going to read some instructions on how to fight fires. To keep burning, a fire needs air, fuel, and heat. Remove one of these three elements, and you put out the fire.

Take away the fuel: if possible, remove the burning material before the fire spreads.

Take away air: smother the fire with a wet rug or blanket, or shovel sand or dirt onto it.

Take away heat: cool the fire by pouring water on it. If, however, the fire is caused by electric wires that have shorted out because of bad insulation, do not use water until you have switched off the current. If that is impossible to do, smother the fire with sand or dirt.

(3) Get directions straight.

Following directions, like following any instructions, often seems complicated. You can easily learn to follow directions, however, by observing three rules:

1. Listen alertly.
2. Memorize the steps.
3. Repeat the steps aloud to make sure you know them in the right order.

● EXERCISE 6.   In pairs, act out the following situations. The person receiving the directions should listen carefully, repeat them aloud, and take notes if necessary.

1. Tell a friend who doesn't know your neighborhood how to go from school to your home.
2. In the corridor of your school, a woman, wearing a hat and coat, stops you. She wants to find the music teacher. Tell her how to find that person.
3. Using a map of your state, tell a friend how to drive from your town to the state capital. If you live in the state capital, tell him how to drive to a city over one hundred miles away that is not on a main route.
4. Tell a friend where he can get a bicycle tire patched, and how to get there.
5. Tell a friend how to find a novel written by Rose Wilder Lane in the main library of your town.

23d. Learn to listen critically.

There is no point in listening attentively unless you also cultivate the habit of evaluating what you hear. You should examine critically any speech that is intended to influence your thoughts or actions. Ask yourself —

1. Who says so? Is the person an authority? Does he know what he is talking about?

2. Is the information up to date?

3. Do the statements seem reasonable? Do they agree with what I already know about the subject?

4. Does the speaker have anything to gain by his position? May he have a motive that prevents him from being objective?

23d

(1) Distinguish between fact and opinion.

When you listen to someone talking on a subject on which opinions differ, distinguish between words that report facts and words that express feelings or opinions. You can check facts to find out whether or not you should accept them. Do not accept another person's *opinions* without doing some thinking of your own.

A fact can be verified. Opinions, however, are personal. They are neither true nor false. In forming your own opinions, you should listen to the factual evidence, listen to the opinions of others, and think about the subject yourself.

Examine the following statements of fact and opinion. What might result if a careless listener took some of the opinions to be facts?

FACT   There are more students taking typing this year than last.

OPINION   All sensible students are taking typing nowadays.

FACT   There are more boys than girls on the Student Council.

OPINION   Boys make better Student Council members than girls do.

FACT   Some sharks are not dangerous to man.

OPINION   The danger from sharks in these waters has been greatly exaggerated.

As a listener you should be alert to statements that are *partly* factual and may be misleading. Careful speakers will use such words as *often*, *probably*, *many*, and so on, to qualify their assertions. They will be precise rather than vague in telling where their information comes from.

MISLEADING   Everybody thinks that the new school is too crowded.

CLEAR   Many people think that the new school is too crowded.

VAGUE   Experts say that one-way traffic will reduce tie-ups at rush hours.

CLEAR   Commissioner Harris and other members of the mayor's traffic control board predict that one-way traffic will reduce tie-ups at rush hours.

(2) Evaluate the reasoning.

When someone expresses an opinion, you have a right and a responsibility to think about the reasoning behind it. You should ask—

1. Is the speaker's thinking logical?
2. Is it supported by examples or other evidence?

Suppose you heard someone say, "Don't vote for Jeanne for class president. She wouldn't be any good; she's a girl." Examine the reasoning. Does the job require qualities that a girl cannot possess? Does being a boy or a girl make any difference at all in this job? Before you accept a speaker's reasoning, make sure that it is based on sound logic.

● **EXERCISE 7.** Imagine yourself listening to the following remarks. Which opinions seem to be based on sound reasoning? Discuss your answers in class.

1. "In my experiments I found that white mice require a balanced diet. Those that were deprived of certain vitamins became nervous and irritable and showed other signs of malnutrition."
2. "No wonder he has such a good voice; he's Italian."
3. "Our neighbor's police dog bit a child once, but I don't think all police dogs are vicious."
4. "Cars made in the United States are the best in the world."
5. "A lake is much better than the ocean for swimming."
6. "Boys always hate piano lessons."
7. "Being on a debating team is good training in logical thinking."
8. "Anyone would rather play ball than study in the library all afternoon."
9. "Parents always forget what it's like to be young."
10. "Her father is a doctor, so she must like science."

PART SEVEN

Aids
to Good
English

CHAPTER 24

Using the Library

The Card Catalogue, the Dewey Decimal System, Reference Books

You are already well acquainted with one important service your library provides—that of supplying you with books for your spare-time reading. Your library should certainly continue to be a source of pleasure for you, but more and more as you get on in school you will be using it as a source of information as well.

A library is a storehouse of human knowledge. It has books of one kind or another on most of the subjects that men have found worth thinking about. No one person can learn all of these things. But it is the mark of an educated person to know how to find out a particular fact or piece of information when he needs it. In most cases, the library is the answer.

THE ARRANGEMENT OF YOUR LIBRARY

Probably there is more than one library available that you can use. There is your school library, and there is the library in your community. If you live in a large city, you can use the large main library as well as the branch library in your neighborhood. Become familiar with these libraries so that you can take full advantage of their resources. If you are not already familiar with your school library, get acquainted with it by using it. Learn where the fiction and nonfiction books, the reference books, and the magazines are kept. Learn the location of the card catalogue. Your school librarian will answer your questions, but the more you use the library, the better you will be able to locate books by yourself. Your community library is likely to be larger than your school library, and there you will be able to find books not available at school. There, too, you should become familiar with the different parts of the library by asking questions and, above all, *using* the library.

Fiction

24a. Learn to find books of fiction.

In most libraries, books of fiction can be found in one section, arranged in alphabetical order according to the author's last name. Several books by the same author are further arranged alphabetically by the first word of the title (not counting *A*, *An*, or *The*).

Suppose you want to find *Phantom of the Blockade* by Stephen W. Meader. First you find the fiction section of the library and then those books by authors whose last names begin with M. Among these you will find Meader. After locating novels by the author you want, you then look at titles. Before coming to *Phantom of the Blockade*, you may find *Away to Sea, Bulldozer, The Fish Hawk's Nest* (arranged under F, not T), and *Lumberjack*.

♦ NOTE Books by authors (like Robert McCloskey) whose names begin with *Mc* are arranged in most libraries as though the name were spelled *Mac; St.* is arranged as though it were spelled out.

● EXERCISE 1. Number 1–16. After these numbers, write the letters of the following books in the order in which they would be arranged on the library shelves.

A. *Bright Island* by Mabel Louise Robinson
B. *Bob, Son of Battle* by Alfred Ollivant
C. *Homer Price* by Robert McCloskey
D. *The Incredible Journey* by Sheila Burnford
E. *Old Ramon* by Jack Schaefer
F. *Old Yeller* by Fred Gipson
G. *David Balfour* by Robert Louis Stevenson
H. *National Velvet* by Enid Bagnold
I. *Johnny Tremaine* by Esther Forbes
J. *Call It Courage* by Armstrong Sperry
K. *The Time Machine* by H. G. Wells
L. *Jim Davis* by John Masefield
M. *Treasure Island* by Robert Louis Stevenson
N. *Charlotte's Web* by E. B. White
O. *Hie to the Hunters* by Jesse Stuart
P. *The Return of Silver Chief* by Jack O'Brien

Nonfiction

24b. **Learn to understand the Dewey decimal system of arranging nonfiction.**

As you use your library, you will learn that nonfiction books are arranged primarily not by author and title but according to the numbers of the Dewey decimal system.

24
a·b

The Dewey decimal system gets its name from Melvil Dewey, the American librarian who developed it. According to this system, all books except fiction are classified under ten headings and arranged by numbers. These numbers and headings are as follows:

000–099 General works (encyclopedias and other reference materials)
100–199 Philosophy
200–299 Religion
300–399 Social sciences (economics, government, etc.)
400–499 Language
500–599 Science
600–699 Technology (engineering, aviation, inventions, etc.)
700–799 The Arts (architecture, music, sports, etc.)
800–899 Literature
900–999 History (including geography, travel books, and biography)

All of the following books about science would be in the 500 series of the Dewey decimal system and could be found in the same section of the library:

> *The Story of Atomic Energy* by Laura Fermi
> *A Dipper Full of Stars: a Beginner's Guide to the Heavens* by Lou Page Williams
> *The Mysterious Earth* by Lester Del Ray
> *Plants That Changed the World* by Bertha S. Dodge

Every book of nonfiction has a call number printed on its spine. This number places the book under one of the ten headings of the Dewey decimal system and then into still smaller categories. For example, *A Dipper Full of Stars* may be found on the 500 shelves under the special category 520–529, *astronomy*. Its specific call number, 523.8, narrows the category even more. All books numbered 523 belong under *descriptive astronomy*, while 523.8 indicates that the book is about *the stars*.

◆ NOTE While biographies dealing with the lives of several persons may be found under the number 920, individual biographies are in a special section of the library and are marked with a B on their spines. (In some libraries they are marked 92.) Under the B appears the initial of the last name of the biography's subject. For example, *Abe Lincoln: Log Cabin to White*

House by Sterling North would be marked $\overset{B}{L}$. Still another way of classifying biographies is to spell out the name of the person who is the subject of the biography, with the number above it.

The Card Catalogue

You don't have to remember the headings of the Dewey decimal system to find a book in the library. You can find out the call number of a nonfiction book and much other information besides from the card catalogue of the library.

24c. Learn to use the card catalogue.

In some prominent place in your library, you will find a cabinet with small drawers. Each drawer is filled with cards arranged in alphabetical order by the information on the top line. This cabinet and its contents is called the *card catalogue*.

The card catalogue contains at least three cards for each book of nonfiction in the library: an *author*

24c

card, a *title card*, and a *subject card*. There may be several subject cards and, in the case of joint authors, several author cards.

The Author Card

If you are looking for a book by a particular author, you would look for the card with the author's name, last name first, printed at the top. If there is more than one author, there will be a card for each name. All books by an author are arranged in the alphabetical order of the titles under his name.

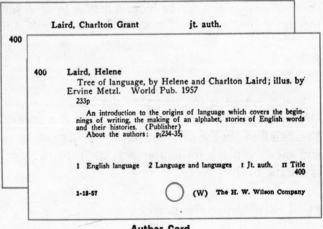

Author Card

The Title Card

If you know the title of a book but do not know the name of the author, you can find the book listed on the *title card*. On this card, the title of the book is

printed at the top. This card is placed alphabetically
in the card catalogue according to the first word in the
title, unless the first word is *a*, *an*, or *the*, in which case
the card is filed alphabetically according to the second
word in the title.

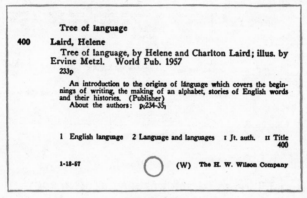

Title Card

The Subject Card

If you do not have a book in mind but are looking
for any available information on a particular subject,
you hunt up the *subject card*. Subject cards refer you to
specific books on the subject. Like author cards and
title cards, they are arranged alphabetically in the card
catalogue.

The Call Number

The number 400 that appears in the upper left corner
of all the sample cards shown above is the *call number*.
It gives you the Dewey decimal number of the book.

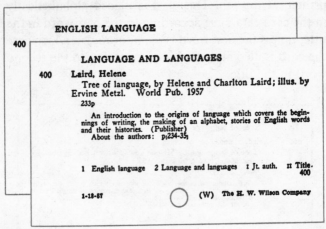

Subject Card

Other Information

In addition to the information discussed above, the card catalogue tells you the publisher and date of publication of a book, how many pages it has, and whether or not it is illustrated. All of this information can be important. Obviously, if you want a book about airplanes, you will look for one published recently enough to include information on the latest developments in jet aircraft. If you want to see what the planes look like, you will choose one that has a number of illustrations rather than one with only a few. The name of the publisher is the least important bit of information on the cards in the card catalogue, but sometimes you will find it useful also. If you are reading up on football, you will probably want a book published in the United States. In England and Canada, football is quite a different game. The place of publication is always given along with the publisher's name.

● EXERCISE 2. List the call number, title, author, and date of publication of one book on each of the following topics.

1. Space travel
2. Thomas A. Edison
3. The sun
4. Football
5. Flowers of North America
6. Fairy tales
7. Early explorations of America
8. Frogs and toads
9. American dramatists
10. Careers

REFERENCE BOOKS

24d. Learn to use reference books.

In addition to its many books on special subjects, a library also has reference books—books which contain information on a wide variety of subjects or which tell you where to find such information. Reference books are always kept together in a special section of the library.

Encyclopedias

When you want a good, detailed introduction to a subject, whether it is fossils, Alexander the Great, or the Battle of Bull Run, the reference book to use is an encyclopedia. An encyclopedia is a collection of articles on many different subjects. Often these articles contain special features like pictures, charts, maps, and lists of facts and figures about population, natural resources, and so on. When you are writing a report, you will probably go to an encyclopedia first for an

24d

overall view of your subject before you go on to more detailed sources of information.

Some encyclopedias most used by persons of your age are:

> *The Book of Knowledge*
> *Compton's Pictured Encyclopedia*
> *World Book Encyclopedia*
> *Collier's Encyclopedia*

All these encyclopedias consist of many volumes, and all except *The Book of Knowledge* arrange their articles alphabetically by title. To find information on a particular subject, use the guide letter or letters on the spine of each volume. An article on *mining* can probably be found near the middle of the volume marked M. To find a specific article in a volume, use the guide words at the top of the pages exactly as you use guide words in a dictionary. (See page 468.) If you cannot find a subject under a particular title, look for similar titles or for a larger subject that includes your subject. For example, information on *doctors* might be found in an article on *medicine*.

If you still cannot find the subject or wish to know if the encyclopedia contains more information on the subject, use the index. The index may be the first volume of the encyclopedia (as in *Britannica Junior*), the last volume (as in *Collier's Encyclopedia*), or at the end of each volume (as in *Compton's Pictured Encyclopedia*). Every encyclopedia has a section on how to use the index, usually at the beginning of the index itself. In addition to volume and page number of a subject, the index will also indicate the location of illustrations, charts, maps, and tables.

● EXERCISE 3.   Look up in an encyclopedia five of the topics listed below. Write down the name of the encyclopedia which contains information about the topic. After the name, write the volume number or letter, and the number of the page on which you found the information. Take brief notes on two of these topics, and be prepared to report on them in class.

EXAMPLE   1. The founding of the Red Cross
          1. *Compton's Pictured Encyclopedia, volume 12, page 117*
             Founded in 1864 in Geneva, Switzerland. Inspired by a pamphlet, "A Memory of Solferino," written by a young Swiss businessman, Henri Dunant.

1. The Pony Express Mail Service
2. The siege of Troy
3. The manufacture of polio vaccine
4. The use of elephants by Hannibal
5. Where amber is found
6. How rice is cultivated
7. Who invented the telescope and when
8. When the last ice age was
9. The mining of diamonds
10. The origin of Halloween
11. How to keep score at bowling
12. How the Amazon River got its name
13. The ransom of Montezuma
14. Why the dinosaur disappeared

Atlases

Atlases are books containing detailed maps and much information about cities and countries. In an atlas you can find such information as the climate, industries, natural resources, and population of a country. You can also learn the location of cities and towns, lakes, mountains, and so on. A few of the common atlases are

> *Goode's School Atlas*
> *Hammond's Library World Atlas and Gazetteer*
> *Lord's Historical Atlas of the United States*
> *Rand McNally Cosmopolitan World Atlas*

An atlas is a valuable book in social studies courses like history and geography. Become thoroughly familiar with at least one atlas.

Almanacs

An almanac is a collection of miscellaneous information. More than anything else, it consists of lists of facts—for example, a list of actors, actresses, and motion pictures that have won Academy Awards; a list of the leading magazines of the United States and Canada; a list of All-Star baseball games, including the dates the games were played, the final scores, and the names of the winning and losing managers; a list of colleges and universities of the United States, the names of their presidents, and the number of students attending them; a list of noted authors, scientists, engineers, and political and military leaders of various nations. Almanacs are published annually and bring you much up-to-date information, but they also present many facts of historical interest.

The two most widely used almanacs are *The World Almanac and Book of Facts* and the *Information Please Almanac, Atlas and Yearbook*. The best way to find information in an almanac is to use the index. In *The*

World Almanac the index is at the front of the **book**, while in the *Information Please Almanac* it is in the back.

Biographical Dictionaries

A biographical dictionary will give you information about the lives of famous persons. Some well-known biographical dictionaries are *Who's Who, Who's Who in America, Webster's Biographical Dictionary,* and *Twentieth Century Authors.*

● EXERCISE 4. Number 1–10 on your paper. After the appropriate number, indicate whether you would look first in an atlas, an almanac, or a collection of biographies for information about the items listed below. Use the abbreviations *At* for atlas, *Al* for almanac, and *B* for a collection of biographies.

1. The birthplace of Robert Browning, the nine-teenth-century English poet
2. The population of Portland, Oregon
3. The continent on which Timbuctoo is located
4. The winner of the 1963 World Series
5. The chief industries of Sweden
6. The principal novels of Jack London
7. The total vote cast in the presidential election of 1952
8. The approximate distance from New York to Moscow by the shortest air route
9. The newspaper career of Richard Harding Davis, the American short story writer
10. The number of tons of natural rubber produced in Africa in 1964

The Readers' Guide

Information on many topics, particularly information about recent events, discoveries, and inventions, is likely to be found in magazines rather than in books. Magazine articles may also supply new information or new points of view about people and things of other times.

To help you locate a particular article or find out what has appeared in magazines on a certain project, your library has a special reference book called the *Readers' Guide to Periodical Literature*, which indexes by author and subject the articles in each issue of more than one hundred magazines.

You will find the *Readers' Guide* in two forms: as a paperbound booklet published 22 times a year and as a large volume containing all the booklets published in a two-year period. The magazine articles themselves are listed by subject (like Aviation) and by author (like Azrael, Jeremy). If you look at the sample on page 461, you will see that each entry presents a brief description of the article and employs special abbreviations. A "Key to Abbreviations" is provided at the front of the *Readers' Guide*. Some abbreviations are

abr	abridged	**por**	portrait
arr	arranged	**tr**	translated, translation,
bi-m	bimonthly		or translator
cond	condensed	**w**	weekly
F	February		

Suppose you are writing a composition on avalanches and wish to find a magazine article on the subject. The *Readers' Guide* would lead you to the February

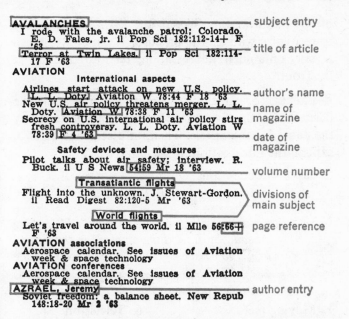

AVALANCHES — subject entry
I rode with the avalanche patrol; Colorado. E. D. Fales, jr. il Pop Sci 182:112-14+ F '63
Terror at Twin Lakes. il Pop Sci 182:114-17 F '63 — title of article
AVIATION
    International aspects
Airlines start attack on new U.S. policy. L. L. Doty. Aviation W 78:44 F 18 '63 — author's name
New U.S. air policy threatens merger. L. L. Doty. Aviation W 78:38 F 11 '63 — name of magazine
Secrecy on U.S. international air policy stirs fresh controversy. L. L. Doty. Aviation W 78:39 F 4 '63 — date of magazine
    Safety devices and measures
Pilot talks about air safety; interview. R. Buck. il U S News 54:59 Mr 18 '63 — volume number
    Transatlantic flights
Flight into the unknown. J. Stewart-Gordon. il Read Digest 82:120-5 Mr '63 — divisions of main subject
    World flights
Let's travel around the world. il Mlle 56:66+ F '63 — page reference
AVIATION associations
Aerospace calendar. See issues of Aviation week & space technology
AVIATION conferences
Aerospace calendar. See issues of Aviation week & space technology
AZRAEL, Jeremy — author entry
Soviet freedom; a balance sheet. New Repub 148:18-20 Mr 2 '63

Reproduced by permission of the H. W. Wilson Company.

1963 issue of *Popular Science*, which has two articles on avalanches, one by E. D. Fales, Jr., and the other unsigned. The entry in the *Readers' Guide* on the first article gives the following information:

> An article about avalanches called "I Rode with the Avalanche Patrol" by E. D. Fales, Jr., may be found in *Popular Science*. The article, which is illustrated (il), is in volume 182; it begins on pages 112–114 and is continued on later pages (182:112-14+) of the February 1963 issue (F '63).

At first, entries in the *Readers' Guide to Periodical Literature* may seem difficult to read, but actually most of the abbreviations (like *il* for *illustrated*) are easy to recognize with a little practice. When you come to a new, unfamiliar abbreviation, refer to the key at the front.

● EXERCISE 5.   In the *Readers' Guide*, find an article listed under any five of the following subjects. Copy the entry for the article. Then, in a sentence or two, explain the information in the entry.

EXAMPLE   Occupations
           Getting ahead. L. R. Fibel. Pop Sci 182:24+ F '63
           An article about occupations called "Getting Ahead" by L. R. Fibel appears in the February, 1963 issue of Popular Science *(volume 182). The article begins on page 24 and is continued on later pages of the issue.*

1. Moving pictures   6. Television
2. United States Congress   7. Astronauts
3. Gardening   8. Automobile racing
4. Wildlife conservation   9. Photography
5. Brazil   10. Yachts

● REVIEW EXERCISE.   Answer the following questions. If necessary, look up information in the chapter.

1. Under which of the ten number ranges of the Dewey decimal system would the following books be found?
   A. *Our Literary Heritage: a Pictorial History of the Writer in America*
   B. *Know Your Government*
   C. *Your Art Heritage*
   D. *All About Language*
2. What is the quickest way to find the call number of a book?

3. Name two different kinds of books in which the following information might be found:
   A. The birth and death dates of Abraham Lincoln
   B. A map of New Hampshire
   C. A biography of Ralph Waldo Emerson, the essay writer
   D. A list of men in the Hall of Fame

4. Name the three kinds of cards in a card catalogue. Which kind would you use most in gathering information for a report?

5. A book has $\overset{B}{W}$ on its spine. What kind of book is it? What or whom might the book be about?

6. Which of these fiction books would come first on a library shelf? Which second? Which last? Identify them by letter.
   A. *Frozen Fire* by Armstrong Sperry
   B. *Winter Danger* by William O. Steele
   C. *Danger to Windward* by Armstrong Sperry

7. You probably would not find an article on the World Series in an encyclopedia. Under what topic might you find information on this subject?

8. What part of an encyclopedia can be used to locate information quickly? Where is this part located in *Compton's Pictured Encyclopedia?* in *Collier's Encyclopedia?*

9. In which reference book would the following entry be found? In a sentence, explain the entry.

   DANCING, Korean

   Folk dances for today. Recreation 56:63
   F '63

10. Give the names of two widely used almanacs. List five different kinds of information that you find in an almanac.

CHAPTER 25

Using the Dictionary

What a Dictionary Tells You about Words

If you are like most people, you use a dictionary mainly to find out the spelling or meaning of a word. Your dictionary is certainly the right place to look for spellings and meanings, but it contains a wealth of other information as well. It tells you what part of speech a word is, how it is pronounced, how it is used, and many other things about it.

There is probably no other single reference book that you will consult so often while you are in school and afterward. But like any tool, a dictionary is most useful to those who know how to use it well. This chapter reviews some of the important features of dictionaries. Since dictionaries differ in their practices, a chapter like this one can only be a general guide. For specific help with your own dictionary, study carefully the introductory instructions it contains. All dictionaries designed for students of your age contain a guide of this kind. You will find the reading of it well worthwhile and interesting, too.

The sample column on the opposite page illustrates some important features to be found in all dictionaries. You will find it helpful to refer to this page from time to time as you work through this chapter.

favorable — guide word

fa vor a ble (fā′vər ə bəl), **1.** favoring; approving: *a favorable answer.* **2.** being to one's advantage; helping: *a favorable wind.* **3.** boding well; promising: *It was a favorable time for our trip, since business was light.* —**fa′vor a ble ness,** *n.*

fa vor a bly (fā′vər ə bli), with consent or approval; kindly. *adv.*

fa vored (fā′vərd), **1.** treated with favor. **2.** having special advantages; talented. **3.** having a certain appearance. *adj.*

fa vor ite (fā′vər it), **1.** liked better than others; liked very much: *What is your favorite flower?* **2.** one liked better than others; person or thing liked very much: *Dick is a favorite with everybody.* **3.** person treated with special favor. **4.** person, horse, etc., expected to win a contest. **1** *adj.,* **2-4** *n.*

fa vor it ism (fā′vər ə tiz′əm), **1.** a favoring of one or some more than others; having favorites. **2.** state of being a favorite. *n.*

fa vour (fā′vər), *Esp. Brit.* favor. *n.*

fawn (fôn), **1.** deer less than a year old. **2.** light, yellowish brown. **1,2** *n.,* **2** *adj.* —**fawn′-like′,** *adj.*

fawn (fôn), **1.** cringe and bow; act slavishly: *Many flattering relatives fawned on the rich old man.* **2.** of dogs, etc., show fondness by crouching, wagging the tail, licking the hand, etc. *v.* —**fawn′er,** *n.*

Fawn of the
Virginia deer

fay (fā), fairy. *n.*

faze (fāz), *U.S. Informal.* disturb; worry; bother. *v.,* **fazed, faz ing.**

FBI, Federal Bureau of Investigation, a bureau of the Department of Justice established to investigate Federal crimes and safeguard national security.

FCC or **F.C.C.,** Federal Communications Commission.

F clef, the bass clef in music. See **clef** for diagram.

Fe, iron.

fe al ty (fē′əl ti), **1.** loyalty and duty owed by a vassal to his feudal lord: *The nobles swore fealty to the king.* **2.** loyalty; faithfulness; allegiance. *n., pl.* **fe al ties.**

fear (fēr), **1.** being afraid; feeling that danger or evil is near; dread: *The knight felt no fears in the midst of battle.* **2.** feel fear. **3.** feel fear of: *Our cat fears big dogs. Those small monkeys fear big snakes. Our baby brother*

entry word — pronunciation — part of speech — numbered definitions — different words with same spelling — illustrative example — usage label — spelling of principal parts — abbreviations — spelling of plural

ARRANGEMENT OF A DICTIONARY

25a. Learn how to find a word in the dictionary.

Although there are thousands of words in a dictionary, the words defined are arranged in such a way that you can easily find the particular word you are looking for. Two devices help you: *alphabetical arrangement* and the *guide words* on each page.

Alphabetical Order

Since the words in a dictionary are entered in alphabetical order, your speed in locating any particular one of them will depend on how well you know your alphabet. The exercises that follow require you to put words in alphabetical order. If you find this slow going, it may be a good idea to spend a little time reviewing the order of letters. The best way to do this is to divide the alphabet into three parts:

abcde   fghijklmnop   qrstuvwxyz

If you divide the alphabet in this way, you will also be learning in which part of the dictionary a given word appears, for the letters *a* through *e* take up roughly the first third of all dictionaries, *f* through *p* the middle third, and *q* through *z* the last third.

Remember that you are not through with alphabetical order when you find the section of words beginning with a particular letter. The words within each section are entered according to the order of the first letter, the next letter, and so on. For example, *pen* comes after *pat*, because *e* follows *a*. In words like *about* and *absent*, you have to go to the third letter in order to place the word. To find out if *basin* comes before or after *basic*, you have to look at the fifth letter.

● EXERCISE 1.   Number your paper 1-20 and arrange the following words in alphabetical order.

ship	explanation
export	reception
industrial	sensation
product	beneficial
shelter	forty
fertile	hindrance
indistinct	transportation
velocity	preposterous
calamity	rhythm
navigation	astonishment

● EXERCISE 2.   Number your paper 1-5. Working as rapidly as you can, put each of the following lists of words in dictionary order after the proper number.

1. boy	butter	boil	bread	build
2. even	envy	evil	ever	event
3. carriage	callow	cartwheel	carried	careful
4. dome	dog	doll	doltish	dominion
5. ski	slight	skillful	sky	skin

Phrase Entries

Most of the entries in a dictionary are single words. Sometimes, however, two or more words are used together with a special meaning (*plum pudding, baker's dozen, Roman numeral,* etc.) Such words are entered in the dictionary as though they were spelled as one word. For example, *Roman numeral* comes after *romance* but before *romantic* because the *n* in *numeral* comes after *c* but before *t*. In this case, it is the sixth letter that decides.

25a

Abbreviations

Some dictionaries include abbreviations in the main body of the book, while others group all of them in a special section at the back. It is likely that the dictionary you are using this year defines abbreviations right along with other words. If this is the case, you will find an abbreviation in the place it would naturally fall in alphabetical order. That is, you will find *lb.*, the abbreviation for *pound*, right after *lazy*, and *LP* (for *long-playing record*) after *lozenge*, or whatever the last word is that begins with *lo*.

● EXERCISE 3.   Number your paper 1–25 and arrange the following words in alphabetical order.

dryer	jackknife	no.	lately	threadbare
another	dry cell	already	dry goods	position
quilt	jack rabbit	thresh	anthem	Dr.
latitude	nuclear	quill	village	nose dive
nosy	boisterous	threat	boiler	villager

Guide Words

As an aid in helping you find the word you want quickly, dictionaries print at the top of each page the first and last word defined on that page. These words, usually printed in heavy type, are called *guide words*. The one at the left shows the first word defined in the left-hand column of the page. The one at the right shows the last word on the page—at the bottom of the right-hand column. If the spelling of the word you are looking for falls alphabetically between these two guide words, the word you want is on that page. Guide words can be great time-savers when you are looking up a word. Get into the habit of using them.

● EXERCISE 4.   Number your paper 1–10. Suppose that the guide words *cafe* and *calamity* appear at the top of a page in your dictionary. Make a plus (+) beside the number of each of the following words that you would expect to find on the page that has these guide words. If the word would appear on an earlier page, write *before*. If it would appear on a later page, write *after*.

EXAMPLES   1. cage
              1. +

             2. cave
             2. *after*

1. cake
2. cattle
3. cafeteria
4. California
5. coke

6. calcium
7. cabbage
8. calamity
9. calf
10. Caesar

● EXERCISE 5.   Using the guide words on each page, look up the following words in your dictionary. On your paper, copy the guide words and the page number from the page on which each of the words appears.

EXAMPLE   1. mature
             1. *matron*   402   *maze*

1. warlike
2. emperor
3. unpredictable
4. frontier
5. tenant
6. lb

7. protection
8. chief
9. superhuman
10. government
11. heartily
12. birthright

INFORMATION IN A DICTIONARY

25b. Learn how to find the meaning you want.

Many English words have more than one meaning. In fact, some common words like *point* and *run* may have twenty, or even more, depending upon the size and completeness of the dictionary. However many meanings are given for a word, each one is defined separately and numbered. The following example shows how one dictionary defines the different meanings of the word *coast:*

> **coast** (kōst),   **1.** land along the sea; seashore. **2.** region near a coast. **3.** go along or near the coast of. **4.** sail from port to port of a coast. **5.** *U.S.* ride or slide down a hill without using power. You can coast downhill on a sled or bicycle. **6.** a slope for sliding downhill on a sled, etc.   1,2,5,6 *n.*,   3-5 *v.*

From *Thorndike-Barnhart Advanced Junior Dictionary*, by Clarence L. Barnhart.
Copyright © 1957
by Scott, Foresman and Company, Chicago. Used by permission.

When more than one meaning is given for a word, read all of them and decide which definition fits the sentence you have in mind. Frequently, one of the definitions will actually *fit* into your sentences. Suppose, for example, you read the sentence, "The golf course has the best *coast* in town." You know that the town referred to is not near the water and that, therefore, neither of the first two meanings is the one you want. But when you come to the last one, you find "a slope for sliding downhill on a sled, etc." This is the meaning you want and it makes reasonably good sense if you substitute it for *coast* in your original sentence.

Dictionaries often supply a sample phrase or sentence after numbered meanings to help you see the differences among them. Notice how the examples help you to keep straight the several meanings of *luck* in the following definition:

> **luck** \ˈlək\ *n.* **1** That which happens to a person apparently by chance; fortune; fate; chance; as, fortunate people who seem to have nothing but good *luck* in their lives. **2** The accidental way events occur; as, happening by pure *luck*. **3** Good luck; good fortune; as, to have *luck;* to be out of *luck.*

By permission. From Webster's New Secondary School Dictionary
Copyright, 1961
by G. & C. Merriam Co., Publishers of the Merriam-Webster Dictionaries.

● EXERCISE 6. Number your paper 1–8. Look at the italicized words in the following sentences. For each italicized word, write the meaning which best fits the sentence. Use the dictionary if you need to.

1. The damaged vessel is *listing* badly.
2. When you have finished *listing* the names, give your paper to Barbara.
3. Do you know the *fare* to Chicago?
4. At this restaurant, the *fare* is always excellent.
5. This *trail* was blazed by the forest ranger.
6. Don't *trail* behind; you'll be late.
7. Grace found three *quarters* in the sofa.
8. The soldiers were well pleased with their *quarters*.

Synonyms and Antonyms

Words that are similar in meaning are *synonyms*. Words that are opposite in meaning are *antonyms*.

Many definitions employ synonyms. You are very likely to find the word *dry* used in the definition for

25b

arid and the word *deep* used in the definition for *profound*. Some dictionaries give lists of synonyms, and some include short paragraphs discussing the differences in meaning among these synonyms. You may find the abbreviation *Syn.* after the list of meanings given for a word; and after *Syn.* will be the word or words that are similar in meaning to the defined word.

> **rab·ble** (răb′l), *n.* a
> noisy crowd or mob:—
> **the rabble**, the common
> people, especially those of the lowest class.
> *Syn.* populace, throng, crowd, mob.

From the *Winston Dictionary for Schools*, 1963 edition, published by Holt, Rinehart and Winston, Inc., reproduced by special permission.

> **mer·cy** \ˈmər-sē\ *n.; pl.* **mer·cies. 1** Kind and gentle treatment of an offender, an opponent, or some unfortunate person. **2** A kind, sympathetic manner or disposition; a willingness to forgive, to spare, or to help. **3** The power to be merciful; as, to throw oneself on an enemy's *mercy.* **4** An act of kindness; a blessing.
> — The words *clemency* and *leniency* are synonyms of *mercy: mercy* usually refers to a compassionate and forgiving attitude on the part of a person who has the power or right to impose severe punishment on another; *clemency* may indicate a habit or policy of moderation and mildness in one whose duty it is to impose punishment for offences; *leniency* often indicates a deliberate overlooking of mistakes or an overindulgent acceptance of another's faults.

By permission. From Webster's New Secondary School Dictionary
Copyright, 1961
by G. & C. Merriam Co., Publishers of the Merriam-Webster Dictionaries.

If the dictionary treats antonyms, it may handle them similarly, using the abbreviation *Ant.*

● EXERCISE 7. Copy from your dictionary (if it gives them) synonyms for each of the following words.

1. injurious	6. immortal
2. begin	7. drab
3. eternal	8. dislike
4. hideous	9. like
5. false	10. say

Part of Speech

The dictionary tells you what part of speech a word is. Many words may be used as more than one part of speech. In a dictionary, each part of speech is indicated by an abbreviation which comes either before or after the definition of the word:

n.	noun	*pron.*	pronoun
v.	verb	*prep.*	preposition
adv.	adverb	*interj.*	interjection
adj.	adjective	*conj.*	conjunction

● EXERCISE 8. Number your paper 1–10. Notice how the italicized word in each sentence is used. After the number, write the abbreviation showing what part of speech that word is. Use the dictionary if necessary.

1. We're going away *soon.*
2. He delivered a short *address* of welcome.
3. Sometimes a cloudy vapor *rings* the moon.
4. *Smooth* the bottom sheet before you put the top sheet on.
5. *However* we go, it will take a long time.
6. I hear Larry's heavy *tread* on the stairs.
7. How *mellow* this cheese tastes!
8. *When* did Jason get here?
9. We looked up when we heard a familiar *hail.*
10. He will *trick* you if he can.

Related Forms of a Word

For many words, there are closely related words and expressions the meaning of which can easily be seen once the meaning of the main word has been explained. For example, *fawnlike* presents no problem if you know the meaning of *fawn*, nor does *fearlessly* once you know *fearless*. Many dictionaries include such words within the entry for the word to which they are related. For example, see the word in heavy type at the end of the entry for *favorable* on page 465.

Since the related forms are often different parts of speech from the entry word, the new part-of-speech label is given. Some dictionaries give pronunciations for these related words, unless they are very easy to figure out. Most dictionaries at least indicate how the related words are accented.

You will be hearing more about related word forms in Chapter 26. When you are looking up a new word, do not neglect any of these close relatives that may be listed. If you can learn two or three new words at a time, why not do it?

25c. Learn to use your dictionary for spelling and capitalization.

The dictionary shows you how to spell a word. Simply following the principles of alphabetical order and using the guide words will lead you to most spellings that you want. Following these principles will lead you to the information that there are two *r*'s in *occurrence* and that there is an *i* after the *l* in *peculiar*. But if you try to look up *perhaps* and *omission* as though they were spelled as "prehaps" and "ommis-

sion" you naturally will not find them. If you cannot
find a word in your dictionary, the chances are you
have guessed wrong about the spelling. In that case,
you must try to discover your error and look elsewhere. Even very bad spellers can find words in a
dictionary. It just takes them longer.

Variant Spellings

You may find two spellings given for a word; thus
you are likely to find in your dictionary both *rac-
coon/ racoon*, *theater/ theatre*, and *gray/ grey*. In such
situations the dictionary is likely to tell you—often by
printing it first—which form is preferred.

Unusual Plurals

Although most nouns form their plurals by adding
–s or *–es*, some do not. The words *fly* and *dowry*, for
example, form the plural by changing the *y* to *i* and
then adding *–es*. Thus the plural of *fly* is *flies* and that
of *dowry* is *dowries*. When a plural is formed in an
irregular way, the dictionary will show it, placing the
abbreviation *pl.* before the plural form. (Notice the
form *fealties* on page 465.)

Past Tense Forms

Some verbs do not form the past tense in the usual
way by adding *–d* or *–ed*, but in other ways. For example, if you look up the words *draw* and *deal* and
see in your dictionary, you will find the following past
forms given:

draw	**drew**
deal	**dealt**
see	**saw**

25c

The omitting of a final silent *e* before *–ed* or the changing from *y* to *i* before *–ed* is regular but may be troublesome. Therefore, your dictionary is likely to list verb forms involving these operations. (Notice the inclusion of *fazed* on page 465.)

Present Participles

Usually you form the present participle of a verb by adding *–ing*. Thus the present participle of *draw* is *drawing*. Some verbs, however, present special problems. For example, to form the present participle of the verb *starve* you drop the *e* and add *–ing: starving*. Similarly, the present participle of *stare* is *staring;* of *hope* is *hoping*. Other words double the final consonant: *hop, hopping; prefer, preferring*.

Dictionaries usually include forms that involve spelling problems like these. Notice the inclusion of *fazing* on page 465.

Comparatives and Superlatives

The dictionary shows the comparative and superlative forms of adjectives when they present any spelling problems. When we add to *hot* the ending *–er* we must double the *t* to spell *hotter*. When we add *–est* to *merry* we must change the *y* to *i* to form *merriest*.

● EXERCISE 9. Using a dictionary if you need to, follow directions for each of the items below, and write the correctly spelled word on your paper.

EXAMPLE   1. Add *–ing* to *write*
           1. *writing*

1. Add *–s* to *spy*.   3. Add *–s* to *monkey*.
2. Add *–ing* to *dance*.   4. Add *–ing* to *duel*.

5. Add *-ly* to *neutral*.   8. Add *-est* to *happy*.
6. Add *-ence* to *recur*.   9. Add *-er* to *win*.
7. Add *-ed* to *pry*.   10. Add *-s* to *hero*.

● EXERCISE 10. Write the past tense and present participle form of each of the following verbs. Use a dictionary if necessary.

1. write   6. weep
2. sleep   7. fortify
3. begin   8. ski
4. lie   9. hurt
5. lay   10. dive

Capitalization

In general, proper nouns are capitalized in English and common nouns written with lower-case, or small, letters. Most dictionaries print proper nouns with a capital letter and common nouns with a small letter. (See how your dictionary prints the entries for the nouns *Canadian* and *Navaho*.)

Sometimes a word is capitalized in one sense but printed with a lower-case letter in another. (Compare your dictionary entries for *God* as the supreme being and for *god* meaning a Latin or Greek deity.)

If you are in doubt about using a capital, the dictionary will help you. Remember that, in addition to consulting the dictionary, you should know the rules for capitalization (see Chapter 10).

● EXERCISE 11. Look up the following words in a dictionary to see when they are capitalized. Be able to explain in each case why a capital letter should or should not be used.

1. arctic	6. capitol
2. congress	7. pole
3. house	8. roman
4. father	9. catholic
5. president	10. republican

Syllable Division

The term *syllable* is not easy to define simply and clearly, but in general a syllable is a short word or part of a longer word containing a single vowel sound with or without adjacent consonants. A dictionary divides into syllables each defined word that contains more than one syllable.

Some dictionaries separate the syllables by a hyphen: sim-plic-i-ty.

Some dictionaries use a dot in the center of the space between syllables: e·ven·tu·al·ly.

Still others simply leave a space between syllables: dread ful ly.

Knowing the syllables in a word sometimes helps you to pronounce and spell the word correctly. In your writing, if you must divide a word at the end of a line, you need to know the syllables, so that you can divide it between syllables.

● EXERCISE 12. Look up the following words in a dictionary. (Use the guide words.) Copy this list, separating the words into syllables. Leave spaces between the syllables.

1. jewel	6. opportunity
2. monastery	7. profuse
3. industrious	8. invention
4. merchant	9. canal
5. companion	10. knightly

25d. Learn to use your dictionary for pronunciation.

The dictionary gives a pronunciation for every entry word. The pronunciation indication is usually given immediately after the entry word, in parentheses (as on page 465), but sometimes it is given between slant bars (as in the entry for *luck* on page 471). Find out which procedure your dictionary uses.

Notice that the spelling given within the parentheses or slant bars has no necessary connection with the spelling of the word. It is an indication of pronunciation alone. For example, you will probably find in your dictionary the respelling "rīd" after *ride*. This does not mean that you can ever correctly spell *ride* in this way; it means that the three sounds, those connected with *r*, *i*, and *d*, are the only ones used in pronouncing the word.

The Accent Mark

When a word has more than one syllable, one, at least, of its syllables is stressed or accented—that is, uttered with greater force or volume than the others. Notice the difference in pronunciation between *beacon*, with the accent on the first syllable, and *begin*, with the accent on the second.

Sometimes the position of the accent makes a great deal of difference. If we pronounce *entrance* with the accent on the first syllable, we have the noun meaning "act of entering" or "way of entering," but if we pronounce this same combination of letters with the accent on the second syllable we have the verb meaning "to

25d

fill with delight and wonder." Notice the position of the accent in every new word that you learn.

Dictionaries commonly indicate the accented syllable by placing the mark ′ after it: *fav′or a ble*. Some dictionaries use the mark ˡ instead, placing it in front of the syllable accented: ˡ*fav or a ble*.

● EXERCISE 13. Look up the following words in your dictionary. Copy the words, dividing them into syllables and placing the accent mark as your dictionary places it. Leave spaces between the syllables.

1. reduce	11. invent
2. queenly	12. occupation
3. embark	13. machinist
4. diffuse	14. odor
5. consider	15. inflict
6. political	16. resist
7. encourage	17. possess
8. misfortune	18. possessive
9. meander	19. public
10. differential	20. publicity

Sometimes for words of three or more syllables a dictionary indicates two accents, one the primary accent, the other the secondary accent. The word *popularity* has five syllables: *pop*, *u*, *lar*, *i*, and *ty*. When you pronounce this word you will have no doubt that the syllable *lar* is accented, but you will also notice that the syllable *pop* receives greater stress than *u*, *i*, or *ty*. Sometimes the secondary accent is indicated by the mark ˌ before and below the syllable in question.

In many dictionaries the primary accent is given in heavy print (′), the secondary in lighter print (′). The word *popularity*, for example, is marked *pop′u lar′i ty*.

In other dictionaries the secondary accent is shown by two accent marks (″) or by the mark ˌ: *pop″u lar′i ty* or ˌ *pop u ′lar i ty.*

The introductory section of your dictionary will tell which of these systems is used in that book.

● EXERCISE 14.   Look up the following words in your dictionary. Copy the words, dividing them into syllables and placing the accent marks where they belong. Follow the system of your dictionary in showing syllable division and accent. Practice pronouncing the words.

1. ruination
2. tributary
3. photographic
4. opposition
5. luminary
6. fumigation
7. graduation
8. classification
9. optimistic
10. senatorial

Symbols for Sounds

We have in English many more sounds than we have letters to show these sounds. The vowels in the words *cat*, *mate*, and *father* have different sounds but we spell all the words with the letter *a*. The dictionary maker cannot show the difference between these pronunciations without using more symbols.

Diacritical Marks

To solve this problem, dictionaries use diacritical marks—special symbols placed above conventional letters.

Recording of pronunciation is among the dictionary maker's most difficult tasks; few specialists on pronunciation are completely satisfied with any one system of recording pronunciation; and dictionaries vary widely in the systems of diacritical marks they use.

In order to use the pronunciations given in your dictionary, you must familiarize yourself with the diacritical marks it uses. These are explained in a key that usually appears inside the front cover and sometimes on each page as well.

In this chapter you will study only a few of the more important diacritical marks that are common to most systems.

Long Vowels

The long straight mark over a vowel is called the *macron* (pronounced *mā′kron*). When the macron appears over a vowel, the vowel is often said to have the sound of its own name. Such vowels are called long vowels.

EXAMPLES	dāt	date
	sēt	seat
	hī	high
	gōt	goat
	ūnit	unit

● EXERCISE 15.   Look up the following words in a dictionary. Copy each word, dividing it into syllables and using the accent mark. Put a macron over each long vowel. For now, ignore all other diacritical marks.

1. invade
2. slope
3. checkmate
4. exaggerate
5. outline

6. mistake
7. mining
8. useful
9. seaweed
10. metronome

Short Vowels

Vowels customarily called "short" include the following:

a as in bat	*o* as in top
e as in net	*oo* as in wood
i as in pick	*u* as in but

Dictionaries vary in their method of showing the pronunciation of short vowels.

One method is to place a *breve* (pronounced brēv) over the vowel. Thus in the *Winston Dictionary for Schools* the pronunciation of *establish* is shown like this: ĕs-tăb′lĭsh. The curved marks over the vowels are breves. Another method is to leave short vowels unmarked: es thet′iks.

The Schwa

Today's dictionary maker is becoming increasingly aware that he needs other devices than diacritical marks to indicate the truth about English pronunciation, and probably the dictionaries of the future will make more use of special symbols. One pronunciation symbol that is now very commonly used is called the *schwa*. Look at the symbol used in the second, third, and fourth syllables in the pronunciation of *favorable:* fa vər ə bəl. Each of these "upside-down *e*'s" is a schwa. The schwa indicates the blurred, unclear sound of *o*, the second *a*, and *e* in *favorable*—the sound that might be spelled as "uh." Notice the use of the schwa in the pronunciations for *favorite* and *fealty* on page 465.

● EXERCISE 16.   Look up the following words. Copy the dictionary pronunciations of the words.

1. dreadfully
2. drama
3. boa
4. complimentary
5. coverall

6. discontentment
7. fission
8. historical
9. narrative
10. obligation

● REVIEW EXERCISE.   Write out the answers to the following questions. Use complete sentences.

1. What is a synonym?
2. What is an antonym?
3. What does the accent mark tell?
4. What is meant by "guide words"?
5. The words *gave*, *general*, *gear*, and *gasoline* all appear on one page of a dictionary. Two of them are the guide words for that page. Which two?
6. What does the macron tell about a vowel?
7–10. List four kinds of information that the dictionary gives you about a word.

CHAPTER 26

Vocabulary

Learning and Using New Words

The number of words you know and use today is much greater than the number you knew four or five years ago. This is true whether or not you have ever consciously tried to enlarge your vocabulary. You have learned many new words from your parents and friends, from the subjects you have studied in school, from books, movies, television programs, and games. There is almost nothing that you do in school or in your free time that doesn't increase your supply of words.

But though you are always learning some new words just by going about your everyday affairs, the chances are that you can learn many more if you make an effort to do so. This chapter will show you some ways in which you can add to your vocabulary a much larger percentage of the new words that come your way. It is very important that you should learn to do so. A good vocabulary is a great advantage in everything you do. It will help you to succeed in school and in your later life.

Before studying ways of developing a better vocabulary you may be interested to know how your stock of words compares right now with the vocabularies of other seventh-grade students. An average seventh-grade student should score between 65 and 70 percent on the following diagnostic test. Can you do better?

● **EXERCISE 1.** Number your paper 1–25. Each numbered word below is followed by four words. Beside the number on your paper, write the letter of the word that is closest in meaning to the numbered word.

EXAMPLE 1. vacant   a. useless   c. stupid
                    b. empty   d. clean

      1. *b*

1. brawny   a. powerful   c. intelligent
               b. ancient   d. delicate

2. catastrophe   a. magazine   c. store
                    b. disaster   d. outlook

3. combustion   a. group   c. friend
                    b. excitement   d. burning

4. decoy   a. watch   c. vision
               b. copy   d. lure

5. diminish   a. make older   c. make easy
               b. make less   d. finish

6. elicit   a. draw forth   c. exchange
               b. give away   d. unravel

7. fatigue   a. make-believe   c. weariness
               b. door   d. appearance

8. gibberish   a. high fever   c. old song
               b. combination   d. senseless chatter

9. hilt   a. mountain   c. towel
               b. handle   d. doorway

10. inarticulate   a. compact   c. not cheap
                   b. not stated   d. unable to speak

11. inflation   a. suit   c. swelling
               b. revelation   d. confidence

12. isolate
   a. place apart
   b. collect
   c. protect
   d. vote

13. larceny
   a. raft
   b. theft
   c. money
   d. cloud

14. methodical
   a. orderly
   b. tired
   c. religious
   d. modern

15. opaque
   a. not near
   b. liquid
   c. not transparent
   d. gentle

16. predict
   a. deny
   b. ignore
   c. request
   d. prophesy

17. punctual
   a. speedy
   b. tasty
   c. honest
   d. on time

18. ramble
   a. sing
   b. grasp
   c. cover
   d. wander

19. renown
   a. awareness
   b. desire
   c. fame
   d. cabinet

20. seclude
   a. tie up
   b. move
   c. keep apart
   d. unlock

21. sullen
   a. gloomy
   b. white
   c. heavy
   d. lonely

22. tendency
   a. weariness
   b. inclination
   c. tool
   d. balcony

23. tangible
   a. solid
   b. massive
   c. ignorant
   d. imaginary

24. unkempt
   a. snowy
   b. untidy
   c. not known
   d. unready

25. variation
   a. violin
   b. vapor
   c. change
   d. violence

26a. As you learn new words, list them with their meanings in your notebook, and use them in your speech and writing.

26a

Keeping a vocabulary list in your notebook is one of the surest ways to enlarge your knowledge of words. After each new word, write a definition of it. Then write a sentence in which the word is used. Keep a special section of your notebook for this purpose. Add words you learn from day to day in other classes and outside school. Review your list occasionally, and use the words in speech and writing as often as you can in order to make them a permanent part of your vocabulary.

MEANING FROM CONTEXT

One obvious way of learning the meaning of a new word is to look it up in a dictionary. The chances are, however, that you have learned only a small percentage of the words you know by this method. More often you guessed the meaning from the situation in which you heard the new word used, or you recognized that it was formed from other words you already knew. You will be using all three of these methods in this chapter and from now on.

26b. Learn new words from context.

The *context* of a word means the other words and sentences that surround it. From the context, you can sometimes guess at the meaning of an unfamiliar word. For example, if you did not know the meaning of the word *accompanist*, you could probably guess it from the way it is used in the following sentence: *The accompanist played so loudly that he interfered with the singer*. From the context, you can tell that "accompanist" means one who plays (probably the piano) while someone sings. The word can hardly mean anything else. If you look up the word in the dictionary, you will find that your guess is right; that, in fact, anyone who performs with a soloist (whether a singer or an instrumentalist) is an accompanist.

Use of context clues in learning new words is so important that a longer illustration will be worthwhile here. Ernest Lawrence Thayer's poem called "Casey at the Bat" tells how mighty Casey, the star of the Mudville team, comes to bat in the last half of the ninth with two out, runners on second and third, and two runs needed for Mudville to tie the opponents. Casey does not swing at the first pitch, and the umpire calls it a strike.

> From the benches, black with people, there
>   went up a muffled roar,
> Like the beating of the storm waves on the
>   stern and distant shore.
> "Kill him! kill the umpire!" shouted someone
>   on the stand;
> And it's likely they'd have killed him had not
>   Casey raised his hand.
>
> With a smile of Christian charity great Casey's
>   visage shone;
> He stilled the rising tumult, he made the game
>   go on;
> He signaled to the pitcher, and once more the
>   spheroid flew;
> But Casey still ignored it, and the umpire said,
>   "Strike two."

The word *visage*, *tumult*, and *spheroid* may give you some trouble, but if you think about the context you may be able to see that *visage* is unlikely to mean

26b

anything other than "face," that *tumult* may be read as "noisy, threatening agitation," and that *spheroid*, at least in this passage, must mean "ball." The words and sentences that surround these three words lead us to safe guesses about their meanings. (Incidentally, mighty Casey struck out on the next pitch, Mudville lost, and there was no joy whatever in the town that night.)

● EXERCISE 2. Number your paper 1–10. For each numbered word in the paragraph below, select the word closest in meaning from the list preceding the paragraph. Write that word next to the appropriate number. Look for clues to meaning in the context. After you have finished, check your answers with the dictionary, and correct them where necessary. You will not need all of the words in the list.

automobile	realized
beginner	roadway
false impression	scattered
patient acceptance	instruction book
picture	speeded up
pretend	stern

The (1) *novice* got into the (2) *vehicle* with his father, asked his dad to hold his learner's permit, and started up the motor. The car began to move, and the boy (3) *accelerated* slowly and carefully. He tried to keep in mind all the directions in the driver's (4) *manual* and at the same time to control the car. He attempted to (5) *feign* confidence, but the (6) *grim* expression on his face showed the strain. Although he was going only 20 miles per hour, he had the (7) *illusion* of going at high speed. The onlookers saw the father look back, his face a (8) *portrait* of hopeless (9) *resignation*, and then they (10) *dispersed* as the car went out of sight in a cloud of dust.

● EXERCISE 3. Number your paper 1–10. Next to each number, copy from column B the word or phrase that is closest in meaning to the italicized word in column A. Refer to the dictionary if necessary.

A	B
1. an *audition* for the singer	cartoon
2. the *bravado* of the trapped wrongdoer	carry
	false boldness
3. an amusing *caricature*	go on board ship
4. tourists about to *embark*	trial hearing
5. a *humane* judge	make up one's mind
6. *lubricate* the motor	merciful
7. a *partial* count	trivial
8. *resolve* to work harder	incomplete
9. an ancient *scroll*	roll of parchment
10. *transport* the luggage	oil

Often an author knows that he may be using a word unfamiliar to his reader and, accordingly, adds a brief definition himself. Notice how the words in heavy type in the following sentences have been defined by the authors.

The university owns a **seismograph,** a machine for measuring the force of earthquakes.

Leading from the heart are two major **arteries,** vessels that carry blood to other parts of the body.

This plastic is **translucent** in that it permits some light to pass through it but prevents one's seeing through it.

26c. Learn the meaning of new words by looking them up in the dictionary.

You may not always be able to guess the meaning of words from the context. Frequently you must use a dictionary. As you know, the dictionary lists words alphabetically and gives much information about them in addition to their meanings. In this chapter, however, we are concentrating on meanings. When you have found the word you are looking for, there may be several meanings given. You must read all of these meanings to find the one which applies in the sentence you have in mind.

● EXERCISE 4.   Copy column A on your paper, and next to each item copy the item from column B that is closest in meaning. Refer to the dictionary when you need to. You will not use all the words in column B.

A	B
1. authentic	invitation to a contest
2. challenge	put off
3. postpone	agreement
4. harmony	call to mind
5. juvenile	frequent
6. nocturnal	genuine
7. perpetual	hold back
8. restrain	issue
9. sequel	lasting forever
10. utter	of the night
	speak
	that which follows
	youthful

● EXERCISE 5.   Write numbers 1–5 on your paper, corresponding to the numbered questions. Next to each number, copy from the list above the questions the word that answers the question. You will not use all the words. You may refer to the dictionary to find the meanings of the words.

censure   eludes   pompous
confiscates   inert   profound

1. What does a good base runner do when the second baseman tries to tag him with the ball as he slides into second base?
2. How do you describe something that seems inactive and motionless?
3. What does the government do when it needs certain property to build a road?
4. What word describes a person who thinks or feels deeply?
5. What is the manner of a self-important person?

● EXERCISE 6. Follow the directions for Exercise 5.

beneficiary   paternal   phenomenon
farce   migrate   rumor

1. What is a play whose purpose is to make people laugh?
2. What is a piece of news that spreads without proof of its truth?
3. What is a person who receives money through a will or insurance policy?
4. What is the attitude of a father to his children?
5. What do groups of animals sometimes do when food becomes scarce where they live?

● EXERCISE 7. Number your paper 1–10. Next to each number, copy a word from the list below which conveys an idea appropriate to the sentence having that number. Look up the words in the dictionary if you do not know their meanings.

26c

EXAMPLE 1. He was admired by all for his brave and generous nature.

    1. *noble*

controversial	frivolous	rigid
credible	lenient	sallow
desolate	overt	tepid
flawless	weary	noble

1. The steel beam did not bend, in spite of the great weight on it.
2. Robinson Crusoe was shipwrecked alone on a barren island.
3. There was nothing sneaky about the action, which was done in full view of everyone.
4. The subject aroused a great deal of debate, and much was said pro and con.
5. The teacher did not scold the boy, despite his lateness to class.
6. The story was easy to believe when we heard the evidence.
7. His yellowish complexion was caused by lack of sunshine.
8. He was astonished the first time he swam in Florida to find the water almost lukewarm.
9. The club members giggled and refused to be serious at the rehearsal.
10. The perfect diamond glittered in its platinum setting.

● EXERCISE 8. Number your paper 1–5. Next to each number, write a word selected from the list below which correctly completes the sentence of the same number. Refer to your dictionary for word meanings.

antecedent	epitaph	pacifist
debris	manuscript	synopsis

1. The summary of earlier installments of a serial story is called a ——.
2. "O Rare Ben Jonson," the inscription on the poet's tomb, is a famous ——.
3. After the hurricane the streets were littered with ——.
4. Because he regarded war as wrong and useless, he was called a ——.
5. The original copy of Longfellow's "Psalm of Life" is a valuable ——.

● EXERCISE 9.   Follow the directions for Exercise 8.

utility	hermit
enmity	opponent
grandeur	strategy

1. As the traveler looked at the Greek temple, he was impressed by its ——.
2. For a long time Thoreau lived at Walden Pond, away from people, almost as a ——.
3. The chess master won the game by his clever ——.
4. Because of a long-standing —— between their families, Romeo and Juliet were not able to be married.
5. By his speed and volleying, the tennis champion overwhelmed his ——.

● EXERCISE 10.   Number 1–10 on your paper. For each number, choose and copy the word or phrase from column B which has the meaning of the numbered word in column A. Use the dictionary.

A	B
1. antedate	a. shut out
2. bulwark	b. ruler
3. caliber	c. light up
4. exclude	d. thrust one's self in
5. illumine	e. farm

6. incite   f. quality
7. intrude   g. stir up
8. moderate   h. find out
9. envelop   i. happen before
10. terminate   j. not extreme
                       k. cover from all sides
                       l. strong means of defense
                       m. bring to an end

● REVIEW EXERCISE A. The words listed below are selected from the words you have studied so far in this chapter. Number your paper 1–20. Beside each number write the letter of the word that is closest in meaning to the numbered word.

1. tepid
     a. calm   c. weary
     b. lukewarm   d. enclosed

2. bravado
     a. false boldness   c. exploration
     b. volume   d. shallowness

3. caliber
     a. character   c. quality
     b. shade   d. dimensions

4. paternal
     a. fatherly   c. ever-increasing
     b. ancestral   d. anxious

5. epitaph
     a. witty saying   c. puzzle
     b. inscription on   d. short poem
        a tomb

6. credible
     a. believable   c. breakable
     b. obscure   d. not difficult

7. elude
     a. oil thoroughly   c. hit savagely
     b. perceive   d. escape from

8. grandeur
     a. size   c. old age
     b. magnificence   d. location

9. sequel
     a. chapter   c. shrill cry
     b. that which fol-   d. development
        lows

10. terminate
   a. period of weeks
   b. infest with insects
   c. bring to an end
   d. railroad depot

11. partial
   a. incomplete
   b. slightly ill
   c. separately
   d. filled up

12. authentic
   a. antique
   b. literary
   c. genuine
   d. false

13. lenient
   a. not severe
   b. soothing
   c. transparent
   d. melodious

14. inert
   a. repulsive
   b. heavy
   c. unmoving
   d. waxy

15. pompous
   a. noble
   b. self-important
   c. ceremonial
   d. lengthy

16. feign
   a. rule
   b. pretend
   c. hope for
   d. cool quickly

17. debris
   a. proclamation
   b. state of exhaustion
   c. severe cold
   d. rubbish

18. incite
   a. dislike
   b. stir up
   c. make calm
   d. speak to

19. caricature
   a. slight damage
   b. scene in color
   c. cartoon
   d. circus performer

20. illusion
   a. veil
   b. picture
   c. misunderstanding
   d. false impression

WORD ANALYSIS

Some English words can be divided into parts. You can see that *untrue* can be divided into *un-* and *true*, that *foretell* is composed of *fore-* and *tell*, and that *mistrust* is made up of *mis-* and *trust*. You can also see that *wildly* can be divided into *wild* and *-ly*, *coldness* into *cold* and *-ness*, and *golden* into *gold* and *-en*. Many other words can be divided like these examples.

26d. **Learn the meaning of new words by dividing them into their parts.**

Roots

Although English has many words that can be divided, it has some that cannot. *Man* cannot be divided into *m* and *an;* *room* is not made up of *r* and *oom*, *ro* and *om*, or *roo* and *m*. *Water* cannot be divided into *wat* and *er*, nor can *summer* be divided.

Words like *man*, *room*, *water*, and *summer* that cannot be broken up into separate parts are called *roots*. Scan a column of your dictionary, paying attention only to the shorter and simpler words. If you happen to start with *cr*, for instance, you will find that the following words are roots: *crab, crack, craft, crag, cram, crane, crank, crash,* and *crate*.

Now consider once more the words *untrue, foretell, mistrust, wildly, coldness,* and *golden*. *Untrue* divides into *un-* and *true*, but the form *true* cannot be further divided. It is a unit by itself; it is not made up of *t* and *rue*, *tr* and *ue*, or *tru* and *e*. And *wildly* divides into *wild* and *-ly*, but *wild* itself is a unit that cannot be divided. *True* and *wild* are roots. Similarly, *tell* in *foretell*, *trust* in *mistrust*, *cold* in *coldness*, and *gold* in *golden* are roots. *Untrue, foretell,* and *wildly* consist of roots with something more added to them.

Prefixes and Suffixes

The groups of letters *un–* (in *untrue*), *fore–* (in *fore-tell*), and *mis–* (in *mistrust*), are called *prefixes;* they are added to the beginning of the word.

In *wildly*, *coldness*, and *golden*, *–ly*, *–ness*, and *–en* are *suffixes*. They are added to the end of the root. Study this small table:

PREFIX	ROOT	SUFFIX	WORD
un–	true		untrue
en–	courage	–ment	encouragement
re–	create	–ion	recreation
	man	–hood	manhood
un–	happy	–ness	unhappiness

Being able to recognize certain words as made up of roots and prefixes or suffixes almost always helps in learning the spelling and the pronunciation of such words and often, although not always, helps in arriving at their meaning.

● EXERCISE 11. Number your paper 1–10. Write *root* after the number of each root word. Write *root and prefix* or *root and suffix* for words made up of a root and one or the other of these elements.

1. friendless
2. sweeten
3. miscount
4. paper
5. maim
6. dismount
7. father
8. recapture
9. arc
10. picture

● EXERCISE 12. Follow directions for Exercise 11.

1. undo
2. apple
3. deem
4. placement

26d

5. intake
6. booklet
7. unable

8. discard
9. lioness
10. uncle

26e. **Learn the meaning of some common prefixes.**

PREFIX	MEANING	EXAMPLE
anti–	against	antiwar
post–	after	postdated
sub–	under	submarine

You can see how these prefixes affect the meaning of the words in which they occur. An *antiwar* point of view is one that is *against* war. A *postdated* letter is one that is dated *after* the time of writing. A *submarine* is a boat that travels *under* water.

● EXERCISE 13. Each of the ten words below uses one of the prefixes you have learned. Copy the numbers on your paper and write the meaning of the word after the number. Use the dictionary.

EXAMPLE   1. subterranean
            1. *under the surface of the earth*

1. antiseptic
2. postscript
3. subdivide
4. postgraduate
5. subsoil

6. antifreeze
7. subtract
8. antiaircraft
9. postlude
10. antisocial

Here are seven additional prefixes. Learn their meanings and study the examples carefully.

PREFIX	MEANING	EXAMPLE
ante–	before	anteroom
contra–	against	contradict
in–	not	inarticulate
inter–	between	interstate
per–	through	perforate
re–	again, back	recall
trans–	across	transfer

● EXERCISE 14. Using the dictionary if necessary, find the meaning for the words given below. Write each meaning after the proper number.

1. inhospitable
2. retouch
3. perspire
4. inhumane
5. perennial
6. transfusion
7. antecedent
8. contravene
9. contraband
10. antedate
11. intervene
12. reassure
13. incompatible
14. transitional
15. incoherent

26f. Increase your vocabulary by learning the companion forms of a word.

Many nouns, verbs, and adjectives in English have closely related companion forms used as other parts of speech. The noun *boy* has the companion forms *boyish* and *boylike*, which are adjectives. The verb *reflect* has the companion noun *reflection*. The adjective *happy* has for companion forms the noun *happiness* and the adverb *happily*. English is rich in relations of this sort. If you keep this in mind, you will find that you can often learn two or three new words as easily as one.

Knowing the companion forms of a word can also be an aid in spelling. If you have trouble remembering that there are two *a*'s in *capable*, the companion form

26
e-f

capacity gives you the clue you need. *Dividend* should be easier to spell correctly if you remember that it is closely related to *divide*.

● EXERCISE 15.   Number your paper 1–10. For each verb, write the companion noun meaning the action itself or condition.

EXAMPLE   1. place
              1. *placement*

1. abandon   6. impeach
2. accuse   7. inquire
3. alter   8. persist
4. appraise   9. rebel
5. defy   10. seize

● EXERCISE 16.   Number your paper 1–10. For each verb, write the companion noun meaning doer of the action indicated.

EXAMPLE   1. act
              1. *actor*

1. agitate   6. serve
2. assist   7. survey
3. instruct   8. survive
4. pursue   9. torment
5. reflect   10. usurp

● EXERCISE 17.   Number your paper 1–5. For each noun or adjective write the companion verb meaning to cause to be or to be like:

EXAMPLE   1. short
              1. *shorten*

1. active   4. human
2. central   5. sweet
3. diverse

● EXERCISE 18.   Number your paper 1–10. For each noun write a companion adjective.

1. algebra
2. alkali
3. atom
4. caprice
5. circle

6. luxury
7. medicine
8. navy
9. suicide
10. triumph

USING NEW WORDS

26g. Use the exact word to express your meaning in describing people and things.

English has so rich a vocabulary that there are words to describe hundreds of kinds of people and things. It is only a person with a very poor vocabulary who describes everything of which he approves as "nice," and everything of which he disapproves as "terrible." Does he mean pleasant, attractive, agreeable, excellent? Or does he mean ugly, unfortunate, evil, distasteful? Using the word to convey the exact shade of meaning you have in mind makes your speaking and writing more mature and interesting.

● EXERCISE 19.   The following sentences are uninteresting and lack force because the italicized word or words in each one do not convey any particular shade of meaning. Number your paper 1–10. After the proper number, write a word or words which can replace the italicized ones and make the sentences more meaningful. Use your imagination.

EXAMPLE   1. The inquisitive puppy *fell* down the stairs.
　　　　　1. *tumbled*

26g

1. Visiting the Grand Canyon was a *good* experience.
2. The diamond necklace *shone* in the sunlight.
3. We all had a *fine* time at Esther's party.
4. Skiing is a *nice* sport.
5. The column of soldiers *walked* down the road.
6. Yesterday was a *bad* day.
7. What a *terrible* movie!
8. The dancer *moved* across the stage.
9. During the storm thunder *was heard* and lightning *was seen*.
10. *Great* waves splashed against the coast.

26h. Master the special vocabularies of your other school subjects.

In addition to facts and skills, you learn new words in your mathematics, science, and social studies classes. Some of these words are completely new; others are familiar words which have special meanings in a particular subject. It is important that you know the meanings of such words, for often they are essential to understanding the important concepts.

The new words you encounter in your textbooks will often be italicized or in heavy type the first time they appear. Pay special attention to words marked in this way. The writer is showing you that they are important. Often, he will define the new word on the spot. Many textbooks also include glossaries—short dictionaries of the special words of a subject. Be sure to use this feature of your textbooks when it is available. Just because a glossary is in the back of a book, don't conclude that it is not important.

● EXERCISE 20. The words below figure prominently in mathematics books designed for students of your age. Write each word on your paper, and follow it by a short definition. Then write a short sentence using each word correctly. Look up any words you do not know in your textbook or in a desk dictionary.

addend	fraction	operation
cube	dividend	percentage
decimal	divisor	power
equality	multiply	root
equation	multiplicand	set

● EXERCISE 21. The following words are likely to appear in your social studies assignments. Follow the directions for Exercise 20.

History: alien, amendment, caucus, colony, elector, emancipate, embargo, impeach, legislature, ratify, secede, sedition, tariff, territory, veto.

Geography: Arctic, contour, delta, estuary, hemisphere, latitude, longitude, promontory, temperate, torrid.

● EXERCISE 22. The following words are likely to appear in your science assignments. Follow the directions for Exercise 20.

artery	eclipse	molecule
bacteria	environment	nucleus
calorie	hybrid	parasite
cell	invertebrate	vertebrate

26i. Use the words from specialized vocabularies in your everyday speaking and writing.

26
h-i

Many of the words you learn in your study of mathematics, science, and other subjects have extended meanings which are appropriate for use elsewhere. You will often encounter words like *multiply*, *ratio*, and *factor* outside of books on mathematics and *nucleus*, *artery*, and *eclipse* in books that have little to do with science. Learn to use the extended meanings of the words you learn in your school subjects appropriately in the other writing and speaking you do.

● EXERCISE 23. The following words from mathematics, science, and social studies have extended meanings useful in general writing and speaking. Use these words appropriately in the blanks below. You will not use all of the words in the list.

alien	equality	parasite
artery	fraction	temperate
cell	latitude	territory
dividend	multiply	torrid
eclipse	nucleus	veto

1. The name of Graham McNamee, once known to millions of radio listeners, has been ——d by more recent radio and television personalities.
2. Harry sometimes eats too much, but Frank is always —— at the dinner table.
3. I would like to go to the movies tonight, but I am afraid that my father will —— the idea.
4. The American Telephone and Telegraph Company has declared a yearly —— on its stock.
5. Carson Boulevard is the main —— through which the city's traffic flows.
6. A person who enjoys the benefits of this country but contributes nothing to its welfare or improvement is a ——.

7. Because Robert does his best when he is allowed to work freely, the teacher gave him much —— in writing his report.

8. Our club's membership will quickly —— after we give our first party.

9. I could look in my sister's room, but she tells me that it is forbidden ——.

10. Only a small —— of the people are familiar with the political platforms of the two candidates.

● REVIEW EXERCISE B. The words listed below are selected from the words you have studied in this chapter. Number your paper 1–20. Beside each number, write the letter of the word that is closest in meaning to the numbered word.

1. alien a. illegal   c. in poor health
     b. foreign d. untruthful

2. deem a. demand c. happen
     b. think   d. regret

3. elude a. hit   c. oil thoroughly
     b. escape from d. perceive

4. veto a. agree   c. invite
     b. delay in making d. refuse to ap-
       up one's mind prove

5. antiseptic a. unsociable c. germicide
     b. ugly   d. illness

6. paternal a. fatherly c. anxious
     b. ever-increasing d. ancestral

7. temperate a. quick-tempered c. moderate
     b. tropical d. too cold

8. contra- a. illegal goods c. unlikely
 band b. disliking music d. mysterious

9. caliber
   a. dimensions
   b. character
   c. shade
   d. quality

10. contro-versial
    a. open to debate
    b. unanimous
    c. disliked
    d. complicated

11. profound
    a. bookish
    b. difficult
    c. foolish
    d. deep

12. parasite
    a. telescope
    b. one that lives at the expense of another
    c. native of Paris
    d. an insulating material

13. illusion
    a. picture
    b. veil
    c. false impression
    d. misunderstand-ing

14. maim
    a. cripple
    b. capture
    c. frighten
    d. threaten

15. perpetual
    a. wearing away
    b. desirable
    c. seldom
    d. lasting forever

16. lenient
    a. melodious
    b. transparent
    c. soothing
    d. not severe

17. novice
    a. expert
    b. something new and strange
    c. beginner
    d. priest

18. humane
    a. living
    b. conscientious
    c. valuable
    d. kind

19. authentic
    a. antique
    b. literary
    c. genuine
    d. false

20. carica-ture
    a. scene in color
    b. circus per-former
    c. slight damage
    d. cartoon

WORD LIST

In your reading you will frequently encounter the words in the following list. Make this list the basis of your vocabulary work throughout the year, and learn about ten words a week. The following plan is one way to study the list. Your teacher may have additional suggestions.

1. *List the words* in your notebook, ten at a time, leaving a space of two lines between words.

2. *Look up each word* in the dictionary, and write after the word a short definition or a synonym. If a word has several meanings, your teacher will tell you which meaning or meanings to record and learn.

3. *Write* on the lines below the definition a sentence in which you use the word correctly.

4. *Copy in your notebook* any sentences showing good context clues to the meanings of these words.

5. *Take a test.* When your teacher dictates the words, write them correctly spelled, and after each word write its meaning.

VOCABULARY LIST

abate	advocate	approximate
abhor	aggravate	assail
abominable	alien	audible
abridge	ally	austere
abrupt	alternate	authentic
abstain	amends	avarice
accord	anguish	avert
acute	anticipate	banish
adhere	antiseptic	beguile
adopt	appease	blemish

bravado	diligent	grandeur
burnish	diminish	gratify
caliber	discretion	grimace
candid	disperse	grotesque
caricature	distort	guarantee
challenge	distract	haggard
cherish	dubious	homage
clamber	economical	hostile
coincide	elaborate	hover
compassion	eloquent	humane
compensate	elude	hypocrite
competent	emancipate	hysterical
comply	enhance	illusion
compute	entice	illustrious
condescend	era	impair
confirm	eventual	impartial
conform	exclude	incompatible
congregate	exotic	incredible
conspire	expand	indispensable
contemplate	exultant	inert
contraband	faculty	infinite
controversial	fascinating	intolerable
credible	feign	intricate
crucial	fluctuate	irritable
debris	frivolous	jostle
deem	frugal	judicial
defiant	furtive	languish
deliberate	futile	legacy
delusion	gaudy	legitimate
deplore	genial	lenient

loiter

lucid

lure

maim

malicious

manuscript

maternal

meditate

mercenary

moderate

mythology

nocturnal

notorious

novice

nurture

obsolete

obstinate

omen

opponent

parasite

partial

paternal

perennial

perilous

perpetual

pestilence

pious

placid

plausible

pompous

ponderous

prate

precarious

prestige

profound

protrude

prudent

quell

query

rapture

rebuke

recoil

refrain

refute

relent

renounce

repel

replenish

resolve

retaliate

sanction

satellite

segregation

sequel

signify

speculate

spontaneous

subsequent

subside

subtle

sumptuous

surmise

temperate

temporary

terminate

tranquil

transgress

transient

turmoil

uncanny

uncouth

unscrupulous

utility

valiant

vanquish

velocity

versatile

veto

vivacious

zealous

Topics
to Write About

Topics
to Write About

The only way to improve your performance in a sport is to practice. Similarly, the only way to improve your writing is to write. In school you get your writing practice by writing compositions. A major problem for all young writers is finding something to write about. You may wish to improve your writing; you may be quite willing to write compositions; but unless you have a topic to write about, you can do neither. The purpose of this supplementary chapter is to help you find topics to write about.

Words are only one of the many means of communicating. Pictures are another. Some pictures—photographs and cartoons, for example—may tell a story. They may not be able to tell a whole story, but they can suggest a story. Cartoons and photographs can also suggest ideas. Other pictures—graphs and charts— provide you with information. In the following pages, most of the topics for writing are suggested by pictures. After studying these cartoons, photographs, charts, and graphs, you will have a chance to write compositions, transforming the pictures into words. You will also be able to give your reactions to these pictures and the ideas they express.

A BRIEF STORY SUGGESTED
BY A CARTOON

A story, like a movie or a play, consists of a series of scenes. A picture of one scene may suggest what the entire play or movie is about. The "stills" frequently posted outside theaters are intended to interest a prospective playgoer in seeing the play. By closely studying a picture, you can create a story in which this picture will represent one scene. The story you create will probably be quite different from the stories your classmates create about the same picture, but the differences will add interest and fun to the whole assignment.

Study the cartoon below (figure 1).

Reprinted with permission from The Saturday Evening Post © 1968, The Curtis Publishing Company.

FIGURE 1

"What's a good name for a muskrat?"

Discuss the following questions about the cartoon:

1. What do you think the mother's reply will be?
2. What problems is this boy obviously going to face? What problems is the mother going to face?
3. Does the cartoon remind you of an experience of your own—perhaps a time when you brought home a stray kitten or puppy and asked to keep it?
4. Do you think the scene pictured would most likely be the opening or the ending of a story?
5. What events do you imagine preceded or followed this scene?
6. Would a story based on this cartoon have to be funny, or could it be serious, even tragic?
7. What opportunities for dialogue, description, and characterization would a story based on this scene afford?

In planning a story suggested by a cartoon or a photograph, you should follow the steps recommended in Chapter 17 for planning any story. These steps as detailed on page 316 include deciding on the following: the time, the place, the people, what happened, and how you felt about it. When you have made these decisions, you should plan your story so that it will have a beginning, a middle, and an end. See page 319 for an explanation of what you should include in each of these three parts.

● COMPOSITION 1. Write the story suggested to you by the cartoon on page 516 (figure 1).

● COMPOSITION 2. Without the aid of class discussion, plan and write a story based on the cartoon on page 518 (figure 2).

Drawing by Weber; © 1967, The New Yorker Magazine, Inc.

FIGURE 2

"<u>Now</u> what do I do?"

A STORY SUGGESTED BY A PHOTOGRAPH

Almost any picture showing people in action will suggest a story to an imaginative person. The photograph (figure 3) on page 520 will surely challenge your imagination.

What you see is a beach scene with two children coming out of the water, but it is the elephant that makes this situation intriguing and makes you wonder what is going on here. The following questions, included here for discussion, may help you to imagine a story in which this picture would be one scene.

1. What events do you imagine preceded the moment recorded by the camera?   What events do you imagine followed it?
2. What do you think you would see happening on this beach if you could see the beach further to the right and to the left?
3. Do you think the boy and girl are at all worried about the elephant? Is the elephant aware of the boy and girl? Is there any connection between the children and the elephant or is their presence together on the beach just a coincidence?
4. An elephant, even though apparently free, must belong to somebody. Who owns the elephant, and why is the elephant allowed to go freely into the water?
5. Where do you think this beach is? Would the country in which the picture was taken make any difference in explaining the picture?

● COMPOSITION 3. Following the suggestions for story writing in Chapter 17, write a carefully planned story suggested by the picture of the children and the elephant. You may want to tell your story as though you were a person in it, or you may want to keep yourself out of the story and tell it as though you were an outsider observing other people. The first way is called the first-person, or "I," point of view. The second is called the third-person point of view.

Other matters you will have to consider in planning your story are the names of the characters, the possible use of conversation, or dialogue, the opening scene and concluding scene, and where in the story the action shown in the photograph will occur. Rather than merely explaining the photograph, try to write an interesting story about it.

Cartier-Bresson, Magnum.

● COMPOSITION 4. Carefully study the following photograph (figure 4). Plan and write a story based on it.

Mobil Oil Corporation.

FIGURE 4

● COMPOSITION 5.   Look through a magazine that you own and find a cartoon or a photograph that suggests an interesting story to you. Write the story. Cut the cartoon or the photograph from the magazine and clip it to your composition so that your teacher and classmates can see the origin of the story.

A "WORD PARAGRAPH" BASED ON A "PICTURE PARAGRAPH"

Like a number of examples used to develop a topic sentence into a paragraph (see page 343), a number of related pictures may be used to develop an idea. Read the caption that stands, like a topic sentence, above the group of sketches below. Note that each sketch is an example that supports the idea in the caption.

EVERYONE ACCEPTS GOVERNMENT SERVICES

© 1967 by Harcourt, Brace & World, Inc. Reproduced from Our American Economy, Third Edition, by Lindholm and Driscoll.

FIGURE 5

● COMPOSITION 6. Using the caption above the pictures (figure 5) as your topic sentence, write a paragraph which says the same thing the group of sketches says. In other words, try to write a paragraph describing what the artist may have had in mind when he made these sketches.

A good way would be to express each of the six examples of government services in a complete sentence. Before you write the final draft of your paragraph, review on page 310 the ways to correct a monotonous style. Resist the tendency to make all your sentences structurally alike. Try to think of one or two additional examples of government services and include them in your paragraph.

Earlier in this chapter, you saw that a picture may suggest a story. In the preceding composition, you saw that a paragraph, which is a series of sentences developing an idea, may be expressed as a series of related drawings. Not only, then, may pictures suggest stories, but they may also express ideas. The fact is that serious cartoonists and great photographers are more concerned with ideas than with stories.

PARAGRAPHS DEVELOPING IDEAS EXPRESSED IN CARTOONS

Examine the three cartoons (figures 6, 7, and 8) and prepare to discuss, in class, answers to the questions following the cartoons.

FIGURE 6   *"His mother wants to know if you'll give him a haircut after you remove his tonsils."*

FIGURE 7

Drawing by Robert Kraus: © 1967, The New Yorker Magazine, Inc.
FIGURE 8

1. With what important fact of family life are all these cartoons concerned?
2. You will probably agree that the cartoons are funny. Is there also a serious side to them? Do they have universal appeal? Explain.
3. Is the boy's refusal to have his hair cut (figure 6) the important thing, or is this refusal only an example of a larger idea? What is this idea? What actions of the man's son (figure 7) do you imagine might have led the father to make this ridiculous addition to the sign on his office door?
4. In figures 6, 7, and 8, are the sympathies of the cartoonists with the parents or with their children? How can you tell?
5. What are some other common causes of conflict between parents and children (between generations)?

● COMPOSITION 7. Write a paragraph in which you develop the idea you think the cartoonists in figures 6, 7, and 8 are trying to express. State this idea first in a topic sentence. You may use as examples the situations pictured in the cartoons or, better yet, you may make up examples of your own.

● COMPOSITION 8. Write a paragraph in which you state what you think are the best means of solving the common conflicts between parents and children.

Study the two cartoons (figures 9 and 10) on pages 526–27. Prepare to discuss, in class, answers to the following questions.

Reprinted with permission from The Saturday Evening Post © *1967, The Curtis Publishing Company.*

FIGURE 9 *"Hey, folks, there's no more woods."*

Drawing by Donald Reilly; © *1967, The New Yorker Magazine, Inc.*

FIGURE 10

1. With what truth about the modern world is the cartoonist concerned in figure 9?
2. What is the cartoonist's attitude toward this truth? How can you tell? Has he succeeded in arousing your sympathy for his attitude? Judging by your own experience, do you think his attitude is justified?
3. What common truth about the behavior of human beings concerns the cartoonist in figure 10? Is the cartoon intended to be funny or not?
4. Does this cartoon remind you of places you know or experiences you have had?
5. Do you see any meaningful relationship between the ideas expressed in these two cartoons?

● COMPOSITION 9.   Write a paragraph in which you put into words the concern expressed in one or both of these cartoons (figures 9 and 10). Begin with your topic sentence. Then, using the example in the cartoons and two other examples of your own, develop the paragraph.

PARAGRAPHS DEVELOPING IDEAS EXPRESSED IN PHOTOGRAPHS

Photographs express ideas, but they are likely to do so less pointedly than cartoons. Whereas a cartoon is usually drawn to present a single unmistakable idea, a great photograph may suggest a number of ideas or interpretations. In other words, you can make more use of your imagination in the interpretation of a photograph than in your interpretation of a cartoon.

You will probably agree that the picture (figure 11) on page 529 is a great photograph. Examine it at length and prepare answers to the following questions for discussion.

1. What things can you point out about this photograph that make it great?
2. Is the man young, middle-aged, or old? What bearing does the man's age have on the meaning of the picture? How old do you think the dog is? Is the dog's age important? Explain.
3. How does the picture make clear the kind of relationship that exists between man and dog? What is the attitude of each toward the other?
4. In what ways do you imagine the dog to be important to this man?
5. What reasons for owning a pet does this photograph suggest?

FIGURE 11

Jim Theologos

● COMPOSITION 10. Write a paragraph in which you state your own beliefs about the value of owning a pet. You need not refer to the photograph; instead, use experiences and examples from your own life to develop your ideas.

● COMPOSITION 11. Write a paragraph describing the way of life of this man and his dog as you imagine it. Tell about them as though you knew them, perhaps as neighbors.

● COMPOSITION 12. Earlier in this chapter (pages 519–21), you were asked to write a story suggested by a picture. Write a story suggested by this photograph of a man and his dog.

● COMPOSITION 13. Take a long look at the photographs on page 531. Select the photograph that suggests an idea you could write about, and write a fully developed paragraph on this idea. Note that this assignment calls for development of an idea, not writing a story.

INFORMATION FROM DIAGRAMS— CHARTS AND GRAPHS·

Facts may be presented to a reader in the form of a diagram (chart or graph) as well as in writing. Charts and graphs are often used to supplement writing, for they are a clear and quick way to help a reader understand what the writing says. In your next compositions, you will be given charts and graphs to study, and you will be asked to write paragraphs giving in words the information conveyed by the charts and graphs.

Examine carefully the three graphs (figures 14, 15,

Photographs on this page by Jim Theologos.

FIGURE 12

FIGURE 13

and 16). Answer the following questions about them:

1. What important change in the American family income has occurred since 1929? Approximately what percent of families have been affected by this change?
2. What important change in the number of hours Americans work in a week has occurred since 1900?
3. What significant change in the production of goods and services has been occurring in the United States?
4. Do any of the facts revealed by these graphs seem inconsistent with one another?

● COMPOSITION 14.   Write a general statement stating the three facts expressed by the three graphs on page 533. Use this statement as a topic sentence and support it with as many specific facts and figures as you can gather from the graphs. In a second paragraph, give your own explanation of the facts shown by the graphs. Explain how Americans can make more money by working fewer hours and how they can, at the same time, produce more goods and services.

●COMPOSITION 15.   The five graphs on pages 534–35 present related facts about changes in farming in the United States. Examine each graph to discover what fact it states. When you have decided what the facts are and discovered how they are related, draw a conclusion from this information and state the conclusion in a sentence. Use this sentence as a topic sentence and develop it into a paragraph, using the details revealed by the graphs as the supporting material of your paragraph.

If you wish, you may write two paragraphs. In the first, give the facts shown by figures 17, 18 and 19. In the second, use the facts in figures 20 and 21 to explain the facts shown in figures 17, 18, and 19.

FIGURE 14

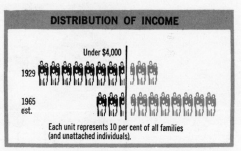

FIGURE 15

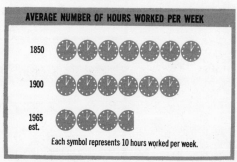

FIGURE 16

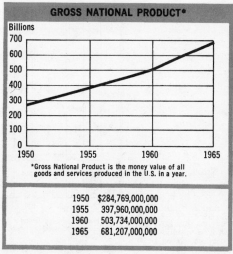

Harbrace Illustration

FIGURE 17

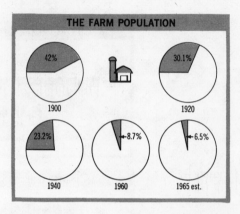

THE FARM POPULATION

1900 — 42%
1920 — 30.1%
1940 — 23.2%
1960 — 8.7%
1965 est. — 6.5%

FIGURE 18

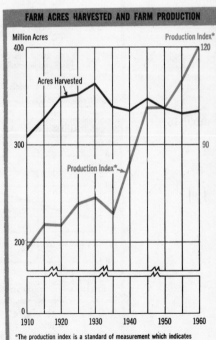

FARM ACRES HARVESTED AND FARM PRODUCTION

Million Acres — Production Index*

Acres Harvested

Production Index*

400 — 120
300 — 90
200
0
1910 1920 1930 1940 1950 1960

*The production index is a standard of measurement which indicates the increase or decrease of total farm production. Farm production for 1947-49 = 100.

Figures 14–15 and 17–21 © 1968 by Harcourt Brace Jovanovich, Inc. Reproduced from Rise of the American Nation, *Volume 1, by Todd and Curti.*

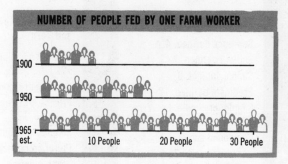

FIGURE 19

FIGURE 20

FIGURE 21

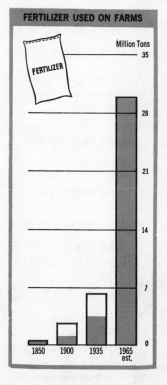

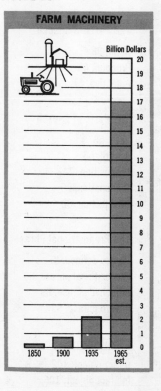

MECHANICS

CORRECTION SYMBOLS

ms	error in manuscript form or neatness
cap	error in use of capital letters
p	error in punctuation
sp	error in spelling
frag	sentence fragment
ss	error in sentence structure
k	awkward sentence
nc	not clear
rs	run-on sentence
gr	error in grammar
w	error in word choice
¶	You should have begun a new paragraph here.
t	error in tense
⌃	You have omitted something.

Index

KEY TO ENGLISH WORKSHOP DRILL

If additional drill is required, see **ENGLISH WORKSHOP, Fourth Edition,** Grade 7, by Greiffenberg, Blumenthal, and Warriner. The rule numbers in this text are keyed below to appropriate lessons in the Workshop.

Text Rule No.	Workshop Lesson No.	Text Rule No.	Workshop Lesson No.	Text Rule No.	Workshop Lesson No.
1a	1	9c	28	16c	9
1b	2	10a	1	16f	120
1c	4	10c	62–64	16g	120
1d	2	10d	64	17c	32,207
1e	3	10f	65	17e	59
1f	5			17f	59
1g	5	11a	1	17g	59
1h	6	11b	1	17h	50,82
1i	6	11c	1	18a	114
		11f	43	18b	114,119
2a	11	11g	43	18c	118
2b	12	11h	44	18d	118
2c	13	11i	45	18e	118
3a	14	11j	46	18f	114,118, 120
3b	15	12c	123		
3c	17	12d	65	19a	115
4a	34	12e	108	19b	115,116
4b	34	12f	108	19c	116
4c	35	12g	109	19d	115,116
4d	36	12h	108	19f	117,119
5a	26	12i	108	19g	120
5c	27	12k	109	20a	69
6a	71	12l	109	20b	69
6b	72	12o	105	20c	69
6c	72	12p	105	20h	120
6d	74	12q	105	21a	121
6e	74	12r	106	21b	121
6g	78	13a	33	21c	121
6h	78	13c	51	21d	122
6k	76	13d	70	21e	123
6n	77	13e	70	25b	40,49, 68,81
7a	84	13f	70		
7b	85	13g	70	25c	40
7c	85–90	13h	95	25d	40
8a	96	13i	83	26a	40
8b	97	15a	52–55	26b	8,21,31
8c	98	15b	56	26c	40,49
8d	99	16a	9	26g	93,102
9b	28	16b	9